Gentleman at Paris

Napoleon's Court and Cabinet of St. Cloud

In a series of letters. Vol. 1

Gentleman at Paris

Napoleon's Court and Cabinet of St. Cloud
In a series of letters. Vol. 1

ISBN/EAN: 9783337350642

Printed in Europe, USA, Canada, Australia, Japan

Cover: Foto ©ninafisch / pixelio.de

More available books at **www.hansebooks.com**

Courts of Europe

NAPOLEON'S COURT

AND

CABINET OF ST. CLOUD

IN A

SERIES OF LETTERS FROM A GENTLEMAN AT
PARIS TO A NOBLEMAN IN LONDON

VOL. I

Illustrated

PHILADELPHIA
GEORGE BARRIE & SON   PUBLISHERS.

INTRODUCTORY LETTER

PARIS, *November 10th*, 1805.

MY LORD,—The Letters I have written to you were intended for the private entertainment of a liberal friend, and not for the general perusal of a severe public. Had I imagined that their contents would have penetrated beyond your closet or the circle of your intimate acquaintance, several of the narratives would have been extended, while others would have been compressed; the anecdotes would have been more numerous, and my own remarks fewer; some portraits would have been left out, others drawn, and all better finished. I should then have attempted more frequently to expose meanness to contempt, and treachery to abhorrence; should have lashed more severely incorrigible vice, and oftener held out to ridicule puerile vanity and outrageous ambition. In short, I should then have studied more to please than to instruct, by addressing myself seldomer to the reason than to the passions.

I subscribe, nevertheless, to your observation, "that the late long war and short peace, with the enslaved state of the Press on the Continent, would occasion a chasm in the most interesting period of modern history, did not independent and judicious travellers or visitors abroad collect and forward to Great Britain (the last refuge of freedom) some materials which, though scanty and insufficient upon the whole, may, in part, rend the veil of destructive politics, and enable future ages to penetrate into mysteries which crime in power has interest to render impenetrable to the just reprobation of honour and of virtue."—If, therefore, my humble labours can preserve loyal subjects from the seduction of traitors, or warn lawful sovereigns and civilized society of the alarming conspiracy against them, I shall not think either my time thrown away, or fear the dangers to which publicity might expose me, were I only suspected here of being an Anglican author. Before the Letters are sent to the press I trust, however, to your discretion the removal of everything that might produce a discovery, or indicate the source from which you have derived your information.

Although it is not usual in private correspondence to quote authorities, I have sometimes done so; but satisfied, as I hope you are, with my veracity, I should have thought the frequent productions of any better pledge than the word of a man of honour an insult to your feelings. I have, besides, not related a fact that is not recent and well-known in our fashionable and political societies; and of ALL the portraits I have delineated, the originals not only exist, but are yet occupied in the present busy scene of the Continent, and figuring either at Courts, in camps, or in Cabinets.

CONTENTS

PAGE

Introductory Letter ix

LETTER I

Bonaparte's political character contrasted with his military education and life—Governed by courtiers and favourites. General Duroc—His character—The causes of his advancement—His military exploits in Italy and Egypt, and political missions to Berlin and St. Petersburg—Visits Madame Bonœil, a female intriguer—His blunder in consequence. The Polish Count S——tz—His character—Dupes Duroc—Duroc's marriage 1

LETTER II

Joseph Bonaparte—His character as a negotiator—The puppet of Talleyrand. Talleyrand's intrigues, and motives for employing the brothers of Bonaparte. Lucien's embassy to Spain. Joseph's rapacity—Connection with an army contractor and stock-jobbing. Secret articles of the Treaty of Luneville—Bonaparte's offence at them—Reproaches Talleyrand. Departure of Lord Whitworth in 1803—Bonaparte's rage and speech to Talleyrand on the occasion, and violent conduct towards his mother, wife, &c. . . . 10

LETTER III

Debates on the religious concordat—Opposed by different factions—Bonaparte's mother, how far instrumental in procuring the restoration of religious worship. Cardinal Gonsalvi and Bishop Bernier—Their intrigues and characters. Madame Bonaparte's astonishment on being ordered to attend Mass, &c.—Her hypocrisy—Watched

by spies—Her mode of passing her time at chapel discovered—
Regulations in consequence. Conversation at Viscount de Segur's
on the religious principles of the French—Imprudent remark of a
young officer the cause of his transportation to Cayenne . . 16

LETTER IV

The assumption of the imperial dignity, long determined on by
Bonaparte — Delayed by the rupture with England—His good
fortune mistaken for political foresight. The disgrace of Moreau,
the murder of the Duke of Enghien, Pichegru, and Georges, and
the treachery towards Mr. Drake not necessary steps to his elevation. Moreau not dangerous as a rival to Bonaparte—Why
not assassinated. Honourable conduct of Pichegru the day before
his death. Murat the executioner of the Duke of Enghien . 24

LETTER V

The characters of the principal emigrants well known to the French
government—Mehée de la Touche—His perfidy and ingratitude—
His mission and intrigues in England—Refused the wages of his
infamy by Talleyrand. Real—A forgery committed by him in 1788
—Strange mixture of society at his house. Madame de Soubray—
Her severe reproof of Mehée de la Touche 32

LETTER VI

Unhappiness of Madame Napoleon on the day of her coronation—
Discipline of the Court of St. Cloud entirely military—Formation
of the household entrusted to Madame Napoleon—Consequent embarrassment—Extricated by an expedient proposed by De Segur.
Madame Napoleon confined—Released at the intercession of her
daughter 39

LETTER VII

Religious discussion tolerated — Why — Remonstrance of Cardinal
Caprara on the subject. Two authors transported to Cayenne—

Pigault Le Brun owes his escape to Madame Murat—Cardinal Caprara's influence over Bonaparte—Defeats a cabal formed against him, and turns it to his advantage—Employed by the Pope in his secret negotiations at Paris—Teases Bonaparte and is confined by him, but obtains his object—Trick attempted to be played on him ends unfortunately for the contrivers 46

LETTER VIII

Grave dress and puritanical demeanour of the company at Madame Napoleon's last levée previous to meeting the Pope—Bonaparte surrounded by Cardinals and Priests—Remark of General Kellerman —Occasions his disgrace—Conduct of the company on quitting the levée—Princess Borghese's ideas respecting a parrot and an almoner, monkeys and chaplains 54

LETTER IX

The reception of Bonaparte as Emperor by the army of England not flattering—Ascribed by him to the adherents of Pichegru and Moreau—His conduct in consequence—Orders a grenadier to be shot, and disbands a regiment. Effect produced on the military by the distribution of the ribands, &c., of the Legion of Honour. The French ports declared to be in a state of blockade by the English—Bonaparte's rage and agitation—Fires at some British cruisers—Breaks six officers of artillery and assaults another— Quits the camp in disgust 59

LETTER X

Count Cobentzel advises his Sovereign to assume the title of Emperor of Austria—His political employments and character—His passion for women—Talleyrand's opinion of him—Invited by Bonaparte to visit the camps of the army of England. Talleyrand's note proscribing all British agents and ambassadors. Bonaparte's arrival at Aix-la-Chapelle—Is met there by the foreign ambassadors— Presented with relics of Charlemagne, and punishes a German professor for proving them forgeries 66

CONTENTS

LETTER XI

Bonaparte finds his wife involved in gambling debts and surrounded by Jews and other creditors—Talleyrand's mode of settling their demands—Count de Segur completes Bonaparte's household establishment—His character and public employments—His domestic misfortunes. Character of the members of Bonaparte's civil list—Methods adopted to augment it with Prussian and German Nobles . 72

LETTER XII

Bonaparte's intention to seize on the Empire of Germany—His secret treaties with the petty German princes at Mentz—The French Revolution not looked on as dangerous in Germany—Why. The Elector of Bavaria—His character and obligations to Louis XVI. —Governed by Montgelas, the idol of Illuminati and patron of Atheists—The progress of illumination in Bavaria—Montgelas concerned in the plot against Mr. Drake—His character . . . 79

LETTER XIII

Attendance of German Princes and Princesses on the Empress Josephine at Mentz, and rich presents to her—Bribery and corruption openly practised there—Disappointment of the German Princes—High price demanded by Talleyrand for indemnities—His intrigue with the Countess de L—— and the Baroness de S——z—Repulsed by the Princess of H——. Bonaparte's jealousy —Mistakes the object of Count de L——ge's attention to the Empress Josephine—His proceedings in consequence. The avarice of the Empress 86

LETTER XIV

Former intimacy of the Writer with Madame Napoleon and her daughter—Their friendly behaviour on his first introduction to them since their elevation—Subsequent change—The Writer declines the offer of a public situation—Arrested—Interview with General Murat—Sentenced to be transported to Cayenne on the

CONTENTS

report of Fouché, but protected by Princess Louis — Cause of Fouché's enmity—His infamous character and unbounded authority—The *oubliettes*, his invention—His immense property—Bonaparte's reasons for employing him 91

Letter XV

The poverty and dependent situation of the foreign ambassadors at Paris—Invited by Talleyrand to a diplomatic dinner—His manœuvre to obtain their declarations respecting the pretended correspondence of Mr. Drake—Servility of the Danish and American ambassadors—Their characters—Baron de Dreyer's reasons for wishing to maintain his situation. Count de Haugwitz—His birth, political life and character 101

Letter XVI

The Writer accepts an invitation from Princess Louis Bonaparte to dinner—The conquest of Great Britain the subject of conversation—Different opinions respecting the proper mode of treating the inhabitants when vanquished. Imprudent observations of Marquis de F——Exiled to Blois in consequence, and saved from severer punishment only by the interference of Princess Louis—Her good nature—Character of Louis 110

Letter XVII

Violent debates in the Sacred College on the journey of the Pope to France—The members bribed by Cardinal Fesch. Birth of Cardinal Fesch—His life and adventures—His marriage and desertion of his wife—Her application to the Pope—His libertinism and adventure at Lyons—His wealth, dignities and expectations . 118

Letter XVIII

The Margrave of Baden made an Elector by the intrigues of Talleyrand and Baron Edelsheim. Character and political life of Edelsheim. Haughty and indecent conduct of Bonaparte to the Elector at Mentz—Secret treaty signed there. The vanity and affected consequence of Edelsheim played on and exposed by Talleyrand—His fondness for Orders of Knighthood—Fawns on Bonaparte to obtain admission into the Legion of Honour . 125

LETTER XIX

The journey of the Pope to France unfavourable to the cause of religion—The restoration of Christianity the most popular act of Bonaparte's Government—The opinion of the people respecting the act of inauguration by the Pope—Their faith in his infallibility shaken. Manners and character of the Pope—Promises made to him by Bonaparte not performed—Refuses to admit De Lalande to see him—De Lalande's atheism—Enmity between him and Talleyrand. The Pope's aversion to Fouché—Fouché's impious conduct at Lyons 133

LETTER XX

Bonaparte's mother the favourite of the Pope—Family parties invited to meet him—Ceremony observed on such occasions. Superstition of Madame Letitia Bonaparte—Her fondness for relics—Buys the shoulder-bone of St. John the Baptist—Robbed of her relics—Fouché applied to—Who discovers pieces of them all in the possession of a favourite servant—The rest found on Madame de Genlis, who had bought them of a priest—The priest arrested—Claims the protection of Madame Letitia—Threatened with the rack and confesses his imposture 141

LETTER XXI

Decrease in the population of Paris not to be lamented—The crimes committed there not suffered to be published. The system of espionage. Immense number of spies—How paid. Bonaparte's private spies under the direction of Duroc. Dispute between Fouché and Talleyrand. Ducroux employed as a spy by Bonaparte and Fouché on each other—His blunder and execution . . . 149

CONTENTS

Letter XXII

The Pope's manner of passing his time at Paris—Great stress laid on his performing the ceremony of inauguration, and sacrifices intended to have been made had he refused—All promises to him disregarded—His blind partiality for Bonaparte. Caprara dissuades Bonaparte from being crowned by the Pope as King of Italy . 157

Letter XXIII

King and Queen of Naples—Their firm and dignified conduct. Chevalier Acton—His birth—Political character—Enemy of the French Revolution. Neutrality of Naples violated. The removal of Acton insisted on by the French Government. Marquis de Gallo—His public employments—A favourite with Bonaparte—Suspected of being tainted with modern philosophy. The Neapolitan Revolution in 1799 favoured by the Nobles. Character of Marquis de Gallo 163

Letter XXIV

Bonaparte and all his family married by the Pope—His courtiers and grand functionaries by the Cardinals—Their regular attendance at Mass and Vespers—Trick of Salmatoris to expose their hypocrisy—Is punished. Fouché's visit to the Imperial Chapel—His discovery there. The indifference of the common people to religious worship—The military compelled to attend Mass—Singular occurrence in consequence, and injustice of Bonaparte 169

Letter XXV

Seizure of Sir George Rumbold—Intended to have been tortured and put to death—Why he was not—Rheinhard officially disavows the outrage—Is disgraced in consequence—His political life and character. Bourrienne—His employment under Bonaparte—His dispute with him and imprisonment—Released and pensioned—His extortions and stock-jobbing—His character . . . 175

Letter XXVI

Joseph Bonaparte's retired mode of life at Paris—His hospitality at Morfontaine—Amusements there, and freedom allowed to the guests. Montaigne, a young poet, a visitor there—His drunkenness—Writes a poem against it. Madame Joseph's gallantries—Duel between her gallants. Eugenius de Beauharnais forbidden the house of Joseph. Madame Miot detected by her husband in an intrigue with Captain d'Horteuil—The gallant beats Miot, who begs pardon—Miot's infamous life and character 184

Letter XXVII

Conduct of the King of Spain—His weak character. The present the age of upstarts. The Prince of Peace—His former occupation—His want of talents—Cause of his advancement—His intrigue with the Queen and favour with the King—Weakness and ignorance of his administration—Disgrace and misfortunes produced by it. Gravina—His character and ambition—His military exploits—Intrigue with an opera girl—His marriage mania involves him in a disagreeable scrape 192

Letter XXVIII

Vicious morals, gross manners, and open corruption of the Court of St. Cloud. Anecdotes. Merlin of Douai—His public employments—Infamous character and great wealth . . . 204

Letter XXIX

Immense number of Bonaparte's household troops—Regularly paid and strictly disciplined—Their privileges, &c. Military reviews—Their use—Less frequent since Bonaparte's coronation. Number of military posted in and near Paris. Army of Invalids—Their prejudices—How employed. Mode of enforcing payment of taxes at Paris. Houses of the invalids—Their reading-rooms, libraries, &c.—Their licentiousness and crimes—Screened from punishment by the orders of Bonaparte. Rabais, a horse grenadier — His amours and debaucheries—Accused before Thuriot, and acquitted—His intrigue with Madame Thuriot—Discovered by her jealousy—Thuriot applies in vain for redress. Rabais' intrigue with Madame Bacciochi — Denounced by Thuriot — Arrest and punishment of Rabais—Curious effects discovered in his trunk—Thuriot's rage and violence in consequence—His employment and crimes . . 211

LETTER XXX

The Writer visits Lucien Bonaparte at his country seat—Lucien's valuable collection of pictures — His hospitality and engaging manners contrasted with those of Napoleon and Joseph — His liberality — Anecdotes — His republicanism — His vices compared with those of Napoleon—His immense wealth, how acquired—Instance of his generosity and perversity 222

LETTER XXXI

Reasons for not incorporating the Batavian Republic with the French Empire—Partition Treaty of Holland offered by France to Prussia—Why declined. Bonaparte displeased with the Batavian Government—Violates its neutrality—Remonstrance of Count Markoff, how answered by Bonaparte—His determination to change the form of Government in Holland—Difficulty of finding fit magistrates—Holland not lately productive of great men. Admiral de Winter—His character—Political connections and employments. Generals Daendels and Dumonceau—Their lives and characters . . . 232

LETTER XXXII

Bonaparte advises Prussia of his intention to change the form of Government in Holland—Chief Magistrates thought of—Young Prince of Orange—Elector of Bavaria. Bonaparte's increasing displeasure with the Batavian Directory—Intention to make his brother Jerome Stadtholder. Schimmelpenninck—His education—Want of talents—Political connections and opinions—His embassy to France—Bribes Talleyrand to procure him the appointment of

Grand Pensionary—His character. Madame Schimmelpenninck—
Her talents and amiable manners—Schimmelpenninck's female
friends of the Palais Royal 240

LETTER XXXIII

Bonaparte's cool reception at Milan—Ascribed by him to the intrigues
of England and Russia—Measures of security adopted—Frequency
of conspiracies in France since the Revolution—Bonaparte's reasons
for concealing them. Plot of Charlotte Encore—Attempts to stab
Bonaparte, prevented by Duroc—Expires on the rack, refusing to
name her accomplices—Their plan and names—How discovered . 250

LETTER XXXIV

All women forbidden to approach Bonaparte without permission—A
female servant of Cardinal Fesch, whom Bonaparte had seduced,
attempts to poison him—Discovered, and poisons herself—Plot to
assassinate him at Milan—His agitation on the discovery—Speech
of one of the conspirators, who stabs himself—The others torn to
pieces on the rack—Proceedings in consequence of this conspiracy.
Bonaparte an object of ridicule in Italy—League of generals against
him—Its object—The generals disgraced 257

LETTER XXXV

Vanity and caprice of Bonaparte—His rage on the Emperor of
Germany refusing to become a member of the Legion of Honour
—His threat and violent conduct towards the Austrian ambassador
—Determines to incorporate the Ligurian Republic with France.
Salicetti, the French minister at Genoa—His birth—Employments
—A terrorist—Recommends Bonaparte to Barras—Displeases him
by his familiarity. Lucien Bonaparte intended to have been made
Sovereign of the Ligurian Republic—Why he was not—The change
of Government—How effected—The Doge and Ligurian Deputation
do homage to Bonaparte as Sovereign at Milan—Their grief and
indignation. The PATRIOTIC ROBBERS stop Salicetti and seize
his papers—PATRIOTIC AVENGERS 265

CONTENTS xxiii

LETTER XXXVI

PAGE

Exchange of Orders of Knighthood between Bonaparte and Sovereign Princes. Foreign ambassadors invited to his coronation at Milan —Some decline to attend. Expenses of the journey to Milan and coronation. General Jourdan—His marriage and military appointments—Cause of his enmity to Pichegru—His military and political exploits—His quarrel with Massena—His character . . . 273

LETTER XXXVII

Conservative Senate, its heterogeneous composition—Character of its members. Senatorial Commission of Personal Liberty—Its members. Lenoin Laroche, Boissy d'Anglas, Sers—Their lives and characters. Senatorial Commission of the Liberty of the Press—Garat and Rœderer its principal members—Pedantry and inhumanity of Garat—An enemy to the liberty of the Press—Rœderer unprincipled and profligate—Rejected by all factions —Employed first by Bonaparte—His incest—His wealth, libertinism and foppery 283

LETTER XXXVIII

Turkish Empire preserved by the mutual jealousies of Austria, France and Russia—Its weakness and anarchy—Political intrigues at Constantinople—The neutrality of the Porte more useful than its alliance—Intrigue of the Brissot faction in 1792 to engage it in a war with Austria—Counteracted by Count de Choiseul-Gouffier, then French ambassador there—De Semonville sent on an embassy thither in 1793 with rich presents—Made prisoner by the Austrians—The Sultan declares war against France—Peace concluded. Sebastiani's mission to Egypt and Syria. General Brune appointed ambassador to the Porte—His character—His vices—Political intrigues and military employments . . . 294

LETTER XXXIX

Brune's numerous suite—Of what composed—Real object of his mission avowed by Talleyrand—Markoff remonstrates. Count

Italinski—His character—Warns the Divan against Brune—Libelled by him in the *Moniteur*. Brune's reception at Constantinople—His chagrin—Demands his recall, upon the Porte's refusal to acknowledge Bonaparte as Emperor. Joubert the bearer of a letter from Bonaparte to the Grand Seignior—His education and employments. Young men educated at the expense of the French Government in foreign countries—For what purpose. Joubert's interview with the Sultan—How obtained—Its result—His second message, and failure. French emissaries in Austria, Hungary and Servia—French officers in the service of Czerni George and Paswan Oglou. Brune quits Constantinople—Appointed to the command of the army of observation opposite the English coast —His instructions—His wealth, ostentation and vanity . . 303

Letter XL

Madame de C——n—Her fashionable parties—Her marriage with Count de C——n disputed—Character of Count de C——n—His physiognomical pursuits—Trick played on him—Purchases Madame de C——n from a Circassian merchant, and sends her to be educated in France—His death—Madame de C——n's numerous suitors and gallants—Her pretended brother—Her own story—Birth and splendid christening of the son of Count de P——t. Villetard—His crimes and violence—His sacrilege and infamous conduct at Loretto—Treachery and hypocrisy. Cardinal de Bellois —His birth—Governed by his grand vicaries. Treilhard steals Madame de C——n's gold plates—His political life. Madame François de Nantes—Her theft, gambling and prostitution . . 313

THE SECRET HISTORY

OF THE

COURT AND CABINET

OF

ST. CLOUD

LETTER I

PARIS, *August*, 1805.

My Lord,—I promised you not to pronounce in haste on persons and events passing under my eyes: thirty-one months have quickly passed away since I became an attentive spectator of the extraordinary transactions, and of the extraordinary characters of the extraordinary Court and Cabinet of St. Cloud. If my talents to delineate equal my zeal to enquire and my industry to examine; if I am as able a painter as I have been an indefatigable observer, you will be satisfied, and with your approbation at once sanction and reward my labours.

With most princes, the supple courtier and the fawning favourite have greater influence than the profound statesman and subtle minister; and the determinations of Cabinets are, therefore, frequently prepared in drawing-rooms, and discussed in the closet. The politician and the counsellor are frequently applauded or censured for transactions which the intrigues of ante-chambers conceived, and which cupidity and favour gave power to promulgate.

It is very generally imagined, but falsely, that Napoleon Bonaparte governs, or rather tyrannizes, by himself, according to his own capacity, caprices or interest; that all his acts, all his changes, are the sole consequence of his own exclusive, unprejudiced will, as well as unlimited authority; that both his greatness and his littleness, his successes and his crimes, originate entirely with himself; that the fortunate hero, who marched triumphant over the Alps, and the dastardly murderer that disgraced human nature at Jaffa, because the same person, owed victory to himself alone, and by himself alone commanded massacre; that the same genius, unbiased and unsupported, crushed factions, erected a throne, and reconstructed racks; that the same mind restored and protected Christianity, and proscribed and assassinated a d'Enghien.

All these contradictions, all these virtues and vices, may be found in the same person; but Bonaparte, individually or isolated, has no claim to them. Except on some sudden occasions that call for immediate decision, no sovereign rules less by himself than Bonaparte; because no sovereign is more surrounded by favourites and counsellors, by needy adventurers and crafty intriguers.

What sovereign has more relatives to enrich, or more services to recompense; more evils to repair, more jealousies to dread, more dangers to fear, more clamours to silence; or stands more in need of information and advice? Let it be remembered that he, who now governs empires and nations, ten years ago commanded only a battery; and five years ago was only a military chieftain. The difference is as immense, indeed, between the sceptre of a monarch and the sword of a general, as between the wise legislator who protects the lives and property of his contemporaries, and the hireling robber who wades through rivers of blood to obtain plunder at the expense and misery of generations. The lower classes of all countries have produced persons who have distinguished themselves as warriors; but what subject has yet usurped a throne, and by his eminence and achievements, without infringing on the laws and liberties of his country, proved himself worthy to reign? Besides, the education which Bonaparte received was entirely military; and a man (let his innate abilities be ever so surprising or excellent) who, during the first thirty years of his life, has made either military or political tactics or exploits his only study, certainly cannot excel equally in the Cabinet and in the camp. It would be as foolish to believe, as absurd to expect, a perfection almost beyond the reach of any man; and of Bonaparte more than of anyone else. A man who, like him, is the continual slave of his own passions, can neither be a good nor a just, an independent nor immaculate master.

Among the courtiers who, ever since Bonaparte was made First Consul, have maintained a great ascendency over him, is the present grand marshal of his Court, the general of division, Duroc. With some parts, but greater presumption, this young man is destined by his master to occupy the most confidential places near his person; and to his care are entrusted the most difficult and secret missions at foreign Courts. When he is absent from France, the liberty of the Continent is in danger; and when in the Tuileries, or at St. Cloud, Bonaparte thinks himself always safe.

Gerard Christhophe Michel Duroc was born at Ponta-Mousson, in the department of Meurthe, on the 25th of October, 1772, of poor but honest parents. His father kept a petty chandler's shop; but by the interest and generosity of Abbé Duroc, a distant relation, he was so well-educated that, in March, 1792, he became a sub-lieutenant of the artillery. In 1796 he served in Italy, as a captain, under

General Andreossy, by whom he was recommended to General l'Espinasse, then commander of the artillery of the army of Italy, who made him an aide-de-camp. In that situation Bonaparte remarked his activity, and was pleased with his manners, and therefore attached him as an aide-de-camp to himself. Duroc soon became a favourite with his chief, and, notwithstanding the intrigues of his rivals, he has continued to be so to this day.

It has been asserted, by his enemies no doubt, that by implicit obedience to his general's orders, by an *unresisting* complacency, and by executing, without hesitation, the most cruel mandates of his superior, he has fixed himself so firmly in his good opinion that he is irremovable. It has also been stated that it was Duroc who commanded the drowning and burying alive of the wounded French soldiers in Italy, in 1797; and that it was he who inspected their poisoning in Syria, in 1799, where he was wounded during the siege of St. Jean d'Acre. He was among the few officers whom Bonaparte selected for his companions when he quitted the army of Egypt, and landed with him in France in October, 1799.

Hitherto Duroc had only shown himself as a brave soldier and obedient officer; but after the revolution which made Bonaparte a First Consul, he entered upon another career. He was then, for the first time, employed in a diplomatic mission to Berlin, where he so far insinuated himself into the good graces of their Prussian Majesties, that the King admitted him to the royal table, and on the parade at Potsdam presented him to his generals and officers as an aide-de-camp *du plus grand homme que je connais;* whilst the Queen gave him a scarf knitted by her own fair hands.

The fortunate result of Duroc's intrigues in Prussia, in 1799, encouraged Bonaparte to despatch him, in 1801, to Russia; where Alexander I. received him with that noble condescension so natural to this great and good prince. He succeeded at St. Petersburg in arranging the political and commercial difficulties and disagreements between France and Russia; but his proposal for a defensive alliance was declined.

An anecdote is related of his political campaign in the North, upon the barren banks of the Neva, which, in causing much entertainment to the inhabitants of the fertile banks of the Seine, has not a little displeased the military diplomatist.

Among Talleyrand's female agents sent to cajole Paul I. during the latter part of his reign, was a Madame Bonœil, whose real name is de F——. When this unfortunate prince was no more, most of the French male and female intriguers in Russia thought it necessary to shift their quarters, and to expect, on the territory of neutral Prussia, farther instructions from Paris, where and how to proceed. Madame Bonœil had removed to Königsberg. In the second week of May, 1801, when Duroc passed through that town for St. Petersburg, he visited this lady, according to the orders of Bonaparte, and obtained from her a list of the names of the principal persons who were inclined to be serviceable to France, and might be trusted by him upon the present occasion. By inattention or mistake she had mispelled the name of one of the most trusty and active adherents of Bonaparte; and Duroc, therefore, instead of addressing himself to the Polish Count de S——lz, went to the Polish Count de S——tz. This latter was as much flattered as surprised, upon seeing an aide-de-camp and envoy of the First Consul of France enter his apartments, seldom visited before but by usurers, gamesters and creditors; and on hearing the object of this visit, began to think either the envoy mad or himself dreaming. Understanding, however, that money would be of little consideration, if the point desired by the First Consul could be carried, he determined to take advantage of this fortunate hit, and invited Duroc to sup with him the same evening; when he promised him he should meet with persons who could do his business, provided his pecuniary resources were as ample as he had stated.

This Count de S———tz was one of the most extravagant and profligate subjects that Russia had acquired by the partition of Poland. After squandering away his own patrimony, he had ruined his mother and two sisters, and subsisted now entirely by gambling and borrowing. Among his associates, in similar circumstances with himself, was a Chevalier de Gausac, a French adventurer, pretending to be an emigrant from the vicinity of Toulouse. To him was communicated what had happened in the morning, and his advice was asked how to act in the evening. It was soon settled that de Gausac should be transformed into a Russian Count de W———, a nephew and confidential secretary of the Chancellor of the same name; and that one Caumartin, another French adventurer, who taught fencing at St. Petersburg, should act the part of Prince de M———, an aide-de-camp of the Emperor; and that all three together should strip Duroc, and share the spoil. At the appointed hour Bonaparte's agent arrived, and was completely the dupe of these adventurers, who plundered him of twelve hundred thousand livres—£50,000. Though not many days passed before he discovered the imposition, prudence prevented him from denouncing the impostors; and this blunder would have remained a secret between himself, Bonaparte and Talleyrand, had not the unusual expenses of Caumartin excited the suspicion of the Russian police minister, who soon discovered the source from which they had flowed. De Gauzac had the imprudence to return to this capital last spring, and is now shut up in the Temple, where he probably will be forgotten.

As this loss was more ascribed to the negligence of Madame Bonœil than to the mismanagement of Duroc, or his want of penetration, his reception at the Tuileries, though not so gracious as on his return from Berlin, nineteen months before, was, however, such as convinced him that if he had not increased, he had at the same time not lessened, the confidence of his master; and, indeed, shortly afterwards, Bonaparte created him first prefect of his palace, and procured him for a wife the only daughter of a rich Spanish banker. Rumour, however, says that Bonaparte was not quite disinterested when he commanded and concluded this match, and that the fortune of Madame Duroc has paid for the expensive supper of her husband with Count de S——tz at St. Petersburg.

LETTER II

PARIS, *August*, 1805.

MY LORD,—Though the Treaty of Luneville will pro bably soon be buried in the rubbish of the Treaty of Amiens, the influence of their parents in the Cabinet of St. Cloud is as great as ever: I say *their* parents, because the crafty ex-bishop Talleyrand, foreseeing the short existence of these bastard diplomatic acts, took care to compliment *the innocent* Joseph Bonaparte with a share in the parentage, although they were his own exclusive offspring.

Joseph Bonaparte, who in 1797, from an attorney's clerk at Ajaccio, in Corsica, was at once transformed into an ambassador to the Court of Rome, had hardly read a treaty, or seen a despatch written, before he was himself to conclude the one, and to dictate the other. Had he not been supported by able secretaries, government would soon have been convinced that it is as impossible to confer talents as it is easy to give places to men to whom Nature has refused parts, and on whom a scanty or neglected education has bestowed no improvements. Deep and reserved, like a true Italian, but vain and ambitious like his brothers, under the character of a statesman, he has only been the political puppet of Talleyrand. If he has sometimes been applauded upon the stages where he has been placed, he is also exposed to the hooting and hisses of the suffering multitude; while the minister pockets undisturbed all the entrance-money, and conceals his wickedness and art under the cloak of Joseph; which protects him besides against the anger and fury of Napoleon. No negotiation of any consequence is undertaken, no diplomatic arrangements are under consideration, but Joseph is always consulted, and Napoleon informed of the consultation. Hence none of Bonaparte's ministers have suffered less from his violence and resentment than Talleyrand, who, in the political department, governs him who governs France and Italy.

As early as 1800, Talleyrand determined to throw the odium of his own outrages against the law of nations, upon the brother of his master. Lucien Bonaparte was that year sent ambassador to Spain, but not sharing with the minister the large profits of his appointment, his diplomatic career was but short. Joseph is as greedy and as ravenous as Lucien, but not so frank or indiscreet. Whether he knew or not of Talleyrand's immense gain by the pacification at Luneville in February, 1801, he did not neglect his own individual interest. The day previous to the signature of this treaty, he despatched a courier to the rich army contractor Collot, acquainting him in secret of the issue of the negotiation, and ordering him at the same time to purchase six millions of livres—£250,000—in the stocks on his account. On Joseph's arrival at Paris, Collot sent him the state bonds for the sum ordered, together with a very polite letter; but though he waited on the grand pacificator several times afterwards, all admittance was refused, until a douceur of one million of livres—nearly £42,000—of Collot's private profit opened the door. In return, during the discussions between France and England in the summer of 1801, and in the spring of 1802, Collot was continued Joseph's private agent, and shared with his patron, within twelve months, a clear gain of thirty-two millions of livres.

Some of the secret articles of the Treaty of Luneville gave Austria, during the insurrection in Switzerland, in the autumn of 1802, an opportunity and a right to make representations against the interference of France; a circumstance which greatly displeased Bonaparte, who reproached Talleyrand for his want of foresight, and of having been outwitted by the Cabinet of Vienna. The minister, on the very next day, laid before his master the correspondence that had passed between him and Joseph Bonaparte, during the negotiation concerning these secret articles, which were found to have been entirely proposed and settled by

Joseph; who had been induced by his secretary and factotum (a creature of Talleyrand) to adopt sentiments for which that minister had been paid, according to report, six hundred thousand livres—£25,000. Several other tricks have in the same manner been played upon Joseph, who, notwithstanding, has the modesty to consider himself (much to the advantage and satisfaction of Talleyrand) the first statesman in Europe, and the good fortune to be thought so by his brother Napoleon.

When a rupture with England was apprehended, in the spring of 1803, Talleyrand never signed a despatch that was not previously communicated to, and approved by Joseph, before its contents were sanctioned by Napoleon. This precaution chiefly continued him in place when Lord Whitworth left this capital, a departure that incensed Napoleon to such a degree, that he entirely forgot both the dignity of his rank amidst his generals, a becoming deportment to the members of the diplomatic corps, and his duty to his mother and brothers, who all more or less experienced the effects of his violent passions. He thus accosted Talleyrand, who purposely arrived late at his circle: "Well! the English ambassador is gone; and we must again go to war. Were my generals as great fools as some of my ministers, I should despair indeed of the issue of my contest with these insolent islanders. Many believe that had I been more ably supported in my Cabinet, I should not have been under the necessity of taking the field, as a rupture might have been prevented." "Such, Citizen First Consul!" answered the trembling and bowing minister, "is not the opinion of the counsellor of state, Citizen Joseph Bonaparte."—"Well, then," said Napoleon, as recollecting himself, " England wishes for war, and she shall suffer for it. This shall be a war of extermination, depend upon it." The name of Joseph alone moderated Napoleon's fury, and changed its object. It is with him what the harp of David was with Saul. Talleyrand knows it, and is no loser by that knowledge. I must, however, in justice say that, had Bonaparte followed his minister's advice, and suffered himself to be entirely guided by his counsel, all hostilities with England at that time might have been avoided; her government would have been lulled into security by the cession of Malta and some commercial regulations, and her future conquest, during a time of peace, have been attempted upon plans duly organized, that might have ensured success. He never ceased to repeat, " Citizen First Consul! some few years longer peace with Great Britain, and the *Te Deums* of modern Britons for the conquest and possession of Malta, will be considered by their children as the funeral hymns of their liberty and independence."

It was upon this memorable occasion of Lord Whitworth's departure, that Bonaparte is known to have betrayed the most outrageous acts of passion; he rudely forced his mother from his closet, and forbade his own sisters to approach his person; he confined Madame Bonaparte for several hours to her chamber; he dismissed favourite generals; treated with ignominy members of his council of state; and towards his physician, secretaries and principal attendants, he committed unbecoming and disgraceful marks of personal outrage. I have heard it affirmed that though her husband, when shutting her up in her dressing-room, put the key in his pocket, Madame Napoleon found means to resent the ungallant behaviour of her spouse, with the assistance of Madame Remusat.

LETTER III

PARIS, *August*, 1803.

MY LORD,—No act of Bonaparte's government has occasioned so many, so opposite, and so violent debates, among the remnants of revolutionary factions comprising his senate and council of state, as the introduction and execution of the religious concordat signed with the Pope. Joseph was here again the ostensible negotiator, though he, on this as well as on former occasions, concluded nothing that had not been prepared and digested by Talleyrand.

Bonaparte does not in general pay much attention to the opinions of others when they do not agree with his own views and interests, or coincide with his plans of reform or innovation; but having in his public career professed himself by turns an atheist and an infidel, the worshipper of Christ and of Mahomet, he could not decently silence those who, after deserting or denying the God of their forefathers and of their youth, continued constant and firm in their apostasy. Of those who deliberated concerning the restoration or exclusion of Christianity, and the acceptance or rejection of the concordat, Fouché, François de

Nantz, Rœderer and Sieyes were for the religion of Nature; Volney, Real, Chaptal, Bourrienne, and Lucien Bonaparte for atheism, and Portalis, Grégoire, Cambacères, Le Brun, Talleyrand, Joseph and Napoleon Bonaparte for Christianity. Besides the sentiments of these confidential counsellors, upwards of two hundred memoirs, for or against the Christian religion, were presented to the First Consul by uninvited and volunteer counsellors; all differing as much from each other as the members of his own privy council.

Many persons do Madame Bonaparte, the mother, the honour of supposing that to her assiduous representations is principally owing the recall of the priests, and the restoration of the altars of Christ. She certainly is the most devout, or rather the most superstitious of her family, and of her name; but had not Talleyrand and Portalis previously convinced Napoleon of the policy of re-establishing a religion which, for fourteen centuries, had preserved the throne of the Bourbons from the machinations ot republicans and other conspirators against monarchy, it is very probable that her representations would have been as ineffective as her piety or her prayers. So long ago as 1796 she implored the mercy of Napoleon for the Roman Catholics in Italy; and entreated him to spare the Pope and the papal territory, at the very time that his soldiers were laying waste and ravaging the legacy of Bologna and of Ravenna, both incorporated with his new-formed Cisalpine Republic; where one of his first acts of sovereignty, in the name of the then sovereign people, was the confiscation of Church lands and the sale of the estates of the clergy.

Of the prelates who with Joseph Bonaparte signed the concordat, the Cardinal Gonsalvi and the Bishop Bernier have, by their labours and intrigues, not a little contributed to the present Church establishment in this country; and to them Napoleon is much indebted for the intrusion of the Bonaparte dynasty among the houses of sovereign princes. The former, intended from his youth for the Church, sees neither honour in this world, nor hopes for any blessing in the next, but exclusively from its bosom and its doctrine. With capacity to figure as a country curate, he occupies the post of the chief secretary of state to the Pope; and though nearly of the same age, but of a much weaker constitution than his sovereign, he was ambitious enough to demand Bonaparte's promise of succeeding to the papal see, and weak and wicked enough to wish and expect to survive a benefactor of a calmer mind and better health than himself. It was he who encouraged Bonaparte to require the presence of Pius VII. in France, and who persuaded this weak pontiff to undertake a journey that has caused so much scandal among the truly faithful; and which, should ever Austria regain its former supremacy in Italy, will send the present Pope to end his days in a convent, and make the successors of St. Peter what this Apostle was himself, a bishop of Rome, and nothing more.

Bernier was a curate in La Vendée before the Revolution, and one of those priests who lighted the torch of civil war in that unfortunate country, under pretence of defending the throne of his King and the altars of his God. He not only possessed great popularity among the lower classes, but acquired so far the confidence of the Vendean chiefs that he was appointed one of the supreme and directing council of the Royalists and Chouans. Even so late as the summer of 1799 he continued not only unsuspected, but trusted by the insurgents in the Western departments. In the winter, however, of the same year he had been gained over by Bonaparte's emissaries, and was seen at his levées in the Tuileries. It is stated that General Brune made him renounce his former principles, desert his former companions, and betray to the then First Consul of the French Republic the secrets of the friends of lawful monarchy, of the faithful subjects of Louis XVIII. His perfidy has been rewarded with one hundred and fifty thousand livres in ready money, with the see of Orleans, and with a promise of a cardinal's hat. He has also, with the Cardinals Gonsalvi, Caprara, Fesch, Cambacères and Mauri, Bonaparte's promise, and, *of course*, the expectation of the Roman tiara. He was one of the prelates who officiated at the late coronation, and is now confided in as a person who has too far committed himself with his legitimate prince, and whose past treachery therefore answers for his future fidelity.

This religious concordat of the 10th September, 1801, as well as all other constitutional codes emanating from revolutionary authorities, proscribes even in protecting. The professors and protectors of the religion of universal peace, benevolence and forgiveness banish in this concordat from France for ever the Cardinals Rohan and Montmorency, and the Bishop of Arras, whose dutiful attachment to their unfortunate prince would, in better times and in a more just and generous nation, have been recompensed with distinctions, and honoured even by magnanimous foes.

When Madame Napoleon was informed by her husband of the *necessity* of choosing her almoner and chaplain, and of attending regularly the Mass, she first fell a-laughing, taking it merely for a joke; the serious and severe looks, and the harsh and threatening expressions of the First Consul soon, however, convinced her how much she was mistaken. To evince her repentance, she on the very next day attended her mother-in-law to church, who was highly edified by the sudden and religious turn of her daughter, and did not fail to ascribe to the efficacious interference of one of her favourite saints this conversion of a profane sinner. But Napoleon was not the dupe of this church-going mummery of his wife, whom he ordered his spies to watch; these were unfortunate enough to discover that she went to the Mass more to fulfil her appointments with her lovers than to pray to her Saviour; and that even by the side of her mother she read *billets-doux* and love-letters when that pious lady supposed that she read her prayers because her eyes were fixed upon her breviary. Without relating to anyone this discovery of his Josephine's frailties, Napoleon, after a violent connubial fracas and reprimand, and after a solitary confinement of her for six days, gave immediate orders to have the chapels of the Tuileries and of St. Cloud repaired; and until these were ready, Cardinal Cambacères and Bernier, by turns, said the Mass in her private apartments; where none but selected favourites or favoured courtiers were admitted. Madame Napoleon now never neglects the Mass, but if not accompanied by her husband is escorted by a guard of *honour*, among whom she knows that he has several agents watching her motions and her very looks.

In the month of June, 1803, I dined with Viscount de Segur, and Joseph and Lucien Bonaparte were among the guests. The latter jocosely remarked with what facility the French Christians had suffered themselves to be hunted in and out of their temples, according to the fanaticism or policy of their rulers; which he adduced as a proof of the great progress of philosophy and *toleration* in France. A young officer of the party, Jacquemont, a relation of the former husband of the present Madame Lucien, observed that he thought it rather an evidence of the indifference of the French people to all religion; the consequence of the great havoc the tenets of infidelity and of atheism had made among the flocks of the faithful. This was again denied by Bonaparte's aide-de-camp, Savary, who observed that, had this been the case, the First Consul (who certainly was as well acquainted with the *religious spirit* of Frenchmen as anybody else) would not have taken the trouble to conclude a religious concordat, nor have been at the expense of providing for the clergy. To this assertion Joseph nodded an assent. When the dinner was over, de Segur took me to a window, expressing his uneasiness at what he called the imprudence of Jacquemont, who, he apprehended, from Joseph's silence and manner, would not escape punishment for having indirectly blamed both the restorer of religion and his plenipotentiary. These apprehensions were justified. On the next day Jacquemont received orders to join the colonial dépôt at Havre; but refusing to obey by giving in his resignation as a captain, he was arrested, shut up in the Temple, and afterwards transported to Cayenne or Madagascar. His relatives and friends are still ignorant whether he is dead or alive, and what is or has been his place of exile. To a petition presented by Jacquemont's sister, Madame de Veaux, Joseph answered "that he never interfered with the acts of the *haute* police of his brother Napoleon's government, being well convinced both of its *justice* and *moderation.*"

LETTER IV

PARIS, *August*, 1805.

MY LORD,—That Bonaparte had, as far back as February, 1803 (when the King of Prussia proposed to Louis XVIII. the formal renunciation of his hereditary rights in favour of the First Consul), determined to assume the rank and title, with the power of a sovereign, nobody can doubt. Had it not been for the war with England, he would in the spring of that year, or twelve months earlier, have proclaimed himself Emperor of the French, and probably would have been acknowledged as such by all other princes To a man so vain and so impatient, so accustomed to command and to intimidate, this suspension of his favourite plan was a considerable disappointment and not a little increased his bitter and irreconcilable hatred of Great Britain.

Here. as well as in foreign countries, the multitude pay homage only to Napoleon's uninterrupted prosperity: without penetrating or considering whether it be the consequence of chance or of well-digested plans; whether he owes his successes to his own merit, or to a blind fortune.

He asserted in his speech to the constitutional authorities, immediately after hostilities had commenced with England, *that the war would be of short duration*, and he firmly believed what he said. Had he by his gunboats, or by his intrigues or threats, been enabled to extort a second edition of the Peace of Amiens, after a warfare of some few months, all mouths would have been ready to exclaim, " Oh, the illustrious warrior! Oh, the profound politician!" Now, after three ineffectual campaigns on the coast, when the extravagance and ambition of our government have extended the contagion of war over the Continent; when both our direct offers of peace, and the negotiations and mediations of our allies, have been declined by, or proved unavailing with, the Cabinet of St. James', the inconsistency, the ignorance, and the littleness of the fortunate great man seem to be not more remembered than the outrages and encroachments that have provoked Austria and Russia to take the field. Should he continue victorious, and be in a position to dictate another Peace of Luneville, which probably would be followed by another pacific overture to or from England, mankind will again be ready to call out, "Oh, the illustrious warrior! Oh, the profound politician! He foresaw, in his wisdom, that a Continental war was necessary to terrify or to subdue his maritime foe; that a peace with England could only be obtained in Germany; and that this war must be excited by extending the power of France on the other side of the Alps. Hence his coronation as a King of Italy; hence his incorporation of Parma and Genoa with France; and hence his donation of Piombino and Lucca to his brother-in-law, Bacchiochi!" Nowhere in history have I read of men of sense being so easily led astray, as in our times, by confounding fortuitous events with consequences resulting from preconcerted plans and well-organized designs.

Only rogues can disseminate and fools believe that the disgrace of Moreau, and the execution of the Duke of Enghien, of Pichegru, and Georges, were necessary as footsteps to Bonaparte's imperial throne; and that without the treachery of Mehée de la Touche, and the conspiracy he pretended to have discovered France would still have been ruled by a First Consul. It is indeed true that this plot is to be counted (as the imbecility of Melas, which lost the battle of Marengo) among those accidents presenting themselves apropos to serve the favourite of fortune in his ambitious views; but without it, he would equally have been hailed an Emperor of the French in May, 1804. When he came from the coast, in the preceding winter, and was convinced of the impossibility of making any impression on the British Islands with his flotilla, he convoked his confidential senators, who then, with Talleyrand, settled the Senatûs Consultum which appeared five months afterwards. Mehée's correspondence with Mr. Drake was then known to him; but he and the minister of police were both unacquainted with the residence and arrival of Pichegru and Georges in France, and of their connection with Moreau; the particulars of which were first disclosed to them in the February following, when Bonaparte had been absent from his army of England six weeks. The assumption of the imperial dignity procured him another decent opportunity of offering his olive-branch to those who had caused his *laurels to wither*, and by whom, notwithstanding his abuse, calumnies and menaces, he would have been more proud to be saluted Emperor, than by all other nations upon the Continent. His vanity, interest and policy, all required this last degree of supremacy and elevation at that period.

Bonaparte had so well penetrated the weak side of Moreau's character that, although he could not avoid doing justice to this general's military talents and exploits, he neither esteemed him as a citizen nor dreaded him as a rival. Moreau possessed great popularity; but so did Dumourier and Pichegru before him: and yet neither of them had found adherents enough to shake those republican governments with which they avowed themselves openly discontented, and against which they secretly plotted. I heard Talleyrand say, at Madame de Montlausier's, in the presence of fifty persons, "Napoleon Bonaparte had never anything to apprehend from General Moreau, and from his popularity, even at the head of an army. Dumourier, too, was at the head of an army when he revolted against the National Convention; but had he not saved himself by flight his own troops would have delivered him up to be punished as a traitor. *Moreau, and his popularity, could only be dangerous to the Bonaparte dynasty were he to survive Napoleon, had not this Emperor wisely averted this danger.*" From this *official* declaration of Napoleon's confidential minister, in a society of known anti-imperialists, I draw the conclusion that Moreau will never more, during the present reign, return to France. How very feeble, and how badly advised must this general have been, when, after his condemnation to two years' imprisonment, he accepted of a perpetual exile, and renounced all hopes of ever again entering his own country. In the Temple, or in any other prison, if he had submitted to the sentence pronounced against him, he would have caused Bonaparte more uneasiness than when at liberty, and been more a point of rally to his adherents and friends than when at his palace of Grosbois, because compassion and pity must have invigorated and sharpened their feelings.

If report be true, however, he did not voluntarily exchange imprisonment for exile; racks were shown him; and by the act of banishment was placed a poisonous draught. This report gains considerable credit when it is remembered that, immediately after his condemnation, Moreau furnished his apartments in the Temple in a handsome manner, so as to be lodged well, it not comfortably, with his wife and child, whom, it is said, he was not permitted to see before he had accepted of Bonaparte's proposal of transportation.

It may be objected to this supposition that the man in power, who did not care about the barefaced murder of the Duke of Enghien, and the secret destruction of Pichegru, could neither much hesitate, nor be very conscientious about adding Moreau to the number of his victims. True, but the assassin in authority is also generally a politician. The untimely end of the Duke of Enghien and of Pichegru was certainly lamented and deplored by the great majority of the French people; but though they had many who pitied their fate, but few had any relative interest to avenge it; whilst in the assassination of Moreau, every general, every officer, and every soldier of his former army, might have read the destiny reserved for himself by that chieftain, who did not conceal his preference of those who had fought under him in Italy and Egypt, and his mistrust and jealousy of those who had vanquished under Moreau in Germany; numbers of whom had already perished at St. Domingo, or in the other colonies, or were dispersed in separate and distant garrisons of the mother country. It has been calculated that of eighty-four generals who made, under Moreau, the campaign of 1800, and who survived the Peace of Luneville, sixteen had been killed or died at St. Domingo, four at Guadeloupe, ten in Cayenne, nine at Île de France, and eleven at l'Île Réunion and in Madagascar. The *mortality* among the officers and men has been in proportion.

An anecdote is related of Pichegru, which does honour to the memory of that unfortunate general. Fouché paid him a visit in prison the day before his death, and offered him "Bonaparte's commission as a field-marshal, and a diploma as a grand officer of the Legion of Honour, provided he would turn informer against Moreau, of whose treachery against himself in 1797 he was reminded. On the other hand, he was informed that, in consequence of his former denials, if he persisted in his refractory conduct, he should never more appear before any judge, but that the affairs of state and the safety of the country required that he should be privately despatched in his gaol." "So," answered this virtuous and indignant warrior, "you will only spare my life upon condition that I prove myself unworthy to live. As this is the case, my choice is made without hesitation; I am prepared to become your victim, but I will never be numbered among your accomplices. Call in your executioners; I am ready to die as I have lived, a man of honour, and an irreproachable citizen." Within twenty-four hours after this answer, Pichegru was no more.

That the Duke of Enghien was shot on the night of the 21st of March, 1804, in the wood or in the ditch of the castle of Vincennes, is admitted even by government; but who really were his assassins is still unknown. Some assert that he was shot by the grenadiers of Bonaparte's Italian guard; others say, by a detachment of the Gendarmes d'Élite; and others again, that the men of both these corps refused to fire, and that General Murat, hearing the troops murmur, and fearing their mutiny, was himself the executioner of this young and innocent prince of the House of Bourbon, by riding up to him and blowing out his brains with a pistol. Certain it is that Murat was the first, and Louis Bonaparte the second in command, on this dreadful occasion.

LETTER V

Paris, *August*, 1805.

My Lord,—Thanks to Talleyrand's *political* emigration, our government has never been in ignorance of the characters and foibles of the leading members among the emigrants in England. Otto, however, finished their picture, but added some new groups to those delineated by his predecessor. It was according to his plan that the expedition of Mehée de la Touche was undertaken, and it was in following his instructions that the campaign of this traitor succeeded so well in Great Britain.

Under the ministry of Vergennes, of Montmorin, and of Delessart, Mehée had been employed as a spy in Russia, Sweden and Poland, and acquitted himself perfectly to the satisfaction of his masters. By some accident or other, Delessart discovered, however, in December, 1791, that he had, while pocketing the money of the Cabinet of Versailles, sold its secrets to the Cabinet of St. Petersburg. He, of course, was no longer trusted as a spy, and therefore turned a Jacobin, and announced himself to Brissot as a persecuted patriot. All the calumnies against this minister

LETTER V

PARIS, *August* 1805.

MY LORD,—Thanks to Talleyrand's *political* emigration, our government has never been in ignorance of the characters and foibles of the leading members among the emigrants in England. Otto, however, finished their picture, but added some new features to those delineated by his predecessor. It was according to his plan that the expedition of Mehée de la Touche was undertaken, and it was in following his instructions that the cunning of this traitor succeeded so well in imposing on Drake.

Under the ministry of Vergennes, of Montmorin, and of Delessart, Mehée had been employed as a spy in Russia, Sweden and Poland, and acquitted himself perfectly to the satisfaction of his masters. By some accident or other, Delessart discovered, however, in December 1791, that he had, while pocketing the money of the Cabinet of Versailles, sold its secrets to the Cabinet of St. Petersburg. He, of course, was no longer trusted as a spy, and therefore turned a Jacobin, and announced himself to Brissot as a persecuted patriot. All the calumnies against this minister

LETTER V

PARIS, *August*, 1805.

MY LORD,—Thanks to Talleyrand's *political* emigration, our government has never been in ignorance of the characters and foibles of the leading members among the emigrants in England. Otto, however, finished their picture, but added some new groups to those delineated by his predecessor. It was according to his plan that the expedition of Mehée de la Touche was undertaken, and it was in following his instructions that the campaign of this traitor succeeded so well in Great Britain.

Under the ministry of Vergennes, of Montmorin, and of Delessart, Mehée had been employed as a spy in Russia, Sweden and Poland, and acquitted himself perfectly to the satisfaction of his masters. By some accident or other, Delessart discovered, however, in December, 1791, that he had, while pocketing the money of the Cabinet of Versailles, sold its secrets to the Cabinet of St. Petersburg. He, of course, was no longer trusted as a spy, and therefore turned a Jacobin, and announced himself to Brissot as a persecuted patriot. All the calumnies against this minister

LETTER V.

PARIS, August 1805.

MY LORD,—Thanks to Talleyrand's political emigration, our government has never been in ignorance of the characters and foibles of the leading members among the emigrants in England. Otto, however, finished their picture, but added ~~several~~ ~~~~ those delineated by his predecessor. It was ~~~~ plan that the expedition of Mehée de la Touche was ~~~~, and it was in ~~~~ his instructions that the campaign of this traitor ~~~~.

Under the ministry of Vergennes, of Montmorin, and of Delessart, Mehée had been employed as a spy in Russia, Sweden and Poland, and acquitted himself perfectly to the satisfaction of his masters. By some or other, Delessart discovered however, in December, 1791, that he had, while pocketing the money of the Cabinet of Versailles, sold its secrets to the Cabinet of St. Petersburg. He, of course, was no longer trusted as a spy, and therefore turned a Jacobin, and announced himself to Brissot as a persecuted patriot. All the calumnies against this minister

LETTER V

PARIS, August, 1815.

MY LORD,—Thanks to Talleyrand's *political* emigration, our government has never been in ignorance of the characters and foibles of the leading members among the emigrants in England. Otto, however, finished their picture, but added some new traits to those delineated by his predecessors. It was, according to his plan, that the expedition of ⸺ ⸺ ⸺ ⸺ ⸺ was undertaken, and it was on following his instructions that the espionage of this ⸺ ⸺ ⸺ ⸺ ⸺ ⸺ ⸺ ⸺ ⸺ ⸺ ⸺.

Under the name of the Count of Montmorin, and of Descart, Mehée de ⸺ ⸺ ⸺ employed as a spy in Russia, Sweden and Poland, and acquitted himself perfectly to the satisfaction of his masters. By some accident or other, Delessart discovered, however, in the month of ⸺, 1791, that he had, while pocketing the money of the Cabinet of Versailles, sold its secrets to the Cabinet of St. Petersburg. He, of course, was no longer trusted as a spy, and therefore turned a Jacobin, and announced himself to Brissot as a persecuted patriot. All the calumnies against this minister

in Brissot's daily paper, *Le Patriote François*, during January, February and March, 1792, were the productions of Mehée's malicious heart and able pen. Even after they had sent Delessart a state prisoner to Orleans, his inveteracy continued, and in September the same year he went to Versailles to enjoy the sight of the murder of his former master. Some go so far as to say that the assassins were headed by this monster, who aggravated cruelty by insult, and informed the dying minister of the hands that stabbed him, and to whom he was indebted for a premature death.

To these and other infamous and barbarous deeds, Talleyrand was not a stranger when he made Mehée his secret agent, and entrusted him with the mission to England. He took, therefore, such steps that neither his confidence could be betrayed, nor his money squandered. Mehée had instructions how to proceed in Great Britain, but he was ignorant of the object government had in view by his mission; and though large sums were promised if successful, and if he gave satisfaction by his zeal and discretion, the money advanced him was a mere trifle, and barely sufficient to keep him from want. He was therefore really distressed, when he fixed upon some necessitous and greedy emigrants for his instruments to play on the credulity of the English ministers in some of their unguarded moments. Their generosity in forbearing to avenge upon the deluded French exiles the slur attempted to be thrown upon their official capacity, and the ridicule intended to be cast on their private characters, has been much approved and admired here by all liberal-minded persons; but it has also much disappointed Bonaparte and Talleyrand, who expected to see these emigrants driven from the only asylum which hospitality has not refused to their misfortunes and misery.

Mehée had been promised by Talleyrand double the amount of the sums which he could swindle from your government· but though he did more mischief to your country than was expected in this, and though he proved that he had pocketed upwards of ten thousand English guineas, the wages of his infamy, when he hinted about the recompense he expected here, Durant, Talleyrand's *chef du bureau*, advised him, *as a friend*, not to remind the minister of his presence in France, as Bonaparte never pardoned a Septembrizer, and the English guineas he possessed might be claimed and seized as national property, to compensate some of the sufferers by the *unprovoked* war with England. In vain did he address himself to his fellow-labourer in revolutionary plots, the counsellor of state, Real, who had been the intermedium between him and Talleyrand, when he was first enlisted among the secret agents; instead of receiving money he heard threats, and, therefore, with as good grace as he could, he made the best of his disappointment; he sported a carriage, kept a mistress, went to gambling-houses, and is now in a fair way to be reduced to the *status quo* before his brilliant exploits in Great Britain.

Real, besides the place of a counsellor of state, occupies also the office of a director of the internal police. Having some difference with my landlord, I was summoned to appear before him at the prefecture of the police. My friend, M. de Sab—r, formerly a counsellor of the parliament at Rouen, happened to be with me when the summons was delivered, and offered to accompany me, being acquainted with Real. Though thirty persons were waiting in the ante-chamber at our arrival, no sooner was my friend's name announced than we were admitted, and I obtained not only *more justice* than I expected, or dared to claim, but an invitation to Madame Real's tea party the same evening. This *justice* and this politeness surprised me, until my friend showed me an act of forgery in his possession, committed by Real in 1788, when an advocate of the parliament, and for which the humanity of my friend alone prevented him from being struck off the rolls and otherwise punished.

As I conceived my usual societies and coteries could not approve my attendance at the house of such a personage, I was intent upon sending an apology to Madame Real. My friend, however, assured me that I should meet in her saloon persons of all classes and of all ranks, and many I little expected to see associating together. I went late, and found the assembly very numerous: at the upper part of the hall were seated Princesses Joseph and Louis Bonaparte, with Madame Fouché, Madame Rœderer, the *ci-devant* Duchess de Fleury, and Marchioness de Clermont. They were conversing with M. Mathew de Montmorency, the contractor (a *ci-devant* lackey) Collot, the *ci-devant* Duke Fitzjames, and the legislator Martin, a *ci-devant* porter: several groups in the several apartments were composed of a similar heterogeneous mixture of *ci-devant* nobles and *ci-devant* valets, of *ci-devant* princesses, marchionesses, countesses and baronesses, and of *ci-devant* chambermaids, mistresses and *poissardes*. Round a gambling table, by the side of the *ci-devant* Bishop of Autun, Talleyrand, sat Madame Hounguenin, whose husband, a *ci-devant* shoeblack, has, by the purchase of *national* property, made a fortune of nine millions of livres — £375,000. Opposite them were seated the *ci-devant* Prince de Chalais, and the present Prince Cambacères, with the *ci-devant* Countess de Beauvais, and Madame Fauve, the daughter of a fishwoman, and the wife of a tribune, a *ci-devant* barber. In another room, the Bavarian minister Cetto was conferring with the spy Mehée de la Touche; but observed at a distance by Fouché's secretary, Desmarets, the son of a tailor at Fontainebleau, and for years a known police spy. When I was just going to retire, the handsome Madame Gillot, and her sister Madame de Soubray, joined me. You have perhaps known them in England, where, before their marriage, they resided for five years with their parents, the Marquis and Marchioness de Courtin; and were often admired by the loungers in Bond Street. The one married for money, Gillot, a *ci-devant* drummer in the French Guard, but who, since the Revolution, has, as a general, made a large fortune; and the other united herself to a *ci-devant* abbé, from love; but both are now divorced from their husbands, who passed them without any notice while they were chatting with me. I was handing Madame Gillot to her carriage, when, from the staircase, Madame de Soubray called to us not to quit her, as she was pursued by a man whom she detested, and wished to avoid. We had hardly turned round, when Mehée offered her his arm, and she exclaimed with indignation, "How dare you, infamous wretch, approach me, when I have forbidden you ever to speak to me! Had you been reduced to become a highwayman, or a housebreaker, I might have pitied your infamy — but a spy is a villain who aggravates guilt by cowardice and baseness, and can inspire no noble soul with any other sentiment but abhorrence, and the most sovereign contempt.' Without being disconcerted, Mehée silently returned to the company, amidst bursts of laughter from fifty servants, and as many masters, waiting for their carriages. M. de Cetto was among the latter, but, though we all fixed our eyes steadfastly upon him, no alteration could be seen on his diplomatic countenance: his face must surely be made of brass, or his heart of marble.

LETTER VI

PARIS, *August*, 1805.

MY LORD,—The day on which Madame Napoleon Bonaparte was elected an Empress of the French by the constitutional authorities of her husband's empire, was, contradictory as it may seem, one of the most uncomfortable in her life. After the show and ceremony of the audience and of the drawing-room were over, she passed it entirely in tears, in her library, where her husband shut her up and confined her.

The discipline of the Court of St. Cloud is as singular as its composition is unique. It is, by the regulation of Napoleon, entirely military. From the Empress to her lowest chambermaid, from the Emperor's first aide-de-camp down to his youngest page, any slight offence or negligence is punished with confinement, either public or private. In the former case the culprits are shut up in their own apartments, but in the latter they are ordered into one of the small rooms, constructed in the dark galleries at the Tuileries and St. Cloud, near the kitchens, where they are guarded day and night by sentries, who answer for their persons, and that nobody visits them.

When, on the 28th of March, 1804, the Senate had determined on *offering* Bonaparte the imperial dignity, he immediately gave his wife full powers, with order to form her household of persons who, from birth and from their principles, might be worthy, and could be trusted to encompass the imperial couple. She consulted Madame Remusat, who in her turn consulted her friend de Segur, who also consulted his *bonne amie*, Madame de Montbrune. This lady determined that if Bonaparte and his wife were desirous to be served, or waited on, by persons above them by ancestry and honour, they should pay liberally for such sacrifices. She was not therefore idle, but wishing to profit herself by the pride of upstart vanity, she had at first merely reconnoitred the ground, or made distant overtures to those families of the ancient French nobility who had been ruined by the Revolution, and whose minds she expected to have found on a level with their circumstances. These, however, either suspecting her intent and her views, or preferring honest poverty to degrading and disgraceful splendour, had started objections which she was not prepared to encounter. Thus the time passed away; and when, on the 18th of the following May, the Senate proclaimed Napoleon Bonaparte Emperor of the French, not a chamberlain was ready to attend him, nor a maid-of-honour to wait on his wife.

On the morning of the 20th May, the day fixed for the constitutional *republican* authorities to present their homage as *subjects*, Napoleon asked his Josephine who were the persons, of both sexes, she had engaged, according to his *carte blanche* given her, as necessary and as unavoidable decorations of the drawing-room of an Emperor and Empress, as thrones and as canopies of state. She referred him to Madame Remusat, who, though but half-dressed, was instantly ordered to appear before him. This lady avowed that his grand master of the ceremonies, de Segur, had been entrusted by her with the whole arrangement, but that she feared that he had not yet been able to complete the full establishment of the Imperial Court. The aide-de-camp Rapp was then despatched after de Segur, who, as usual, presented himself smiling and cringing. "Give me the list," said Napoleon, "of the ladies and gentlemen you have no doubt engaged for our household."—"May it please your Majesty," answered de Segur (trembling with fear), "I humbly supposed that they were not requisite before the day of your Majesty's coronation."—"You supposed!" retorted Napoleon. "How dare you suppose differently from our commands? Is the Emperor of the Great Nation not to be encompassed with a more numerous retinue, or with more lustre, than a First Consul? Do you not see the immense difference between the sovereign monarch of an empire, and the citizen chief magistrate of a commonwealth? Are there not starving nobles in my empire enough to furnish all the Courts in Europe with attendants, courtiers and valets? Do you not believe that with a nod, with a single nod, I might have them all prostrated before my throne? What can, then, have occasioned this impertinent delay?"—"Sire!" answered de Segur, "it is not the want of numbers, but the difficulty of the choice among them. I will never recommend a single individual upon whom I cannot depend; or who, on some future day, may expose me to the greatest of all evils, the displeasure of my Prince."—"But," continued Napoleon, "what is to be done to-day that I may augment the number of my suite, and by it impose upon the gaping multitude and the attending deputations?"—"Command," said de Segur, "all the officers or your Majesty's staff, and of the staff of the Governor of Paris, General Murat, to surround your Majesty's sacred person, and order them to accoutre themselves in the most shining and splendid manner possible. The presence of so many military men will also, in a political point of view, be useful. It will lessen the pretensions of the constituted authorities, by telling them indirectly it is not to your Senatus Consultum, to your decrees, or to your votes, that I am indebted for my present sovereignty: I owe it exclusively to my own merit and valour, and to the valour of my brave officers and men, to whose arms I trust more than to your counsels."

This advice obtained Napoleon's entire approbation, and was followed. De Segur was permitted to retire, but when Madame Remusat made a curtsey also to leave the room, she was stopped with his terrible *aux arrets!* and left under the care and responsibility of his aide-de-camp, Le Brun, who saw her safe into her room, at the door of which he placed two grenadiers. Napoleon then went out, ordering his wife, at her peril, to be in time, ready and brilliantly dressed, for the drawing-room.

Dreading the consequences of her husband's wrath, Madame Napoleon was not only punctual, but so elegantly and tastefully decorated with jewels and ornaments that even those of her enemies or rivals who refused her beauty, honour and virtue, allowed her taste and dignity. She thought that even in the regards of Napoleon she read a tacit approbation. When all the troublesome bustle of the morning was gone through, and when senators, legislators, tribunes, and prefects had complimented her as a model of female perfection, on a signal from her husband she accompanied him in silence through six different apartments before he came to her library, where he surlily ordered her to enter and to remain until further orders. "What have I done, Sire! to deserve such treatment?" exclaimed she, trembling.—"If," answered Napoleon, "Madame Remusat, your favourite, has made a fool of you, this is only to teach you that you shall not make a fool of me. Had not de Segur—fortunately for him—had the ingenuity to extricate us from the dilemma into which my confidence and dependence on you had brought me, I should have made a fine figure indeed on the first day of my Emperorship. —Have patience, Madam; you have plenty of books to divert you, but you must remain where you are until I am inclined to release you." So saying, Napoleon locked the door and put the key in his pocket.

It was near two o'clock in the afternoon when she was thus shut up. Remembering the recent flattery of her courtiers, and comparing it with the unfeeling treatment of her husband, she found herself so much the more unfortunate, as the expressions of the former were regarded by her as praise due to her merit, while the unkindness of the latter was unavailingly resented as the undeserved oppression of a capricious despot.

Business, or perhaps malice, made Napoleon forget to send her any dinner; and when, at eight o'clock, his brothers and sisters came according to invitation to take tea, he said coldly, " Apropos, I forgot it. My wife has not dined yet; she is busy, I suppose, in her philosophical meditations in her study." Madame Louis Bonaparte, her daughter, flew directly towards the study, and her mother could scarcely, for her tears, inform her that she was a prisoner, and that her husband was her gaoler. "Oh, Sire!" said Madame Louis, returning, "even this remarkable day is a day of mourning for my poor mother!"—"She deserves worse," answered Napoleon, "but, for your sake, she shall be released; here is the key, let her out."

Madame Napoleon was, however, not in a situation to wish to appear before her envious brothers and sisters-in-law. Her eyes were so swollen with crying that she could hardly see; and her tears had stained those imperial robes which the unthinking and inconsiderate no doubt believed a certain preservative against sorrow and affliction. At nine o'clock, however, another aide-de-camp of her husband presented himself, and gave her the choice either to accompany him back to the study or to join the family party of the Bonapartes.

In deploring her mother's situation, Madame Louis Bonaparte informed her former governess, Madame Cam—n, of these particulars, which I heard her relate at Madame de M——r's, almost verbatim as I report them to you. Such, and other scenes nearly of the same description, are neither rare nor singular, in the most singular Court that ever existed in *civilized* Europe.

LETTER VII

Paris, *August*, 1805.

My Lord,—Though government suffer a religious, or, rather, anti-religious liberty of the Press, the authors who libel or ridicule the Christian, particularly the Roman Catholic, religion, are excluded from all prospect of advancement, or, if in place, are not trusted or liked. Cardinal Caprara, the nuncio of the Pope, proposed last year, in a long memorial, the same severe restrictions on the discussions or publications in religious matters as were already ordered in those concerning politics. But both Bonaparte and his minister in the affairs of the Church, Portalis, refused the introduction of what they called a tyranny on the conscience. Caprara then addressed himself to the ex-Bishop Talleyrand, who on this occasion was more explicit than he generally is. "Bonaparte," said he, "rules not only over a fickle, but a gossiping (*bavard*) people, whom he has prudently forbidden all conversation and writing concerning government or affairs of state. They would soon (accustomed as they are, since the Revolution, to verbal and written debates) be tired of talking about fine weather or about the opera. To occupy them and their attention, some ample subject of diversion was necessary, and religion was surrendered to them at discretion; because, enlightened as the world now is, even atheists or Christian fanatics can do but little harm to society. They may spend rivers of ink, but they will be unable to shed a drop of blood."—"True," answered the Cardinal, "but only to a certain degree. The licentiousness of the Press, with regard to religious matters, does it not also furnish infidelity with new arms to injure the faith? and have not the horrors from which France has just escaped proved the danger and evil consequences of irreligion, and the necessity of encouraging and protecting Christianity? By the recall of the clergy, and by the religious concordat, Bonaparte has shown himself convinced of this truth."—"So he is," interrupted Talleyrand; "but he abhors intoleration and persecution" (not in politics). "I shall, however, to please your Eminence, lay the particulars of your conversation before him."

Some time afterwards, when Talleyrand and Bonaparte must have agreed about some new measure to indirectly chastise impious writers, the senators Garat, Jaucourt, Rœderer and Demeunier, four of the members of the senatorial commission of the liberty of the Press, were sent for, and remained closeted with Napoleon, his minister

Portalis, and Cardinal Caprara for two hours. What was determined on this occasion has not transpired, as even the Cardinal, who is not the most discreet person when provoked, and his religious zeal gets the better of his political prudence, has remained silent, though seemingly contented.

Two rather insignificant authors, of the name of Varennes and Beaujou, who published some scandalous libels on Christianity, have since been taken up, and after some months' imprisonment in the Temple been condemned to transportation to Cayenne for life; not as infidels or atheists, but as conspirators against the State, in consequence of some unguarded expressions which prejudice or ill-will alone would judge connected with politics. Nothing is now permitted to be printed against religion but with the author's name; but by affixing his name, he may abuse the worship and Gospel as much as he pleases. Since the example of severity alluded to above, however, this practice is on the decline. Even Pigault Le Brun, a popular but immoral novel writer, narrowly escaped lately a trip to Cayenne for one of his blasphemous publications; and owes to the protection of Madame Murat exclusively that he was not sent to keep Varennes and Beaujou company. Some years ago, when Madame Murat was neither so great nor so rich as at present, he presented her with a copy of his works, and she has been unfashionable enough not only to remember the compliment, but wished to return it by nominating him her private secretary; which, however, the veto of Napoleon prevented.

Of Napoleon Bonaparte's religious sentiments, opinions are not divided in France. The influence over him of the petty, superstitious Cardinal Caprara is, therefore, inexplicable. This prelate has forced from him assent to transactions which had been refused both to his mother and his brother Joseph, who now often employ the Cardinal with success, where they either dare not or will not show themselves. It is true his Eminence is not easily rebuked, but returns to the charge unabashed by new repulses; and he obtains by teasing more than by persuasion; but a man by whom Bonaparte suffers himself to be teased with impunity is no insignificant favourite, particularly when, like this Cardinal, he unites cunning with devotion, craft with superstition; and is as accessible to corruption as tormented by ambition.

As most ecclesiastical promotions passed through his *pure* and *disinterested* hands, Madame Napoleon, Talleyrand and Portalis, who also wanted some douceurs for their extraordinary expenses, united together last spring to remove him from France, and Napoleon was cajoled to nominate him a grand almoner of the Kingdom of Italy, and the Cardinal set out for Milan. He was, however, artful enough to convince his Sovereign of the propriety of having his grand almoner by his side; and he is, therefore, obliged to this intrigue of his enemies that he now disposes of the benefices in the Kingdom of Italy, as well as those of the French Empire.

During the Pope's residence in this capital, his Holiness often made use of Cardinal Caprara in his secret negotiations with Bonaparte; and whatever advantages were obtained by the Roman Pontiff for the Gallican Church his Eminence almost extorted; for he never desisted, where his interest or pride were concerned, till he had succeeded. It is said that one day last January, after having been for hours exceedingly teasing and troublesome, Bonaparte lost his patience, and was going to treat his Eminence as he frequently does his relatives, his ministers, and counsellors, that is to say, to kick him from his presence; but suddenly recollecting himself, he said, "Cardinal, remain here in my closet until my return, when I shall have more time to listen to what you have to relate." It was at ten o'clock in the morning, and a day of great military audience and grand review. In going out he put the key in his pocket, and told the guards in his ante-chamber to pay no attention if they should hear any noise in his closet.

It was dark before the review was over, and Bonaparte had a large party to dinner. When his guests retired, he went into his wife's drawing-room, where one of the Pope's chamberlains waited on him with the information that his Holiness was much alarmed about the safety of Cardinal Caprara, of whom no account could be obtained, even with the assistance of the police, to whom application had been made, since his Eminence had so suddenly disappeared. "Oh! how absent I am," answered Napoleon, as with surprise; "I entirely forgot that I left the Cardinal in my closet this morning. I will go myself and make an apology for my blunder." His Eminence, quite exhausted, was found fast asleep; but no sooner was he a little recovered than he interrupted Bonaparte's affected apology with the repetition of the demand he had made in the morning; and so well was Napoleon pleased with him, for neglecting his personal inconvenience only to occupy himself with the affairs of his Sovereign, that he consented to what was asked, and in laying his hand upon the shoulders of the prelate, said, "Faithful minister! was every prince so well served as your Sovereign is by you, many evils might be prevented, and much good effected." The same evening Duroc brought him, as a present, a snuff-box with Bonaparte's portrait, set round with diamonds, worth one thousand louis d'or. The adventures of this day certainly did not lessen his Eminence in the favour of Napoleon or of Pius VII.

Last November, some not entirely unknown persons intended to amuse themselves at the Cardinal's expense. At seven o'clock one evening, a young abbé presented himself at the Cardinal's house, Hôtel de Montmorin, Rue Plumet, as by appointment of his Eminence, and was, by his secretary, ushered into the study and asked to wait there. Hardly half-an-hour afterwards, two persons, pretending to be agents of the police, arrived just as the Cardinal's carriage had stopped. They informed him that the woman introduced into his house in the dress of an abbé was connected with a gang of thieves and housebreakers, and demanded his permission to arrest her. He protested that, except the wife of his porter, no woman in any dress whatever could be in his house, and that, to convince themselves, they were very welcome to accompany his valet-de-chambre into every room they wished to see. To the great surprise of his servant, a very pretty girl was found in the bed of his Eminence's bed-chamber, which joined his study, who, though the pretended police agents insisted on her getting up, refused, under pretence that she was there waiting for her *bon ami*, the Cardinal. His Eminence was no sooner told of this than he shut the gate of his house, after sending his secretary to the commissary of police of the section. In the meantime, both the police agents and the girl entreated him to let them out, as the whole was merely a *badinage;* but he remained inflexible, and they were all three carried by the real police commissary to prison. Upon a complaint made by his Eminence to Bonaparte, the police minister, Fouché, received orders to have those who had dared thus to violate the sacred character of the representative of the holy Pontiff immediately, and without further ceremony, transported to Cayenne. The Cardinal demanded, and obtained, a process verbal of what had occurred, and of the sentence on the culprits, to be laid before his Sovereign. As Eugenius de Beauharnais interested himself so much for the individuals involved in this affair, as both to implore Bonaparte's pardon and the Cardinal's interference for them, many were inclined to believe that he was in the secret, if not the contriver of this unfortunate joke. This supposition gained credit when, after all his endeavours to save them proved vain, he sent them seventy-two thousand livres— £3,000—to Rochefort, that they might, on their arrival at Cayenne, be able to buy a plantation. He procured them also letters of recommendation to the governor, Victor Hughes, to be treated differently from other transported persons.

LETTER VIII

Paris, *August*, 1805.

My Lord,—I was particularly attentive in observing the countenances and demeanour of the company at the last levée which Madame Napoleon Bonaparte held, previous to her departure with her husband to meet the Pope at Fontainebleau. I had heard from good authority "that, to those whose propensities were known, Duroc's information that the Empress was visible was accompanied with a kind of admonitory or courtly hint, that the strictest decency in dress and manners, and a conversation chaste, and rather of an unusually modest turn, would be highly agreeable to their Sovereigns, in consideration of the solemn occasion of a Sovereign Pontiff's arrival in France; an occurrence that had not happened for centuries, and probably would not happen for centuries to come." I went early, and was well rewarded for my punctuality.

There came the senator Fouché, handing his *amiable* and *chaste* spouse, walking with as much gravity as formerly, when a friar, he marched in a procession. Then presented themselves the senators Sieyes and Rœderer, with an air as composed as if the former had still been an abbé and the confessor of the latter. Next came Madame Murat, whom three hours before I had seen in the Bois de Boulogne in all the disgusting display of fashionable nakedness, now clothed and covered to her chin. She was followed by the *pious* Madame Le Clerc, now Princess Borghese, who was sighing deeply and loudly. After her came limping the *godly* Talleyrand, dragging his *pure* moiety by his side, both with downcast and edifying looks; the *Christian patriots*, Gravina and Lima; Dreyer and Beust, Dalberg and Cetto, Malsburgh and Pappenheim, with the *Catholic* Schimmelpenninck and Mohammed Said Halel Effendi, all presented themselves as penitent sinners imploring absolutions, after undergoing mortifications.

But it would become tedious and merely a repetition, were I to depict separately the figures and characters of all the personages at this politico-comical masquerade. Their conversation was, however, more uniform, more contemptible, and more laughable, than their accoutrements and grimaces were ridiculous. To judge from what they said, they belonged no longer to this world; all their thoughts were in heaven, and they considered themselves either on the borders of eternity or on the eve of the day of the Last Judgment. The *truly devout* Madame

Napoleon spoke with rapture of martyrs and miracles, of the Mass and of the vespers, of Agnuses and relics of Christ her Saviour, and of Pius VII., his vicar. Had not her enthusiasm been interrupted by the enthusiastic commentaries of her mother-in-law, I saw every mouth open ready to cry out, as soon as she had finished, "Amen! Amen! Amen!"

Napoleon had placed himself between the old Cardinal de Bellois and the not young Cardinal Bernier, so as to prevent the approach of any profane sinner or unrepentant infidel. Round him and their clerical chiefs, all the curates and grand vicars, almoners and chaplains of the Court, and the capitals of the princess, princesses and grand officers of state, had formed a kind of cordon. "Had," said the young General Kellerman to me, "Bonaparte always been encompassed by troops of this description, he might now have sung hymns as a saint in heaven, but he would never have reigned as an Emperor upon earth." This indiscreet remark was heard by Louis Bonaparte, and on the next morning Kellerman received orders to join the army in Hanover, where he was put under the command of a general younger than himself. He would have been still more severely punished, had not his father, the senator (General Kellerman), been in such great favour at the Court of St. Cloud, and so much *protected* by Duroc, who

Napoleon spoke with rapture of martyrs and miracles, of
the Mass and of the vespers, of Agnuses and relics of
Christ her Saviour, and of Pius VII., his vicar. Had not
her enthusiasm been interrupted by the enthusiastic commentaries of her mother-in-law, I saw every mouth open
ready to cry out, as soon as she had finished, "Amen!
Amen! Amen!"

Napoleon had placed himself between the old Cardinal
de Bellois and the not young Cardinal Bernier, so as to
prevent the approach of any profane sinner or unrepentant
infidel. Round him and their clerical chiefs, all the curates
and grand vicars, almoners and chaplains of the Court, and
the capitals of the princess, princesses, and grand officers
of state had formed a kind of cordon. "Had," said the
young General Kellerman to me, "Bonaparte always been
encompassed by troops of this description, he might now
have sung hymns as a saint in heaven, but he would never
have reigned as an Emperor upon earth." This indiscreet
remark was heard by Louis Bonaparte, and on the next
morning Kellerman received orders to join the army in
Hanover, where he was put under the command of a
general younger than himself. He would have been still
more severely punished, had not his father, the senator
(General Kellerman), been in such great favour at the
Court of St. Cloud, and so much *protected* by Duroc, who

had made, in 1792, his first campaign under this officer, then commander-in-chief of the army of the Ardennes.

When this devout assembly separated, which was by courtesy an hour earlier than usual, I expected every moment to hear a chorus of horse-laughs, because I clearly perceived that all of them were tired of their assumed parts, and, with me, inclined to be gay at the expense of their neighbours. But they all remembered also that they were watched by spies, and that an imprudent look or an indiscreet word, gaiety instead of gravity, noise when silence was commanded, might be followed by an airing in the wilderness of Cayenne. They, therefore, all called out, "Coachman, to our hotel!"—as much as to say, we will to-day, in compliment to the new-born Christian zeal of our Sovereigns, finish our evening as piously as we have begun it. But no sooner were they out of sight of the palace than they hurried to scenes of dissipation, all endeavouring, in the debauchery and excesses so natural to them, to forget their unnatural affectation and hypocrisy.

Well you know the standard of the faith even of the members of the Bonaparte family. Two days before this *Christian* circle at Madame Napoleon's, Madame de Chateaureine, with three other ladies, visited the Princess Borghese. Not seeing a favourite parrot they had often previously admired, they inquired what was become of it. "Oh, the poor creature!" answered the Princess; "I have disposed of it, as well as of two of my monkeys. The Emperor has obliged me to engage an almoner and two chaplains, and it would be too extravagant in me to keep six useless animals in my hotel. I must now submit to hearing the disgusting howlings of my almoner instead of the entertaining chat of my parrot, and to see the awkward bows and kneelings of my chaplains instead of the amusing capering of my monkeys. Add to this, that I am forced to transform into a chapel my elegant and tasty boudoir on the ground-floor, where I have passed so many fortunate moments, so many delicious *tête-à-têtes*. Alas! what a change!—what a shocking fashion, that we are now all again to be Christians!!!"

LETTER IX

PARIS, *August*, 1805.

MY LORD,—Notwithstanding what was inserted in our public prints to the contrary, the reception Bonaparte experienced from his army of England in June last year—the first time he presented himself to them as an Emperor—was far from such as flattered either his vanity or views. For the first days, some few solitary voices alone accompanied the "*Vive l'Empereur!*" of his generals, and of his aides-de-camp. This indifference, or, as he called it, mutinous spirit, was so much the more provoking as it was unexpected. He did not, as usual, ascribe it to the emissaries or gold of England, but to the secret adherents of Pichegru and Moreau amongst the brigades or divisions that had served under these unfortunate generals. He ordered, in consequence, his minister Berthier to make out a list of all these corps. Having obtained this, he separated them by ordering some to Italy, others to Holland, and the rest to the frontiers of Spain and Germany. This act of revenge or jealousy was regarded both by the officers and men as a disgrace and as a doubt thrown out against their fidelity, and the murmur was loud and general. In consequence of this, some men were shot, and many more arrested. Observing, however, that severity had not the desired effect, Bonaparte suddenly changed his conduct, released the imprisoned, and rewarded with the crosses of his Legion of Honour every member of the so lately suspected troops who had ever performed any brilliant or valorous exploits under the proscribed generals. He even incorporated among his own body-guards and guides, men who had served in the same capacity under these rival commanders, and numbers of their children were received in the Prytanees and military free schools. The enthusiastic exclamation that soon greeted his ears convinced him that he had struck upon the right string of his soldiers' hearts. Men who, some few days before, wanted only the signal of a leader to cut an Emperor they hated to pieces, would now have contended who should be foremost to shed their last drop of blood for a chief they adored.

This affected liberality towards the troops who had served under his rivals roused some slight discontent among those to whom he was chiefly indebted for his own laurels. But if he knew the danger of reducing to despair slighted men with arms in their hands, he also was well aware of the equal danger of enduring licentiousness or audacity among troops who had, on all occasions, experienced his preference and partiality; and he gave a sanguinary proof of his opinion on this subject at the grand parade of the 12th of July, 1804, preparatory to the grand fête of the 14th. A grenadier of the 21st Regiment (which was known in Italy under the name of the Terrible), in presenting arms to him, said, "Sire! I have served under you four campaigns, fought under you in ten battles or engagements; have received in your service seven wounds, and am not a member of your Legion of Honour; whilst many who served under Moreau, and are not able to show a scratch from an enemy, have that distinction." Bonaparte instantly ordered this man to be shot by his own comrades in the front of the regiment. The six grenadiers selected to fire seeming to hesitate, he commanded the whole corps to lay down their arms, and after being disbanded, to be sent to the different colonial dépôts. To humiliate them still more, the mutinous grenadier was shot by the gendarmes. When the review was over, "*Vive l'Empereur!*" resounded from all parts, and his popularity among the troops has since rather increased than diminished. Nobody can deny that Bonaparte possesses a great presence of mind, an undaunted firmness, and a perfect knowledge of the character of the people over whom he reigns. Could but justice and humanity be added to his other qualities—but, unfortunately for my nation, I fear that the answer of General Mortier to a remark of a friend of mine on this subject is not problematical : " Had," said this imperial favourite, " Napoleon Bonaparte been just and humane, he would neither have vanquished nor reigned."

All these scenes occurred before Bonaparte, seated on a throne, received the homage, as a Sovereign, of one hundred and fifty thousand warriors, who now bowed as subjects, after having for years fought for liberty and equality, and sworn hatred to all monarchical institutions ; and who hitherto had saluted and obeyed him only as the first among equals. What an inconsistency ! The splendour and show that accompanied him everywhere, the pageantry and courtly pomp that surrounded him, and the decorations of the stars and ribands of the Legion of Honour, which he distributed with bombastic speeches among troops — to whom those political impositions and social cajoleries were novelties — made such an impression upon them, that had a bridge been then fixed between Calais and Dover, brave as your countrymen are, I should have trembled for the liberty and independence of your country. The heads and imagination of the soldiers, I know from the best authority, were then so exalted, that though they might have been cut to pieces, they could never have been defeated or routed. I pity our children when I reflect that their tranquillity and happiness will, perhaps, depend upon such a corrupt and unprincipled people of soldiers; easy tools in the hands of every impostor or mountebank.

The lively satisfaction which Bonaparte must have felt at the pinnacle of grandeur where fortune had placed him, was not, however, entirely unmixed with uneasiness and vexation. Except at Berlin, in all the other great Courts the Emperor of the French was still *Monsieur* Bonaparte; and your country, of the subjugation of which he had spoken with such lightness and such inconsideration, instead of dreading, despised his boasts and defied his threats. Indeed, never before did the Cabinet of St. James' more opportunely expose the reality of his impotency, the impertinence of his menaces, and the folly of his parade for the invasion of your country, than by declaring all the ports containing his invincible armada in a state of blockade. I have heard from an officer who witnessed his fury when in May, 1799, he was compelled to retreat from before St. Jean d'Acre, and who was by his side in the camp at Boulogne when a despatch informed him of this circumstance, that it was nothing compared to the violent rage into which he flew upon reading it. For an hour afterwards not even his brother Joseph dared approach him; and his passion got so far the better of his policy, that what might still have long been concealed from the troops was known within the evening to the whole camp. He dictated to his secretary orders for his ministers at Vienna, Berlin, Lisbon and Madrid, and couriers were sent away with them; but half-an-hour afterwards other couriers were despatched after them with other orders, which were revoked in their turn, when at last Joseph had succeeded in calming him a little. He passed, however, the whole following night full dressed and agitated; lying down only for an instant, but having always in his room Joseph and Duroc, and deliberating on a thousand methods of destroying the insolent islanders; all equally violent, but all equally impracticable.

The next morning, when, as usual, he went to see the manœuvres of his flotilla, and the embarkation and landing of his troops, he looked so pale that he almost excited pity. Your cruisers, however, as if they had been informed of the situation of our hero, approached unusually near, to evince, as it were, their contempt and derision. He ordered instantly all the batteries to fire, and went himself to that which carried its shot farthest; but that moment six of your vessels, after taking down their sails, cast anchors, with the greatest *sang-froid*, just without the reach of our shot. In an unavailing anger he broke upon the spot six officers of artillery, and pushed one, Captain d'Ablincourt, down the precipice under the battery, where he narrowly escaped breaking his neck as well as his legs; for which injury he was compensated by being made an officer of the Legion of Honour. Bonaparte then convoked upon the spot a council of his generals of artillery and of the engineers, and, within an hour's time, some guns and mortars of still heavier metal and greater calibre were carried up to replace the others; but, fortunately for the generals, before a trial could be made of them the tide changed, and your cruisers sailed.

In returning to breakfast at General Soult's, he observed the countenances of his soldiers rather inclined to laughter than to wrath; and he heard some jests, significant enough in the vocabulary of encampments, and which informed him that contempt was not the sentiment with which your navy had inspired his troops. The occurrences of these two days hastened his departure from the coast for Aix-la-Chapelle, where the cringing of his courtiers consoled him, in part, for the want of *respect* or *gallantry* in your English tars.

LETTER X

PARIS, *August*, 1805.

MY LORD, — According to a general belief in our diplomatic circles, it was the Austrian ambassador in France, Count Cobentzel, who principally influenced the determination of Francis II. to assume the hereditary title of Emperor of Austria, and to acknowledge Napoleon Emperor of the French.

Jean Philippe, Count de Cobentzel, enjoys, not only in his own country, but through all Europe, a great reputation as a statesman, and has for a number of years been employed by his Court in the most intricate and delicate political transactions. In 1790 he was sent to Brabant to treat with the Belgian insurgents; but the States of Brabant refusing to receive him, he retired to Luxembourg, where he published a proclamation, in which Leopold II. revoked all those edicts of his predecessor, Joseph II., which had been the principal cause of the troubles; and re-established everything upon the same footing as during the reign of Maria Theresa. In 1791 he was appointed ambassador to the Court of St. Petersburg, where his conduct obtained the approbation of his own Prince and of the Empress of Russia.

In 1793 the Committee of Public Safety nominated the intriguer, De Semonville, ambassador to the Ottoman Porte. His mission was to excite the Turks against Austria and Russia, and it became of great consequence to the two Imperial Courts to seize this incendiary of regicides. He was therefore stopped, on the 25th of July, in the village of Novate, near the lake of Chiavenne. A rumour was very prevalent at this time that some papers were found in De Semonville's portfolio implicating Count de Cobentzel as a correspondent with the revolutionary French generals. The continued confidence of his Sovereign contradicts, however, this inculpation, which seems to have been merely the invention of rivalry or jealousy.

In October, 1795, Count de Cobentzel signed, in the name of the Emperor, a treaty with England and Russia; and in 1797 he was one of the Imperial plenipotentiaries sent to Udine to negotiate with Bonaparte, with whom, on the 17th of October, he signed the Treaty of Campo Formio. In the same capacity he went afterwards to Rastadt, and when this congress broke up, he returned again as an ambassador to St. Petersburg.

After the Peace of Luneville, when it required to have a man of experience and talents to oppose to our so *deeply* able minister, Talleyrand, the Cabinet of Vienna removed him from Russia to France, where, with all other representatives of princes, he has experienced more of the frowns and rebukes, than of the dignity and good grace, of our present Sovereign.

Count de Cobentzel's foible is said to be a passion for women; and it is reported that our worthy minister, Talleyrand, has been kind enough to assist him frequently in his amours. Some adventures of this sort, which occurred at Rastadt, afforded much amusement at the Count's expense. Talleyrand, from envy, no doubt, does not allow him the same political merit as his other political contemporaries, having frequently repeated, "that the official dinners of Count de Cobentzel were greatly preferable to his official notes."

So well pleased was Bonaparte with this ambassador when at Aix-la-Chapelle last year, that, as a singular favour, he permitted him, with the Marquis de Gallo (the Neapolitan minister and another plenipotentiary at Udine), to visit the camps of his army of England on the coast. It is true that this condescension was, perhaps, as much a boast, or a threat, as a compliment.

The famous diplomatic note of Talleyrand, which, at Aix-la-Chapelle, proscribed *en masse* all your diplomatic agents, was only a slight revenge of Bonaparte's for your mandate of blockade. Rumour states that this measure was not approved of by Talleyrand, as it would not exclude any of your ambassadors from those Courts not immediately under the whip of our Napoleon. For fear, however, of some more extravagant determination, Joseph Bonaparte dissuaded him from laying before his brother any objections or representations. "But what absurdities do I not sign!" exclaimed the pliant minister.

Bonaparte, on his arrival at Aix-la-Chapelle, found there, according to command, most of the members of the foreign diplomatic corps in France, waiting to present their new credentials to him as Emperor. Charlemagne had been saluted as such, in the same place, about one thousand years before; an inducement for the modern Charlemagne to set all these ambassadors travelling some hundred miles, without any other object but to gratify his impertinent vanity. Every spot where Charlemagne had walked, sat, slept, talked, eaten or prayed, was visited by him with great ostentation; always dragging behind him the foreign representatives, and by his side his wife. To a peasant who presented him a *stone* upon which Charlemagne was said to have once knelt, he gave nearly half its weight in gold; on a priest who offered him a small crucifix, before which that Prince was reported to have prayed, he bestowed an episcopal see; to a manufacturer he ordered one thousand louis for a portrait of Charlemagne, said to be drawn by his daughter, but which, in fact, was from the pencil of the daughter of the manufacturer; a German *savant* was made a member of the National Institute for an old diploma, supposed to have been signed by Charlemagne, who many believe was not able to write; and a German baron, Krigge, was registered in the Legion of Honour for a ring presented by this Emperor to one of his ancestors, though his nobility is well known not to be of sixty years' standing. But woe to him who dared to suggest any doubt about what Napoleon believed, or seemed to believe! A German professor, Richter, more a pedant than a courtier, and more sincere than wise, addressed a short memorial to Bonaparte, in which he proved, from his intimacy with antiquity, that most of the pretended relics of Charlemagne were impositions on the credulous; that the portrait was a drawing of this century, the diploma written in the last; the crucifix manufactured within fifty, and the ring, perhaps, within ten years. The night after Bonaparte had perused this memorial, a police commissary, accompanied by four gendarmes, entered the professor's bedroom, forced him to dress, and ushered him into a covered cart, which carried him under escort to the left bank of the Rhine; where he was left with orders, under pain of death, never more to enter the territory of the French empire. This expedition and summary justice silenced all other connoisseurs and antiquarians; and relics of Charlemagne have since poured in, in such numbers, from all parts of France, Italy, Germany, and even Denmark, that we are here in hope to see one day established a museum Charlemagne, by the side of the museums Napoleon and Josephine. A ballad, written in monkish Latin, said to be sung by the daughters and maids of Charlemagne at his Court on great festivities, was addressed to Duroc by a Danish professor, Cranener, who in return was presented, on the part of Bonaparte, with a diamond ring worth twelve thousand livres—£500. This ballad may, perhaps, be the foundation of a future *Bibliothèque* or *Lyceum* Charlemagne

LETTER XI

Paris, *August*, 1805.

My Lord,—On the arrival of her husband at Aix-la-Chapelle, Madame Napoleon had lost her money by gambling, without recovering her health by using the baths and drinking the waters; she was, therefore, as poor as low-spirited, and as ill-tempered as dissatisfied. Napoleon himself was neither much in humour to supply her present wants, provide for her extravagances, or to forgive her ill-nature; he ascribed the inefficacy of the waters to her excesses, and reproached her for too great condescension to many persons who presented themselves at her drawing-room and in her circle, but who, from their rank in life, were only fit to be seen as supplicants in her ante-chambers, and as associates with her valets or chambermaids.

The fact was that Madame Napoleon knew as well as her husband that these gentry were not in their place in the company of an Empress; but they were her creditors, some of them even Jews; and as long as she continued debtor to them she could not decently — or rather, she dared not — prevent them from being visitors to her. By confiding her situation to her old friend, Talleyrand, she was, however, soon released from those troublesome personages. When the minister was informed of the occasion of the attendance of these impertinent intruders, he humbly proposed to Bonaparte not to pay their demands and their due, but to make them examples of severe justice in transporting them to Cayenne, as the only sure means to prevent, for the future, people of the same description from being familiar or audacious.

When, thanks to Talleyrand's interference, these *family* arrangements were settled, Madame Napoleon recovered her health with her good-humour; and her husband, who had begun to forget the English blockade, only to think of the papal *accolade* (dubbing), was more *tender* than ever. I am assured that, during the fortnight he continued with his wife at Aix-la-Chapelle, he only shut her up or confined her twice, kicked her three times, and abused her once a day.

It was during their residence in that capital that Count de Segur at last completed the composition of their household, and laid before them the list of the ladies and gentlemen who had consented to put on their livery. This de Segur is a kind of amphibious animal, neither a royalist nor a republican, neither a democrat nor an aristocrat, but a disaffected subject under a king, a dangerous citizen of a commonwealth, ridiculing both the friend of equality and the defender of prerogatives; no exact definition can be given, from his past conduct and avowed professions, of his real moral and political character. One thing is only certain—he was an ungrateful traitor to Louis XVI., and is a submissive slave under Napoleon the First.

Though not of an ancient family, Count de Segur was a nobleman by birth, and ranked among the ancient French nobility because one of his ancestors had been a field-marshal. Being early introduced at Court, he acquired, with the common corruption, also the pleasing manners of a courtier; and by his assiduities about the ministers, Counts de Maurepas and de Vergennes, he procured from the latter the place of an ambassador to the Court of St. Petersburg. With some reading and genius, but with more boasting and presumption, he classed himself among French men of letters, and was therefore as such received with distinction by Catharine II., on whom, and on whose Government, he in return published a libel. He was a valet under La Fayette, in 1789, as he has since been under every succeeding king of faction. The partisans of the Revolution pointed him out as a fit ambassador from Louis XVI. to the late King of Prussia; and he went in 1791 to Berlin, in that capacity; but Frederick William II. refused him admittance to his person, and after some ineffectual intrigues with the illuminati and *philosophers* at Berlin, he returned to Paris as he left it; provided, however, with materials for another libel on the Prussian Monarch, and on the House of Brandenburgh, which he printed in 1796. Ruined by the Revolution which he had so much admired, he was imprisoned under Robespierre, and was near starving under the Directory, having nothing but his literary productions to subsist on. In 1799, Bonaparte made him a legislator, and in 1803, a counsellor of state; a place which he resigned last year for that of a grand master of the ceremonies at the present Imperial Court. His ancient inveteracy against your country has made him a favourite with Bonaparte. The indelicate and scandalous attacks, in 1796 and 1797, against Lord Malmesbury, in the then official journal, *Le Redacteur*, were the offspring of his malignity and pen; and the philippics and abusive notes in our present official *Moniteur*, against your government and country, are frequently his *patriotic* progeny, or rather, he often shares with Talleyrand and Hauterive their paternity.

The Revolution has not made Count de Segur more happy with regard to his family, than in his circumstances, which, notwithstanding his brilliant grand-mastership, are far from being affluent. His amiable wife died of terror, and broken-hearted from the sufferings she had experienced, and the atrocities she had witnessed; and when he had enticed his eldest son to accept the place of a sub-prefect under Bonaparte, his youngest son, who never approved our present regeneration, challenged his brother to fight, and, after killing him in a duel, destroyed himself. Count de Segur is therefore, at present, neither a husband nor a father, but only a grand master of ceremonies! What an indemnification!

Madame Napoleon and her husband are both certainly under much obligation to this nobleman for his care to procure them comparatively decent persons to decorate their levées and drawing-rooms, who, though they have no claim either to morality or virtue, either to honour or chastity, are undoubtedly a great acquisition at the Court of St. Cloud, because none of them has either been accused of murder, or convicted of plunder; which is the case with some of the ministers, and most of the generals, senators and counsellors. It is true that they are a mixture of beggared nobles and enriched valets, of married courtesans and divorced wives, but, for all that, they can with justice demand the places of honour of all other Imperial courtiers of both sexes.

When Bonaparte had read over the names of these Court recruits, engaged and enlisted by de Segur, he said, "Well, this lumber must do until we can exchange it for better furniture." At that time, young Count d'Arberg (of a German family, on the right bank of the Rhine), but whose mother is one of Madame Bonaparte's maids-of-honour, was travelling for him in Germany and in Prussia, where, among other *negotiations*, he was charged to procure some persons of both sexes, of the most ancient nobility, to augment Napoleon's suite, and to figure in his livery. More individuals presented themselves for this *honour* than he wanted, but they were all without education, and without address: ignorant of the world as of books; not speaking well their own language, much less understanding French or Italian; vain of their birth, but not ashamed of their ignorance, and as proud as poor. This project was therefore relinquished for the present; but a number of the children of the principal *ci-devant* German nobles, who, by the Treaty of Luneville and Ratisbon had become subjects of Bonaparte, were, by the advice of Talleyrand, *offered* places in French Prytanees, where the Emperor promised to take care of their future advancement. Madame Bonaparte, at the same time, selected twenty-five young girls of the same families, whom she also *offered* to educate at her expense. Their parents understood too well the meaning of these generous *offers* to dare decline their acceptance. These children are the plants of the Imperial nursery, intended to produce future pages, chamberlains, equerries, maids-of-honour and ladies-in-waiting, who for ancestry may bid defiance to all their equals of every Court in Christendom. This act of *benevolence*, as it was called in some German papers, is also an indirect chastisement of the refractory French nobility, who either demanded too high prices for their degradation, or abruptly refused to disgrace the names of their forefathers.

LETTER XII

PARIS, *August*, 1805.

MY LORD,—Bonaparte has been as profuse in his disposal of the imperial diadem of Germany, as in his promises of the papal tiara of Rome. The Houses of Austria and Brandenburgh, the Electors of Bavaria and Baden, have by turns been cajoled into a belief of his exclusive support towards obtaining it at the first vacancy. Those, however, who have paid attention to his machinations, and studied his actions; who remember his pedantic affectation of being considered a modern, or rather a second Charlemagne; and who have traced his steps through the labyrinth of folly and wickedness, of meanness and greatness, of art, corruption and policy, which have seated him on his present throne, can entertain little doubt but that he is seriously bent on seizing and adding the sceptre of Germany to the crowns of France and Italy.

During his stay last autumn at Mentz, all those German Electors who had spirit and dignity enough to refuse to attend on him there in person, were obliged to send extraordinary ambassadors to wait on him, and to compliment him on their part. Though hardly one corner of the veil that covered the intrigues going forward there is yet lifted up, enough is already seen to warn Europe and alarm the world. The secret treaties he concluded there with most of the petty Princes of Germany, against the Chief of the German empire (which not only entirely detached them from their country and its legitimate Sovereign, but made their individual interests hostile and totally opposite to that of the German commonwealth, transforming them also from independent princes into vassals of France), both directly increased his already gigantic power, and indirectly encouraged him to extend it beyond what his most sanguine expectation had induced him to hope. I do not make this assertion from a mere supposition in consequence of ulterior occurrences. At a supper with Madame Talleyrand last March, I heard her husband, in a gay, unguarded, or perhaps *premeditated* moment, say, when mentioning his proposed journey to Italy, " I prepared myself to pass the Alps last October at Mentz. The first ground-stone of the throne of Italy was, strange as it may seem, laid on the banks of the Rhine : with such an extensive foundation, it must be difficult to shake, and impossible to overturn it." We were, in the whole, twenty-five persons at table when he spoke thus, many of whom, he well knew, were intimately acquainted both with the Austrian and Prussian ambassadors, who, by-the-by, both on the next day sent couriers to their respective Courts.

The French Revolution is neither seen in Germany in that dangerous light which might naturally be expected from the sufferings in which it has involved both princes and subjects; nor are its future effects dreaded from its past enormities. The cause of this impolitic and anti-patriotic apathy is to be looked for in the palaces of sovereigns, and not in the dwellings of their people. There exists hardly a single German prince whose ministers, courtiers and counsellors are not numbered, and have long been notorious among the anti-social conspirators, the Illuminati: most of them are knaves of abilities, who have usurped the easy direction of ignorance, or forced themselves as guides on weakness or folly, which bow to their charlatanism as if it was sublimity, and hail their sophistry and imposture as inspiration.

Among princes thus encompassed, the Elector of Bavaria must be allowed the first place. A younger brother of a younger branch, and a colonel in the service of Louis XVI., he neither acquired by education, nor inherited from nature, any talent to reign, nor possessed any one quality that fitted him for a higher situation than the head of a regiment or a lady's drawing-room. He made himself justly suspected of a moral corruption, as well as of a natural incapacity, when he announced his approbation of the Revolution against his benefactor, the late King of France, who, besides a regiment, had also given him a yearly pension of one hundred thousand livres—£4,000. Immediately after his unexpected accession to the Electorate of Bavaria, he concluded a subsidiary treaty with your country, and his troops were ordered to combat rebellion, under the standard of Austrian loyalty. For some months it was believed that the Elector wished by his conduct to obliterate the memory of the errors, vices and principles of the Duke of Deux-Ponts (his former title). But placing all his confidence in a political adventurer and revolutionary fanatic, Montgelas, without either consistency or firmness, without being either bent upon information or anxious about popularity, he threw the whole burden of state on the shoulders of this dangerous man, who soon showed the world that his master, by his first treaties, intended only to pocket your money without serving your cause or interest.

This Montgelas is, on account of his cunning and long standing among them, worshipped by the gang of German Illuminati as an idol rather than revered as an apostle. He is their Baal, before whom they hope to oblige all nations upon earth to prostrate themselves as soon as infidelity has entirely banished Christianity; for the Illuminati do not expect to reign till the last Christian is buried under the rubbish of the last altar of Christ. It is not the fault of Montgelas if such an event has not already occurred in the Electorate of Bavaria.

Within six months after the Treaty of Luneville, Montgelas began in that country his political and religious innovations. The nobility and the clergy were equally attacked; the privileges of the former were invaded, and the property of the latter confiscated; and had not his zeal carried him too far, so as to alarm our *new* nobles, our *new* men of property, and *new* Christians, it is very probable that Atheism would have already, without opposition, reared its head in the midst of Germany, and proclaimed there the rights of man, and the code of liberty and equality.

The inhabitants of Bavaria are, as you know, all Roman Catholics, and the most superstitious and ignorant Catholics of Germany. The step is but short from superstition to infidelity; and ignorance has furnished in France more sectaries of Atheism than perversity. The Illuminati, *brothers* and *friends* of Montgelas, have not been idle in that country. Their writings have perverted those who had no opportunity to hear their speeches, or to witness their example; and I am assured by Count de Beust, who travelled in Bavaria last year, that their progress among the lower classes is astonishing, considering the short period these emissaries have *laboured*. To anyone looking on the map of the Continent, and acquainted with the spirit of our times, this impious focus of illumination must be ominous.

Among the members of the foreign diplomatic corps, there exists not the least doubt but that this Montgelas, as well as Bonaparte's minister at Munich, Otto, was acquainted with the treacherous part Mehée de la Touche played against your minister, Drake; and that it was planned between him and Talleyrand as the surest means to break off all political connections between your country and Bavaria. Mr. Drake was personally liked by the Elector, and was not inattentive either to the plans and views of Montgelas or to the intrigues of Otto. They were, therefore, both doubly interested to remove such a troublesome witness.

M. de Montgelas is now a grand officer of Bonaparte's Legion of Honour, and he is one of the few foreigners nominated the *most worthy* of such a distinction. In France he would have been an acquisition either to the factions of a Marat, of a Brissot, or of a Robespierre; and the Goddess of Reason, as well as the God of the Theophilanthropists, might have been sure of counting him among their adorers. At the clubs of the Jacobins or Cordeliers, in the fraternal societies, or in a revolutionary tribunal; in the Committee of Public Safety, or in the council chamber of the Directory, he would equally have made himself notorious and been equally in his place. A stoic *sans-culotte* under Du Clots, a staunch republican under Robespierre, he would now have been the most pliant and brilliant courtier of Bonaparte.

LETTER XIII

PARIS, *August*, 1805.

MY LORD,—No Queen of France ever saw so many foreign princes and princesses in her drawing-rooms as the first Empress of the French did last year at Mentz; and no sovereign was ever before so well paid, or accepted with less difficulty donations and presents for her gracious protection. Madame Napoleon herself, on her return to this capital last October, boasted that she was ten millions of livres—£420,000—richer in diamonds; two millions of livres—£62,000—richer in pearls, and three millions of livres —£125,000—richer in plate and china, than in the June before, when she quitted it. She acknowledged that she left behind her some creditors and some money at Aix-la-Chapelle; but at Mentz she did not want to borrow, nor had time to gamble. The gallant *ultra Romans* provided everything, even to the utmost extent of her wishes; and she, on her part, could not but honour those with her company as much as possible, particularly as they required *nothing else* for their *civilities*. Such was the Empress's expression to her lady-in-waiting, the handsome Madame Seran, with whom no confidence, no tale, no story and no scandal expires; and who was in a great hurry to inform, the same evening, the tea party at Madame de Beauvais' of this good news, complaining at the same time of not having had the least share in this rich harvest.

Nowhere, indeed, were bribery and corruption carried to a greater extent, or practised with more effrontery, than at Mentz. Madame Napoleon had as much her fixed price for every favourable word she spoke, as Talleyrand had for every line he wrote. Even the attendants of the former, and the clerks of the latter, demanded, or rather extorted, douceurs from the exhausted and almost ruined German petitioners; who in the end were rewarded for all their meanness and for all their expenses with promises at best; as the new plan of supplementary indemnities was, on the very day proposed for its final arrangement, postponed by the desire of the Emperor of the French, until further orders. This *provoking* delay could no more be foreseen by the Empress than by the minister, who, in return for their presents and money almost overpowered the German Princes with *his* protestations of regret at their disappointments. Nor was Madame Bonaparte less sorry or less civil. She sent her chamberlain, Daubusson la Feuillad, with regular compliments of condolence to every Prince who had enjoyed her protection. They returned to their homes, therefore, if not wealthier, at least happier; flattered by assurances and condescensions, confiding in hope as in certainties. Within three months, however, it is supposed that they would willingly have disposed both of promises and expectations at a loss of fifty per cent.

By the cupidity and selfishness of these and other German Princes, and their want of patriotism, Talleyrand was become perfectly acquainted with the value and production of every principality, bishopric, county, abbey, barony, convent and even village in the German empire; and though most national property in France was disposed of at one or two years' purchase, he required five years' purchase-money for all the estates and lands on the other side of the Rhine, of which, under the name of indemnities, he stripped the lawful owners to gratify the ambition or avidity of intruders. This high price has cooled the *claims* of the bidders, and the plan of the supplementary indemnities is still suspended, and probably will continue so until our minister lowers his terms. A combination is supposed to have been entered into by the chief demanders of indemnities, by which they have bound themselves to resist all farther extortions. They do not, however, know the man they have to deal with; he will, perhaps, find out some to lay claim to their own private and hereditary property whom he will produce and support, and who certainly will have the same right to pillage them as they had to the spoils of others.

It was reported in our fashionable circles last autumn,

and *smiled* at by Talleyrand, that he promised the Countess de L—— an abbey, and the Baroness de S——z a convent, for certain personal favours, and that he offered a bishopric to the Princess of H—— on the same terms, but this lady answered, "that she would think of his offers after he had put her husband in possession of the bishopric." It is not necessary to observe that both the Countess and the Baroness are yet waiting to enjoy his liberal donations, and to be indemnified for their prostitution.

Napoleon Bonaparte was attacked by a fit of jealousy at Mentz. The young nephew of the Elector Arch-Chancellor, Count de L——ge, was very assiduous about the Empress, who, herself, at first mistook the motive. Her confidential secretary, Deschamps, however, afterwards informed her that this nobleman wanted to purchase the place of a co-adjutor to his uncle, so as to be certain of succeeding him. He obtained, therefore, several private audiences, *no doubt* to regulate the price, when Napoleon put a stop to this secret negotiation by having the Count carried by gendarmes, *with great politeness*, to the other side of the Rhine. When convinced of his error, Bonaparte asked his wife what sum had been promised for her *protection*, and immediately gave her an order on his minister of the treasury (Marbois) for the amount. This was an act of justice, and a reparation worthy of a *good* and *tender* husband; but when, the very next day, he recalled this order, threw it into the fire before her eyes, and confined her for six hours in her bedroom, because she was not dressed in time to take a walk with him on the ramparts, one is apt to believe that military despotism has erased from his bosom all connubial affection, and that a momentary effusion of kindness and generosity can but little alleviate the frequent pangs caused by repeated insults and oppression. Fortunately, Madame Napoleon's disposition is proof against rudeness as well as against brutality. If what her *friend* and *consoler*, Madame Deluçay, reports of her is not exaggerated, her tranquillity is not much disturbed nor her happiness affected by these explosions of passionate authority, and she prefers admiring, in undisturbed solitude, her diamond box to the most beautiful prospects in the most agreeable company; and she inspects with more pleasure in confinement, her rich wardrobe, her beautiful china, and her heavy plate, than she would find satisfaction, surrounded with crowds, in contemplating Nature, even in its utmost perfection. "The paradise of Madame Napoleon," says her friend, "must be of metal, and lighted by the lustre of brilliants, else she would decline it for a hell and accept Lucifer himself for a spouse, provided gold flowed in his infernal domains, though she were even to be scorched by its heat."

LETTER XIV

Paris, *August*, 1805.

My Lord,—I believe that I have mentioned to you, when in England, that I was an old acquaintance of Madame Napoleon, and a visitor at the house of her first husband. When introduced to her after some years' absence, during which fortune had treated us very differently, she received me with more civility than I was prepared to expect, and would, perhaps, have spoken to me more than she did, had not a look of her husband silenced her. Madame Louis Bonaparte was still more condescending, and recalled to my memory what I had not forgotten—how often she had been seated, when a child, on my lap, and played on my knees with her doll. Thus they behaved to me when I saw them for the first time in their present elevation; I found them afterwards, in their drawing-rooms or at their routs and parties, more shy and distant. This change did not much surprise me, as I hardly knew anyone that had the slightest pretension to their acquaintance who had not troubled them for employment or borrowed their money, at the same time that they complained of their neglect and their breach of promises. I continued, however, as much as etiquette and decency required, assiduous, but never familiar : if they addressed me, I answered with respect, but not with servility ; if not, I bowed in silence when they passed. They might easily perceive that I did not intend to become an intruder, nor to make the remembrance of what was past an apology or a reason for applying for present favours. A lady, on intimate terms with Madame Napoleon, and once our common friend, informed me, shortly after the untimely end of the lamented Duke of Enghien, that she had been asked whether she knew anything that could be done for me, or whether I would not be flattered by obtaining a place in the Legislative Body or in the Tribunate? I answered as I thought, that were I fit for a public life nothing could be more agreeable or suit me better; but, having hitherto declined all employments that might restrain that independence to which I had accustomed myself from my youth, I was now too old to enter upon a new career. I added that, though the Revolution had reduced my circumstances, it had not entirely ruined me. I was still independent, because my means were the boundaries of my wants.

A week after this conversation General Murat, the governor of this capital, and Bonaparte's *favourite* brother-in-law, invited me to a conversation in a note delivered to me by an aide-de-camp, who told me that he was ordered to wait for my company, or, which was the same, he had orders not to lose sight of me, as I was his prisoner. Having nothing with which to reproach myself, and all my written remarks being deposited with a friend, whom none of the Imperial functionaries could suspect, I entered a hackney coach without any fear or apprehension; and we drove to the governor's hotel.

From the manner in which General Murat addressed me, I was soon convinced that if I had been accused of any error or indiscretion, the accusation could not be very grave in his eyes. He entered with me into his closet, and enquired whether I had any enemies at the police office? I told him not to my knowledge.—"Is the police minister and senator, Fouché, your friend?" continued he. —"Fouché," said I, "has bought an estate that formerly belonged to me; may he enjoy it with the same peace of mind as I have lost it. I have never spoken to him in my life."—"Have you not complained at Madame de la Force's of the execution of the *ci-devant* Duke of Enghien, and agreed with the other members of her coterie to put on mourning for him?"—"I have never been at the house of that lady since the death of the Prince, nor more than once in my life."—"Where did you pass the evening last Saturday?"—"At the hotel, and in the assembly of Princess

Louis Bonaparte."—"Did she see you?"—"I believe that she did, because she returned my salute."—"You have known her Imperial Highness a long time?"—"From her infancy." —"Well, I congratulate you. You have in her a generous protectress. But for her you would now have been on the way to Cayenne. Here you see the list of persons condemned yesterday, upon the report of Fouché, to transportation. Your name is at the head of them. You were not only accused of being an agent of the Bourbons, but of having intrigued to become a member of the Legislature, or of the Tribunate, that you might have so much the better opportunity to serve them. Fortunately for you, the Emperor remembered that the Princess Louis had demanded such a favour for you, and he informed her of the character of her *protégé*. This brought forward your innocence, because it was discovered that, instead of asking for, you had declined the offer she had made you through the Empress. Write the Princess a letter of thanks. You have, indeed, had a narrow escape, but it has been so far useful to you, that Government is now aware of your having some secret enemy in power, who is not delicate about the means of injuring you."

In quitting General Murat, I could not help deploring the fate of a despot, even while I abhorred his unnatural power. The curses, the complaints, and reproaches for all the crimes, all the violence, all the oppression perpetrated in his name, are entirely thrown upon him; while his situation and occupation do not admit the seeing and hearing everything and everybody himself. He is often forced, therefore, to judge according to the report of an impostor; to sanction with his name the hatred, malignity or vengeance of culpable individuals; and to sacrifice innocence to gratify the vile passions of his vilest slave. I have not so bad an opinion of Bonaparte as to think him capable of wilfully condemning any person to death or transportation, of whose innocence he was convinced, provided that person stood not in the way of his interest and ambition; but suspicion and tyranny are inseparable companions, and injustice their common progeny. The unfortunate beings on the long list General Murat showed me were, I dare say, most of them as innocent as myself, and *all certainly condemned unheard.* But suppose, even, that they had been indiscreet enough to put on mourning for a prince of the blood of their former kings, did their imprudence deserve the same punishment as the deed of the robber, the forger or the housebreaker? and, indeed, it was more severe than what our laws inflict on such criminals, who are only condemned to transportation for some few years, after a public trial and conviction; while the exile of these unconvicted, untried, and most probably innocent persons is continued for life, on charges as unknown to themselves as their destiny and residence remain to their families and friends. Happy England! where no one is condemned unheard, and no one dares attempt to make the laws subservient to his passions or caprice.

As to Fouché's enmity, at which General Murat so plainly hinted, I had long apprehended it from what others, in similar circumstances with myself, had suffered. He has, since the Revolution, bought no less than sixteen national estates, seven of the former proprietors of which have suddenly disappeared since his ministry, probably in the manner he intended to remove me. This man is one of the most immoral characters the Revolution has dragged forward from obscurity. It is more difficult to mention a crime that he has not perpetrated than to discover a good or just action that he ever performed. He is so notorious a villain that even the infamous National Convention expelled him from its bosom, and since his ministry no man has been found base enough, in my debased country, to extenuate, much less to defend, his past enormities. In a nation so greatly corrupted and immoral this alone is more than negative evidence.

As a friar before the Revolution *he has avowed*, in his correspondence with the National Convention, that he never believed in a God; and as one of the first public functionaries of a Republic he has *officially denied* the existence of virtue. He is, therefore, as unmoved by tears as by reproaches, and as inaccessible to remorse as hardened against repentance. With him interest and bribes are everything, and honour and honesty nothing. The supplicant or the pleader who appears before him with no other support than the justice of his cause is fortunate indeed if, after being cast, he is not also confined or ruined, and perhaps both; while a line from one of the Bonapartes, or a purse of gold, changes black to white, guilt to innocence, removes the scaffold waiting for the assassin, and extinguishes the faggots lighted for the parricide. His authority is so extensive, that on the least signal, with one blow, from the extremities of France to her centre, it crushes the cot and the palace; and his decisions, against which there is no appeal, are so destructive that they never leave any traces behind them, and Bonaparte, Bonaparte *alone*, can prevent or arrest their effect.

Though a traitor to his former benefactor, the ex-Director Barras, he possesses now the unlimited confidence of Napoleon Bonaparte, and, as far as is known, has not yet done anything to forfeit it; if private acts of cruelty cannot, in the agent of a tyrant, be called breach of trust or infidelity. He shares with Talleyrand the fraternity of the vigilant, immoral and tormenting secret police; and with Real and Dubois, the prefect of police, the reproduction, or rather the invention, of new tortures and improved racks; the *oubliettes*, which are wells or pits dug under the Temple and most other prisons, are the works of his own infernal genius. They are covered with trapdoors, and any person whom the rack has mutilated, or not obliged to speak out; whose return to society is thought dangerous, or whose discretion is suspected; who has been imprisoned by mistake, or discovered to be innocent; who is disagreeable to the Bonapartes, their favourites, or the mistresses of their favourites; who has displeased Fouché, or offended some other placeman; any who have refused to part with their property for the recovery of their liberty, are all precipitated into these artificial abysses—*there to be forgotten*, or worse, to be starved to death, if they have not been fortunate enough to break their necks and be killed by the fall.

The property Fouché has acquired by his robberies within these last twelve years is at the lowest rate valued at fifty millions of livres—£2,100,000—which must increase yearly; as a man who disposes of the liberty of fifty millions of people is also, in a great part, master of their wealth. Except the chiefs of the governments and their officers of state, there exists not an inhabitant of France, Italy, Holland or Switzerland who can consider himself secure for an instant of not being seized, imprisoned, plundered, tortured or exterminated by the orders of Fouché and by the hands of his agents.

You will, no doubt, exclaim, "How can Bonaparte employ, how dares he confide, in such a man?" Fouché is as able as unprincipled, and, with the most unfeeling and perverse heart, possesses great talents. There is no infamy he will not stoop to, and no crime, however execrable, that he will hesitate to commit, if his Sovereign orders it. He is, therefore, a most useful instrument in the hand of a despot who, notwithstanding what is said to the contrary in France, and believed abroad, would cease to rule the day he became just, and the reign of laws and of humanity banished terror and tyranny.

It is reported that some person, pious or revengeful, presented some time ago to the devout mother of Napoleon a long memorial containing some particulars of the crimes and vices of Fouché and Talleyrand, and required of her, if she wished to prevent the curses of Heaven from falling on her son, to inform him of them, that he might cease to employ men so unworthy of him, and so repugnant to a Divinity. Napoleon, after reading through the memorial, is stated to have answered his mother, who was always pressing him to dismiss these ministers: "The memorial, Madam, contains nothing of what I was not previously informed. Louis XVI. did not select any but those whom he hought the most virtuous and moral of men for his ministers and counsellors; and where did their virtues and morality bring him? If the writer of the memorial will mention two honest and irreproachable characters, with equal talents and zeal to serve me, neither Fouché nor Talleyrand shall again be admitted into my presence."

LETTER XV

PARIS, *August*, 1805.

MY LORD, — You have with some reason in England complained of the conduct of the members of the foreign diplomatic corps in France, when the pretended correspondence between Mr. Drake and Mehée de la Touche was published in our official gazette. Had you, however, like myself, been in a situation to study the characters and appreciate the *worth* of most of them, this conduct would have excited no surprise; and pity would have taken the place both of accusation and reproach. Hardly one of them, except Count Philippe de Cobentzel, the Austrian ambassador (and even he is considerably involved), possesses any property, or has anything else but his salary to depend upon for subsistence. The least offence to Bonaparte or Talleyrand would instantly deprive them of their places; and, unless they were fortunate enough to obtain some other appointment, reduce them to live in obscurity, and perhaps in want, upon a trifling pension in their own country.

The day before Mr. Drake's correspondence appeared

in the *Moniteur*, in March, 1804, Talleyrand gave a grand diplomatic dinner; in the midst of which, as was previously agreed with Bonaparte, Duroc called him out on the part of the First Consul. After an absence of near an hour, which excited great curiosity and some alarm among the diplomatists, he returned very thoughtful and seemingly very low-spirited. "Excuse me, gentlemen," said he, "I have been impolite against my inclination. The First Consul knew that you honoured me with your company to-day, and would therefore not have interrupted me by his orders had not a discovery of a most extraordinary nature against the law of nations just been made; a discovery which calls for the immediate indignation against the Cabinet of St. James', not only of France, but of every nation that wishes for the preservation of civilized society. After dinner I shall do myself the honour of communicating to you the particulars, well convinced that you will all enter with warmth into the just resentment of the First Consul." During the repast the bottle went freely round, and as soon as they had drunk their coffee and liqueurs, Talleyrand rang a bell, and Hauterive presented himself with a large bundle of papers. The pretended original letters of Mr. Drake were handed about with the commentaries of the minister and his secretary. Their heads heated with wine, it was not difficult to influence their minds, or to mislead their judgment, and they exclaimed, as in a chorus, "*C'est abominable! Cela fait frémir!*" Talleyrand took advantage of their situation, as well as of their indiscretion. "I am glad, gentlemen," said he, "and shall not fail to inform the First Consul of your *unanimous* sentiments on this disagreeable subject; but verbal expressions are not sufficient in an affair of such great consequence. I have orders to demand your written declarations, which, after what you have already expressed, you cannot hesitate about sending to me to-night, that they may accompany the denunciation which the First Consul despatches, within some few hours, to all the Courts on the Continent. You would much please the First Consul were you to write as near as possible according to the formula which my secretary has drawn up. It states nothing either against *convenance*, or against the customs of Sovereigns, or etiquettes of Courts, and I am certain is also perfectly congenial with your individual feelings." A silence of some moments now followed (as all the diplomatists were rather taken by surprise with regard to a written declaration), which the Swedish ambassador, Baron Ehrensward, interrupted by saying that, "though he personally might have no objection to sign such a declaration, he must demand some time to consider whether he had a right to write in the name of his Sovereign, without his orders, on a subject still unknown to him." This remark made the Austrian ambassador, Count de Cobentzel, propose a private consultation among the members of the foreign diplomatic corps at one of their hotels, at which the Russian chargé d'affaires, d'Oubril, who was not at the dinner party, was invited to assist. They met accordingly, at the Hotel de Montmorency, Rue de Lille, occupied by Count de Cobentzel; but they came to no other unanimous determination than that of answering a written communication of Talleyrand by a written note, according as everyone judged most proper and prudent, and corresponding with the supposed sentiments of his Sovereign.

As all this official correspondence has been published in England, you may, upon reading the notes presented by Baron de Dreyer, and Mr. Livingstone,[1] the *neutral* ambassadors of Denmark and America, form some tolerably just idea of Talleyrand's formula. Their impolitic servility was blamed even by the other members of the diplomatic corps.

Livingstone you know, and perhaps have not to learn that, though a staunch republican in America, he was the most abject courtier in France; and though a violent de-

---

[1] In consequence of this conduct, Livingstone was recalled by his Government, and lives now in obscurity and disgrace in America. To console him, however, in his misfortune, Bonaparte, on his departure, presented him with his portrait, enamelled on the lid of a snuff-box, set round with diamonds, and valued at one thousand louis d'or.

fender of liberty and equality on the other side of the Atlantic, no man bowed lower to usurpation, or revered despotism more, in Europe. Without talents, and almost without education, he thinks intrigues negotiations, and conceives that policy and duplicity are synonymous. He was called here "the courier of Talleyrand," on account of his voyages to England, and his journeys to Holland, where this minister sent him to intrigue, with less ceremony than one of his secret agents. He acknowledged that no government was more liberal, and no nation more free, than the British; but he hated the one as much as he abused the other; and he did not conceal sentiments that made him always so welcome to Bonaparte and Talleyrand. Never over nice in the choice of his companions, Arthur O'Connor, and other Irish traitors and vagabonds, used his house as their own; so much so that, when he invited other ambassadors to dine with him, they, before they accepted the invitation, made a condition that no outlaws or adventurers should be of the party.

In your youth, Baron de Dreyer was an ambassador from the Court of Copenhagen to that of St. James'. He has since been in the same capacity to the Courts of St. Petersburg and Madrid. Born a Norwegian, of a poor and obscure family, he owes his advancement to his own talents; but these, though they have procured him rank, have left him without a fortune. When he came here, in June, 1797, from Spain, he brought a mistress with him, and several children he had had by her during his residence in that country. He also kept an English mistress some thirty years ago in London, by whom he had a son, M. Guillaumeau, who is now his secretary. Thus encumbered, and thus situated, at the age of seventy, it is no surprise if he strives to die at his post, and that fear to offend Bonaparte and Talleyrand sometimes gets the better of his prudence.

In Denmark, as well as in all other Continental States, the pensions of diplomatic invalids are more scanty than those of military ones, and totally insufficient for a man who, during half a century nearly, has accustomed himself to a certain style of life, and to expenses requisite to represent his Prince with dignity. No wonder, therefore, that Baron de Dreyer prefers Paris to Copenhagen, and that the cunning Talleyrand takes advantage of this preference.

It was reported here among our foreign diplomatists, that the English minister in Denmark complained of the contents of Baron de Dreyer's note, concerning Mr. Drake's correspondence; and that the Danish prime minister, Count de Bernstorf, wrote to him in consequence, by the order of the Prince Royal, a severe reprimand. This act of political justice is, however, denied by him, under pretence that the

Cabinet of Copenhagen has laid it down as an invariable rule, never to reprimand, but always to displace those of its agents with whom it has reason to be discontented. Should this be the case, no Sovereign in Europe is better served by his representatives than his Danish Majesty, because no one seldomer changes or removes them.

While I am speaking of diplomatists, I cannot forbear giving you a short sketch of one whose weight in the scale of politics entitles him to particular notice: I mean the Count de Haugwitz, insidiously complimented by Talleyrand with the title of "The Prince of Neutrality, the Sully of Prussia." Christian Henry Curce, Count de Haugwitz, who, until lately, has been the chief director of the political conscience of his Prussian Majesty, as his minister of the foreign department, was born in Silesia, and is the son of a nobleman who was a General in the Austrian service when Frederick the Great made the conquest of that country. At the death of this King, in 1786, Count de Haugwitz occupied an inferior place in the foreign office, where Count de Hertzberg observed his zeal and assiduity, and recommended him to the notice of the late King Frederick William II. By the interest of the celebrated Bishopswerder, he procured, in 1792, the appointment of an ambassador to the Court of Vienna, where he succeeded Baron de Jacobi, the present Prussian minister in your country. In the autumn of the same year he went to Ratisbon, to co-operate with the Austrian ambassador, and to persuade the Princes of the German empire to join the coalition against France. In the month of March, 1794, he was sent to the Hague, where he negotiated with Lord Malmesbury concerning the affairs of France; shortly afterwards, his nomination as a minister of state took place, and from that time his political sentiments seem to have undergone a revolution, for which it is not easy to account; but, whatever were the causes of his change of opinions, the Treaty of Basle, concluded between France and Prussia in 1795, was certainly negotiated under his auspices; and in August, 1796, he signed, with the French minister at Berlin, Citizen Caillard, the first and famous Treaty of Neutrality; and a Prussian cordon was accordingly drawn, to cause the neutrality of the North to be observed and protected. Had the Count de Haugwitz of 1795 been the same as the Count de Haugwitz of 1792, it is probable we should no longer have heard of either a French republic or a French empire; but a legitimate monarch of the kingdom of France would have ensured that security to all other legitimate Sovereigns, the want of which they themselves, or their children, will feel and mourn in vain, as long as unlimited usurpations tyrannize over my wretched country. It is to be hoped, however, that the good sense of the Count will point out to him, before it is too late, the impolicy of his present connections; and that he will use his interest with his Prince to persuade him to adopt a line of conduct suited to the grandeur and dignity of the Prussian monarchy, and favourable to the independence of insulted Europe.

When his present Prussian Majesty succeeded to the throne, Count de Haugwitz continued in office, with increased influence; but he some time since resigned, in consequence, it is said, of a difference of opinion with the other Prussian ministers on the subject of a *family* alliance, which Bonaparte had the *modesty* to propose, between the *illustrious* house of Napoleon the First and the royal line of Brandenburgh.

On this occasion his King, to evince his satisfaction with his past conduct, bestowed on him not only a large pension, but an estate in Silesia, where he before possessed some property. Bonaparte also, to express his regret at his retreat, proclaimed his Excellency a grand officer of the Legion of Honour.

Talleyrand insolently calls the several *cordons*, or ribands, distributed by Bonaparte among the Prussian ministers and generals, "his leading-strings." It is to be hoped that Frederick William III. is sufficiently upon his guard to prevent these *strings* from strangling the Prussian monarchy and the Brandenburgh dynasty.

LETTER XVI

PARIS, *August*, 1805.

MY LORD, — Upwards of two months after my visit to General Murat, I was surprised at the appearance of M. Darjuson, the chamberlain of Princess Louis Bonaparte. He told me that he came on the part of Prince Louis, who honoured me with an invitation to dine with him the day after. Upon my enquiry whether he knew if the party would be very numerous, he answered, between forty and fifty; and that it was a kind of farewell dinner, because the Prince intended shortly to set out for Compiegne to assume the command of the camp formed in its vicinity, of the dragoons and other light troops of the army of England.

The principal personages present at this dinner were Joseph Bonaparte and his wife, General and Madame Murat, the ministers Berthier, Talleyrand, Fouché, Chaptal and Portalis. The conversation was entirely military, and chiefly related to the probable conquest or subjugation of Great Britain, and the probable consequence to mankind in general of such a great event. No difference of opinion was heard with regard to its immediate benefit to France and gradual utility to all other nations; but Berthier seemed to apprehend that before France could have time to organize this valuable conquest, she would be obliged to support another war, with a formidable league, perhaps, of all other European nations. The issue, however, he said, would be glorious to France, who, by her achievements, would force all people to acknowledge her their mother country; and then, first, Europe would constitute but one family.

Chaptal was as certain as everybody else of the destruction of the tyrants of the seas; but he thought France would never be secure against the treachery of modern Carthage until she followed the example of Rome towards ancient Carthage; and, therefore, after reducing London to ashes, it would be proper to disperse round the universe all the inhabitants of the British Islands, and to re-people them with nations less evil-disposed and less corrupted. Portalis observed that it was more easy to conceive than to execute such a vast plan. It would not be an undertaking of five, of ten, nor of twenty years, to transplant these nations; that misfortunes and proscription would not only inspire courage and obstinacy, but desperation. "No people," continued he, "are more attached to their customs and countries than islanders in general; and though British subjects are the greatest travellers, and found everywhere, they all suppose their country the best, and always wish to return to it and finish their days amidst their native fogs and smoke. Neither the Saxons, nor the Danes, nor Norman conquerors transplanted them, but, after reducing them, incorporated themselves by marriages among the vanquished, and in some few generations were but one people. It is asserted by all persons who have lately visited Great Britain, that, though the *civilization* of the lower classes is much behind that of the same description in France, the higher orders, the rich and the fashionable, are, with regard to their manners, more French than English, and might easily be cajoled into obedience and subjection to the sovereignty of a nation whose customs, by free choice, they have adopted in preference to their own, and whose language forms a necessary part of their education, and, indeed, of the education of almost every class in the British empire. The universality of the French language is the best ally France has in assisting her to conquer an universal dominion. He wished, therefore, that when we were in a situation to dictate in England, instead of proscribing Englishmen we should proscribe the English language, and advance and reward, in preference, all those parents whose children were sent to be educated in France, and all those families who voluntarily adopted in their houses and societies exclusively the French language." Murat was afraid that if France did not transplant the most stubborn Britons, and settle among them French colonies, when once their military and commercial navy was annihilated, they would turn pirates, and, perhaps, within half-a-century, lay all other nations as much under contribution by their piracies as they now do by their industry; and that, like the pirates on the coast of Barbary, the instant they had no connections with other civilized nations, cut the throats of each other, and agree in nothing but in plundering, and considering all other people in the world their natural enemies and purveyors. To this opinion Talleyrand, by nodding assent, seemed to adhere; but he added, "Earthquakes are generally dreaded as destructive; but such a convulsion of nature as would swallow up the British Islands, with all their inhabitants, would be the greatest blessing Providence ever conferred on mankind."

Louis Bonaparte then addressed himself to me and to the Marquis de F——: "Gentlemen," said he, "you have been in England; what is your opinion of the character of these islanders, and of the probability of their subjugation?" I answered that, during the fifteen months I resided in London I was too much occupied to prevent myself from starving, to meditate about anything else; that my stomach was my sole meditation as well as anxiety. That, however, I believed that in England, as everywhere else, a mixture of good and bad qualities was to be found; but which prevailed would be presumption in me, from my position, to decide. But I did not doubt that if we cordially hated the English they returned us the compliment with interest, and, therefore, the contest with them would be a severe one. The Marquis de F—— imprudently attempted to convince the company that it was difficult, if not impossible, for our army to land in England, much less to conquer it, until we were masters of the seas by a superior navy. He would, perhaps, have been still more indiscreet, had not Madame Louis interrupted him, and given another turn to the conversation by enquiring about the fair sex in England, and if it was true that handsome women were more numerous there than in France? Here again the Marquis, instead of paying her a compliment, as she perhaps expected, roundly assured her that for one beauty in France, hundreds might be counted in England, where gentlemen were, therefore, not so easily satisfied; and that a woman regarded by them only as an ordinary person would pass for a first-rate beauty among French beaux, on account of the great scarcity of them here. "You must excuse the Marquis, ladies," said I, in my turn; "he has not been in love in England. There, perhaps, he found the belles less cruel than in France, where, for the cruelty of one lady, or for her insensibility of his merit, he revenges himself on the whole sex."—"I apply to M. Talleyrand," answered the

Marquis; "he has been longer in England than myself."
—"I am not a competent judge," retorted the minister;
"Madame Talleyrand is here, and has not the honour of being a Frenchwoman; but I dare say the Marquis will agree with me that in no society in the British Islands, among a dozen of ladies, has he counted more beauties, or admired greater accomplishments or more perfection." To this the Marquis bowed assent, saying that in all his general remarks the party present, of course, was not included. All the ladies, who were well acquainted with his absent and blundering conversation, very good-humouredly laughed, and Madame Murat assured him that if he would give her the address of the belle in France who had transformed a gallant Frenchman into a *chevalier* of British beauty, she would attempt to make up their difference. "She is no more, Madam," said the Marquis; "she was, unfortunately, guillotined two days before——" the father of Madame Louis, he was going to say, when Talleyrand interrupted him with a significant look, and said, "Before the fall of Robespierre, you mean."

From these and other traits of the Marquis's character, you may see that he erred more from absence of mind than any premeditation to give offence. He received, however, the next morning, a *lettre de cachet* from Fouché, which exiled him to Blois, and forbade him to return to

Paris without further orders from the minister of police. I know, from *high* authority, that to the interference of Princess Louis alone is he indebted for not being shut up in the Temple, and, perhaps, transported to our colonies, for having depreciated the power and means of France to invade England. I am perfectly convinced that none of those who spoke on the subject of the invasion expressed anything but what they really thought; and that, of the whole party, none, except Talleyrand, the Marquis and myself, entertained the least doubt of the success of the expedition; so firmly did they rely on the former fortune of Bonaparte, his boastings and his assurance.

After dinner I had an opportunity of conversing for ten minutes with Madame Louis Bonaparte, whom I found extremely amiable, but I fear that she is not happy. Her husband, though the most stupid, is, however, the best-tempered of the Bonapartes, and seemed very attentive and attached to her. She was far advanced in her pregnancy, and looked, notwithstanding, uncommonly well. I have heard that Louis is inclined to inebriation, and when in that situation is very brutal to his wife, and very indelicate with other women before her eyes. He intrigues with her own servants, and the number of his illegitimate children is said to be as many as his years. She asked General Murat to present me and recommend me to Fouché, which he did with great politeness; and the minister assured me that he should be glad to see me at his hotel, which I much doubt. The last words Madame Louis said to me, in showing me a princely crown, richly set with diamonds, and given her by her brother-in-law, Napoleon, were, "Alas! grandeur is not always happiness, nor the most elevated the most fortunate lot."

LETTER XVII

PARIS, *August*, 1805.

MY LORD,—The arrival of the Pope in this country was certainly a grand epoch, not only in the history of the Revolution, but in the annals of Europe. The debates in the Sacred College for and against this journey, and for and against his coronation of Bonaparte, are said to have been long as well as violent, and only arranged according to the desires of Cardinal Fesch by the means of four millions of livres— £166,000—distributed apropos among its pious members. Of this money, the Cardinals Mattei, Pamphili, Dugnani, Maury, Pignatelli, Roverella, Somaglia, Pacca, Brancadoro, Litta, Gabrielli, Spina, Despuig and Galeffi, are said to have shared the greatest part; and from the most violent anti-Bonapartists, they instantly became the strenuous adherents of Napoleon the First, who of course cannot be ignorant of their real worth.

The person entrusted by Bonaparte and Talleyrand to carry on at Rome the intrigue which sent Pius VII. to cross the Alps, was Cardinal Fesch, brother of Madame Letitia Bonaparte by the side of her mother, who, in a second marriage, chose a pedlar of the name of Nicolo Fesch, for her husband.

Joseph, Cardinal Fesch, was born at Ajaccio, in Corsica, on the 8th of March, 1763, and was in his infancy received as a singing boy (*enfant de chœur*) in a convent of his native place. In 1782, whilst he was on a visit to some of his relations in the Island of Sardinia, being on a fishing party some distance from shore, he was, with his companions, captured by an Algerine felucca, and carried a captive to Algiers. Here he turned Mussulman, and, until 1790, was a zealous believer in, and professor of, the Alcoran. In that year he found an opportunity to escape from Algiers, and to return to Ajaccio, when he abjured his renegacy, exchanged the Alcoran for the Bible, and, in 1791, was made a constitutional curate, that is to say, a revolutionary Christian priest. In 1793, when even those were proscribed, he renounced the sacristy of his Church for the bar of a tavern, where, during 1794 and 1795, he gained a small capital by the number and liberality of his English customers. After the victories of his nephew Napoleon in Italy during the following year, he was advised to reassume the clerical habit, and after Napoleon's proclamation of a First Consul he was made Archbishop of Lyons. In 1802, Pius VII. decorated him with the Roman purple, and he is now a pillar of the Roman faith, in a fair way of seizing the Roman tiara. If letters from Rome can be depended upon, Cardinal Fesch, in the name of the Emperor of the French, informed his Holiness the Pope that he must either retire to a convent or travel to France, either abdicate his own sovereignty, or inaugurate Napoleon the First a Sovereign of France. Without the decision of the Sacred College, effected in the manner already stated, the majority of the faithful believe that this Pontiff would have preferred obscurity to disgrace.

While Joseph Fesch was a master of a tavern he married the daughter of a tinker, by whom he had three children. This marriage, according to the republican regulations, had only been celebrated by the municipality at Ajaccio; Fesch, therefore, upon again entering the bosom of the Church, left his municipal wife and children to shift for themselves, considering himself still, according to the canonical laws, a bachelor. But Madame Fesch, hearing, in 1801, of her *ci-devant* husband's promotion to the Archbishopric of Lyons, wrote to him for some succours, being with her children reduced to great misery. Madame Letitia Bonaparte answered her letter, enclosing a draft for six hundred livres—£25—informing her that the same sum would be paid her every six months, as long as she continued with her children to reside at Corsica, but that it would cease the instant she left that island. Either thinking

in a fair way of seizing the Roman tiara. If letters from Rome are to be depended upon, Cardinal Fesch, in the name of the Emperor of the French, informed his Holiness the Pope that he must either retire to a convent or travel to France, either abdicate his own sovereignty, or inaugurate Napoleon the First a Sovereign of France. Without the decision of the Sacred College, effected in the manner already stated, the majority of the faithful believe that this Pontiff would have preferred obscurity to disgrace.

While Joseph Fesch was a master of a tavern he married the daughter of a tinker, by whom he had three children. This marriage, according to the republican regulations, had only been celebrated by the municipality at Ajaccio; Fesch, therefore, upon entering the bosom of the Church, left his municipal wife and children to shift for themselves, considering himself still, according to the canonical laws, a bachelor. But Madame Fesch, hearing, in 1801, of her *ci-devant* husband's promotion to the Archbishopric of Lyons, wrote to him for some succours, being with her children reduced to great misery. Madame Letitia Bonaparte answered her letter, enclosing a draft for six hundred livres—£25—informing her that the same sum would be paid her every six months, as long as she continued with her children to reside at Corsica, but that it would cease the instant she left that island. Either thinking

herself not sufficiently paid for her discretion, or enticed by some enemy of the Bonaparte family, she arrived secretly at Lyons in October last year, where she remained unknown until the arrival of the Pope. On the first day his Holiness gave there his public benediction, she found means to pierce the crowd, and to approach his person, when Cardinal Fesch was by his side. Profiting by a moment's silence, she called out loudly, throwing herself at his feet: "Holy Father! I am the lawful wife of Cardinal Fesch, and these are our children; he cannot, he dares not, deny this truth. Had he behaved liberally to me, I should not have disturbed him in his present grandeur; I supplicate you, Holy Father, not to restore me my husband, but to force him to provide for his wife and children, according to his present circumstances." — "*Matta — ella è matta, santissimo padre!* She is mad—she is mad, Holy Father," said the Cardinal; and the good Pontiff ordered her to be taken care of, to prevent her from doing herself or the children any mischief. She was, indeed, taken care of, because nobody ever since heard what has become either of her or her children; and as they have not returned to Corsica, probably some snug *retreat* has been allotted them in France.

The purple was never disgraced by a greater libertine than Cardinal Fesch: his amours are numerous, and have often involved him in disagreeable scrapes. He had, in 1803, an unpleasant adventure at Lyons, which has since made his stay in that city but short. Having thrown his handkerchief at the wife of a manufacturer of the name of Girot, she accepted it, and gave him an appointment at her house, at a time in the evening when her husband usually went to the play. His Eminence arrived in disguise, and was received with open arms. But he was hardly seated by her side before the door of a closet was burst open, and his shoulders smarted from the lashes inflicted by an offended husband. In vain did he mention his name and rank, they rather increased than decreased the fury of Girot, who pretended it was utterly impossible for a Cardinal and Archbishop to be thus overtaken with the wife of one of his flock; at last Madame Girot proposed a pecuniary accommodation, which, after some opposition, was acceded to; and his Eminence signed a bond for one hundred thousand livres—£4,000—upon condition that nothing should transpire of this intrigue—a high price enough for a sound drubbing. On the day when the bond was due, Girot and his wife were both arrested by the police commissary, Dubois (a brother of the prefect of police at Paris), accused of being connected with coiners, a capital crime at present in this country. In a search made in their house, bad money to the amount of three thousand livres—£125—was discovered; which they had received the day before from a man who called himself a merchant from Paris, but who was a police spy sent to entrap them. After giving up the bond of the Cardinal, the Emperor graciously remitted the capital punishment, upon condition that they should be transported for life to Cayenne.

This is the prelate on whom Bonaparte intends to confer the Roman tiara, and to constitute a successor of St. Peter. It would not be the least remarkable event in the beginning of the remarkable nineteenth century were we to witness the Papal throne occupied by a man who, from a singing boy became a renegade slave, from a Mussulman a constitutional curate, from a tavern-keeper an archbishop, from the son of a pedlar the uncle of an Emperor, and from the husband of the daughter of a tinker, a member of the Sacred College.

His sister, Madame Letitia Bonaparte, presented him, in 1802, with an elegant library, for which she had paid six hundred thousand livres—£25,000—and his nephew, Napoleon, allows him a yearly pension double that amount. Besides his dignity as a prelate, his Eminence is ambassador from France at Rome, a Knight of the Spanish Order of the Golden Fleece, a grand officer of the Legion of Honour, and a grand almoner of the Emperor of the French.

The Archbishop of Paris is now in his ninety-sixth year, and at his death Cardinal Fesch is to be transferred to the see of this capital, in expectation of the triple crown and the keys of St. Peter.

LETTER XVIII

Paris, *August*, 1805.

My Lord, — The amiable and accomplished Amelia Frédérique, Princess Dowager of the late Electoral Prince Charles Louis of Baden, born a Princess of Hesse-Darmstadt, has procured the Electoral House of Baden the singular honour of giving consorts to three reigning and sovereign Princes—to an Emperor of Russia, to a King of Sweden, and to the Elector of Bavaria. Such a distinction, and such alliances, called the attention of those at the head of our Revolution; who, after attempting in vain to blow up hereditary thrones by the aid of *sans-culotte* incendiaries, seated *sans-culottes* upon thrones, that they might degrade what was not yet ripe for destruction.

Charles Frederick, the reigning Elector of Baden, is now near fourscore years of age. At this period of life if any passions remain, avarice is more common than ambition; because treasures may be hoarded without bustle, while activity is absolutely necessary to push forward to the goal of distinction. Having bestowed a new King on

Tuscany, Bonaparte and Talleyrand also resolved to confer new Electors on Germany. A more advantageous fraternity could not be established between the innovators here, and their opposers in other countries, than by incorporating the grandfather-in-law of so many sovereigns with their own revolutionary brotherhood; to humble him by a new rank, and to disgrace him by indemnities obtained from their hands. An intrigue between our minister, Talleyrand, and the Baden minister, Edelsheim, transformed the oldest Margrave of Germany into its youngest Elector, and extended his dominions by the spoils obtained at the expense of the rightful owners. The invasion of the Baden territory in time of peace, and the seizure of the Duke of Enghien, though under the protection of the laws of nations and hospitality, must have soon convinced Baron Edelsheim what return his *friend* Talleyrand expected, and that Bonaparte thought he had a natural right to insult by his attacks those he had dishonoured by his connections.

The minister, Baron Edelsheim, is half an illuminato, half a philosopher, half a politician, and half a revolutionist. He was, long before he was admitted into the council chamber of his Prince, half an atheist, half an intriguer, and half a spy, in the pay of Frederick the Great of Prussia. His entry upon the stage at Berlin, and particularly the first parts he was destined to act, was curious and extraordinary; whether he acquitted himself better in this capacity than he has since in his political one is not known. He was afterwards sent to this capital to execute a commission, of which he acquitted himself very ill; exposing himself rashly, without profit or service to his employer. Frederick II., dreading the tediousness of a proposed congress at Augsburg, wished to send a private emissary to sound the King of France. For this purpose he chose Edelsheim as a person least liable to suspicion. The project of Frederick was to indemnify the King of Poland for his first losses by robbing the ecclesiastical Princes of Germany. This, Louis XV. totally rejected; and Edelsheim returned with his answer to the Prussian Monarch, then at Freyburg. From thence he afterwards departed for London, made his communications, and was once again sent back to Paris, on pretence that he had left some of his travelling trunks there; and the Bailli de Foulay, the ambassador of the Knights of Malta, being persuaded that the Cabinet of Versailles was effectually desirous of peace, was, as he had been before, the mediator. The Bailli was deceived. The Duke de Choiseul, the then prime minister, indecently enough threw Edelsheim into the Bastille, in order to search or seize his papers, which, however, were secured elsewhere. Edelsheim was released on the morrow, but obliged to depart the kingdom

by the way of Turin, as related by Frederick II. in his
"History of the Seven Years' War." On his return he was
disgraced, and continued so until 1778; when he again was
used as emissary to various Courts of Germany. In 1786
the Elector of Baden sent him to Berlin, on the ascension
of Frederick William II., as a complimentary envoy. This
monarch, when he saw him, could not forbear laughing at
the high wisdom of the Court that selected such a personage for such an embassy, and of his own sagacity in
accepting of it. He quitted the capital of Prussia as he
came there, with an opinion of himself that the royal
smiles of contempt had neither altered nor diminished.

You see by this account, that Edelsheim has long
been a partisan of the pillage of Germany called indemnities; and long habituated to affronts, as well as to plots.
To all his other half-qualities, half-modesty can hardly be
added, when he calls himself, or suffers himself to be
called, "the Talleyrand of Carlsruhe." He accompanied
his Prince last year to Mentz; where this old Sovereign
was not treated by Bonaparte in the most decorous or
decent manner, being obliged to wait for hours in his
ante-chamber, and afterwards stand during the levées, or
in the drawing-rooms of Napoleon or of his wife, without
the offer of a chair, or an invitation to sit down. It was
here where, by a secret treaty, Bonaparte became the

Sovereign of Baden, if sovereignty consists in the disposal of the financial and military resources of a State; and they were agreed to be assigned over to him whenever he should deem it proper or necessary to invade the German empire, in return for his protection against the Emperor of Germany, who can have no more interest than intent to attack a country so distant from his hereditary dominions, and whose Sovereign is, besides, the grandfather of the consort of his nearest and best ally.

Talleyrand often amused himself at Mentz with playing on the vanity and affected consequence of Edelsheim, who was delighted if at any time our minister took him aside, or whispered to him as in confidence. One morning, at the assembly of the Elector Arch-Chancellor, where Edelsheim was creeping and cringing about him as usual, he laid hold of his arm and walked with him to the upper part of the room. In a quarter of an hour they both joined the company, Edelsheim unusually puffed up with vanity. "I will lay any bet, gentlemen," said Talleyrand, "that you cannot, with all your united wits, guess the grand subject of my conversation with the good Baron Edelsheim." Without waiting for an answer, he continued: "As the Baron is a much older and more experienced traveller than myself, I asked him which, of all the countries he had visited, could boast the prettiest and kindest women. His reply was really very instructive, and it would be a great pity if justice were not done to his merit by its publicity." Here the Baron, red as a turkey-cock and trembling with anger, interrupted: "His Excellency," said he, "is to-night in a humour to joke; what we spoke of had nothing to do with women."— "Nor with men either," retorted Talleyrand, going away. This anecdote, Baron Dahlberg, the minister of the Elector of Baden to our Court, had the ingenuity to relate at Madame Chapui's as an evidence of Edelsheim's intimacy with Talleyrand; only he left out the latter part, and forgot to mention the bad grace with which this impertinence of Talleyrand was received; but this defect of memory Count de Beust, the envoy of the Elector Arch-Chancellor, *kindly* supplied.

Baron Edelsheim is a great amateur of knighthoods. On days of great festivities his face is, as it were, illuminated with the lustre of his stars; and the crosses on his coat conceal almost its original colour. Every petty prince of Germany has dubbed him a chevalier; but emperors and kings have not been so unanimous in distinguishing his desert, or in satisfying his desires.

At Mentz no prince or minister fawned more assiduously upon Bonaparte than this hero of chivalry. It could not escape notice, but need not have alarmed our great man, as was the case. The prefect of the palace was ordered to give authentic information concerning Edelsheim's *moral* and *political* character. He applied to the police commissary, who, within twenty hours, signed a declaration affirming that Edelsheim was the most inoffensive and least dangerous of all imbecile creatures that ever entered the Cabinet of a prince; that he had never drawn a sword, worn a dagger, or fired a pistol in his life; that the enquiries about his real character were sneered at in every part of the Electorate, as nowhere they allowed him common-sense, much less a character; all blamed his presumption, but none defended his capacity.

After the perusal of this report, Bonaparte asked Talleyrand, "What can Edelsheim mean by his troublesome assiduities? Does he want any indemnities, or does he wish me to make him a German prince? Can he have the impudence to hope that I should appoint him a tribune, a legislator, or a senator in France, or that I would give him a place in my council of state?"—"No such thing," answered the minister; "did not your Majesty condescend to notice at the last fête that this eclipsed moon was encompassed in a firmament of stars. You would, sire, make him the happiest of mortals were you to nominate him a member of your Legion of Honour."—"Does he want nothing else?" said Napoleon, as if relieved at once from an oppressive burden. "Write to my chancellor of the Legion of Honour, Lacépede, to send him a patent, and do you inform him of this favour."

It is reported at Carlsruhe, the capital of Baden, that Baron Edelsheim has composed his own epitaph, in which he claims *immortality*, because under his ministry the Margravate of Baden was elevated into an Electorate ! ! !

LETTER XIX

PARIS, *August*, 1805.

MY LORD,—The sensation that the arrival of the Pope in this country caused among the lower classes of people cannot be expressed, and if expressed, would not be believed. I am sorry, however, to say that, instead of improving their morals or increasing their faith, this journey has shaken both morality and religion to their foundation.

According to our religious notions, as you must know, the Roman Pontiff is the vicar of Christ, and infallible; he can never err. The atheists of the National Convention and the Theophilanthropists of the Directory not only denied his demi-divinity, but transformed him into a satyr; and in pretending to tear the veil of superstition, annihilated all belief in a God. The ignorant part of our nation, which, as everywhere else, constitutes the majority, witnessing the impunity and prosperity of crime, and bestowing on the Almighty the passions of mortals, first doubted of His omnipotence in not crushing guilt, and afterwards of His existence in not exterminating the blasphemers from among the living. Feeling, however, the want of consolation in their misfortunes here, and hope of a reward hereafter for unmerited sufferings upon earth, they all hailed as a blessing the restoration of Christianity; and by this *political* act Bonaparte gained more adherents than by all his victories he had procured admirers.

Bonaparte's character, his good and his bad qualities, his talents and his crimes, are too recent and too notorious to require description. Should he continue successful, and be attended by fortune to his grave, future ages may perhaps hail him a hero and a great man; but by his contemporaries it will always be doubtful whether mankind has not suffered more from his ambition and cruelties than benefited by his services. Had he satisfied himself by continuing the chief magistrate of a commonwealth; or, if he judged that a monarchical government alone was suitable to the spirit of this country, had he recalled our legitimate King, he would have occupied a principal, if not the first, place in the history of France; a place much more exalted than he can ever expect to fill as an Emperor of the French. Let his prosperity be ever so uninterrupted, he cannot be mentioned but as an usurper; an appellation never exciting esteem, frequently inspiring contempt, and always odious.

The crime of usurpation is the greatest and most enormous a subject can perpetrate; but what epithet can there be given to him who, to preserve an authority unlawfully acquired, associates in his guilt a Supreme Pontiff, whom the multitude is accustomed to reverence as the representative of their God, but who, by this act of scandal and sacrilege, descends to a level with the most culpable of men? I have heard, not only in this city but in villages, where sincerity is more frequent than corruption, and where hypocrites are as little known as infidels, these remarks made by the people: "Can the real vicar of Christ, by his inauguration, commit the double injustice of depriving the legitimate owner of his rights, and of bestowing as a sacred donation what belongs to another; and what he has no power, no authority, to dispose of? Can Pius VII. confer on Napoleon the First what belongs to Louis XVIII.? Would Jesus Christ. if upon earth, have acted thus? Would his immediate successors, the Apostles, not have preferred the suffering of martyrdom to the commission of any injury? If the present Roman Pontiff acts differently from what his Master and predecessors would have done, can he be the vicar of our Saviour?" These and many similar reflections the common people have made, and make yet. The step from doubt to disbelief is but short, and those brought up in the Roman Catholic religion, who hesitate about believing Pius VII. to be the vicar of Christ, will soon remember the precepts of atheists and freethinkers, and believe that Christ is not the Son of God, and that a God is only the invention of fear.

The fact is, that by the Pope's performance of the coronation of an Emperor of the French, a religious as well as a political revolution was effected: and the usurper in power, whatever his creed may be, will hereafter, without much difficulty, force it on his slaves. You may perhaps object that Pius VII., in his official account to the Sacred College of his journey to France, speaks with enthusiasm of the Catholicism of the French people. But did not the Goddess of Reason, did not Robespierre as a high priest of a Supreme Being, speak as highly of their sectaries? Read the *Moniteur* of 1793 and 1794, and you will be convinced of the truth of this assertion. They, like the Pope, spoke of what they saw, and they, like him, did not see an individual who was not instructed how to perform his part, so as to give satisfaction to him whom he was to please, and to those who employed him. As you have attended to the history of our Revolution, you have found it in great part a cruel masquerade, where none but the unfortunate Louis XVI. appeared in his native and natural character and without a mask.

The countenance of Pius VII. is placid and benign, and a kind of calmness and tranquillity pervades his address and manners, which are, however, far from being easy or elegant. The crowds that he must have been accustomed to see since his present elevation, have not lessened a timidity the consequence of early seclusion. Nothing troubled him more than the numerous deputations of our Senate, Legislative Body, Tribunate, National Institute, Tribunals, &c., that teased him on every occasion. He never was suspected of any vices, but all his virtues are negative; and his best quality is, not to do good, but to prevent evil. His piety is sincere and unaffected, and it is not difficult to perceive that he has been more accustomed to address his God than to converse with men. He is nowhere so well in his place as before the altar; when imploring the blessings of Providence on his audience he speaks with confidence, as to a friend to whom his purity is known, and who is accustomed to listen favourably to his prayers. He is zealous but not fanatical, but equally superstitious as devout. His closet was crowded with relics, rosaries, &c., but there he passed generally eight hours of the twenty-four upon his knees in prayer and meditation. He often inflicted on himself mortifications, observed fast-days, and kept his vows with religious strictness.

None of the promises made him by Cardinal Fesch, in the name of Napoleon the First, were performed, but were put off until a general pacification. He was promised indemnity for Avignon, Bologna, Ferrara and Ravenna; the ancient supremacy and pecuniary contributions of the Gallican Church, and the restoration of certain religious orders, both in France and Italy; but notwithstanding his own representations, and the activity of his Cardinal, Caprara, nothing was decided, though nothing was refused.

By some means or other he was become perfectly acquainted with the crimes and vices of most of our public functionaries. Talleyrand was surprised when Cardinal Caprara explained to him the reason why the Pope refused to admit some persons to his presence, and why he wished others even not to be of the party when he accepted of the invitations of Bonaparte and his wife to their private societies. Many are, however, of opinion that Talleyrand, from malignity or revenge, often heightened and confirmed his Holiness's aversion. This was at least once the case with regard to De Lalande. When Duroc enquired the cause of the Pope's displeasure against this astronomer, and hinted that it would be very agreeable to the Emperor were his Holiness to permit him the honour of prostrating himself, he was answered, that men of talents and learning would always be welcome to approach his person; that he pitied the errors and prayed for the conversion of this *savant*, but was neither displeased nor offended with him. Talleyrand, when informed of the Pope's answer, accused Cardinal Caprara of having misinterpreted his master's communications; and this prelate, in his turn, censured our minister's bad memory.

You must have read that this De Lalande is regarded in France as the first astronomer of Europe, and hailed as the high priest of atheists; he is said to be the author of a shockingly blasphemous work called "The Bible of a People who acknowledge no God." He *implored* the ferocious Robespierre to *honour* the heavens by bestowing on a new planet pretended to be discovered his *ci-devant* christian-name, Maximilian. In a letter of congratulation to Bonaparte, on the occasion of his present elevation, he also *implored* him to *honour* the God of the Christians by styling himself Jesus Christ the First, Emperor of the French, instead of Napoleon the First. But it was not his known impiety that made Talleyrand wish to exclude him from insulting with his presence a Christian pontiff. In the summer of 1799, when the minister was in a momentary disgrace, De Lalande was at the head of those who imputed to his treachery, corruption and machinations all the evils France then suffered, both from external enemies and internal factions. If Talleyrand has justly been reproached for soon forgetting good offices and services done him, nobody ever denied that he has the best recollection in the world of offences or attacks, and that he is as revengeful as unforgiving.

The only one of our *great* men whom Pius VII. remained obstinate and inflexible in not receiving, was the senator and minister of police, Fouché. As his Holiness was not so particular with regard to other persons who, like Fouché, were both apostate priests and regicide subjects, the following is reported to be the cause of his aversion and obduracy :—

In November, 1793, the remains of a wretch of the name of Challiers—justly called, for his atrocities, the Marat of Lyons—were ordered by Fouché, then a representative of the people in that city, to be produced and publicly worshipped; and, under his particular auspices, a grand fête was performed to the memory of this republican *martyr*, who had been executed as an assassin. As part of this impious ceremony, an ass, covered with a bishop's vestments, having on his head a mitre, and the volumes of Holy Writ tied to his tail, paraded the streets. The remains of Challiers were then burnt, and the ashes distributed among his adorers; while the books were also consumed, and the ashes scattered in the wind. Fouché proposed, after giving the ass some water to drink in a sacred chalice, to terminate the festivity of the day by murdering all the prisoners, amounting to seven thousand five hundred; but a sudden storm prevented the execution of this diabolical proposition, and dispersed the sacrilegious congregation.

LETTER XX

Paris, *August*, 1805.

My Lord, — Though all the Bonapartes were great favourites with Pius VII., Madame Letitia, their mother, had a visible preference. In her apartments he seemed most pleased to meet the *family parties*, as they were called, because to them, except the Bonapartes, none but a few select favourites were invited; a distinction as much wished for and envied as any other Court honour. After the Pope had fixed the evening he would appear among them, Duroc made out a list, under the dictates of Napoleon, of the chosen few destined to partake of the blessing of his Holiness's presence; this list was merely *pro formâ*, or as a compliment, laid before him; and after his *tacit* approbation, the individuals were informed, from the first chamberlain's office, that they would be honoured with admittance at such an hour, to such a company, and in such an apartment. The dress in which they were to appear was also prescribed. The parties usually met at six o'clock in the evening. On the Pope's entrance all persons, of both sexes, kneeled to receive his blessing. Tea, ice, liqueurs and confectionery were then served. In the place of honour were three elevated elbow-chairs, and his Holiness was seated between the Emperor and Empress, and seldom spoke to anyone to whom Napoleon did not previously address the word. The exploits of Bonaparte, particularly his campaigns in Egypt, were the chief subjects of conversation. Before eight o'clock the Pope always retired, distributing his blessing to the kneeling audience, as on his entry. When he was gone, card-tables were brought in, and play was permitted. Duroc received his master's orders how to distribute the places at the different tables, what games were to be played, and the amount of the sums to be staked. These were usually trifling and small compared to what is daily risked in our fashionable circles.

Often, after the Pope had returned to his own rooms, Madame Letitia Bonaparte was admitted to assist at his private prayers. This lady, whose intrigues and gallantry are proverbial in Corsica, has, now that she is old (as is generally the case), turned devotee, and is surrounded by hypocrites and impostors, who, under the mask of sanctity, deceive and plunder her. Her ante-chambers are always full of priests; and her closet and bedroom are crowded with relics, which she collected during her journey to Italy last year. She might, if she chose, establish a Catholic museum, and furnish it with a more curious collection, in its sort, than any of our other museums contain. Of all the saints in our calendar, there is not one of any notoriety who has not supplied her with a finger, a toe, or some other part; or with a piece of a shirt, a handkerchief, a sandal, or a winding-sheet. Even a bit of a pair of breeches, said to have belonged to St. Mathurin, whom many think was a *sans-culotte*, obtains her adoration on certain occasions. As none of her children have yet arrived at the same height of faith as herself, she has, in her will, bequeathed to the Pope all her relics, together with eight hundred and seventy-nine Prayer-Books, and four hundred and forty-six Bibles, either in manuscript or of different editions. Her favourite breviary, used only on great solemnities, was presented to her by Cardinal Maury at Rome, and belonged, as it is said, formerly to St. François, whose commentary, written with his own hand, fills the margins; though many, who with me adore him as a saint, doubt whether he could either read or write.

Not long ago she made, as she thought, an exceedingly valuable acquisition. A priest arrived direct from the Holy City of Jerusalem, well recommended by the inhabitants of the convents there, with whom he pretended to have passed his youth. After prostrating himself before the Pope, he waited on Madame Letitia Bonaparte. He told her that he had brought with him from Syria the famous relic, the shoulder-bone of St. John the Baptist; but that, being in want of money for his voyage, he borrowed upon it from a Grecian Bishop in Montenegro two hundred louis d'or. This sum, and one hundred louis d'or besides, was immediately given him; and within three months, for a large sum in addition to those advanced, this precious relic was in Madame Letitia's possession.

Notwithstanding this lady's care not to engage in her service any person of either sex who cannot produce, not a certificate of *civism* from the municipality as was formerly the case, but a certificate of Christianity, and a billet of confession signed by the curate of the parish, she had often been robbed, and the robbers had made particularly free with those relics which were set in gold or in diamonds. She accused her daughter, the Princess Borghese, who often rallies the devotion of her mamma, and who is more an *amateur* of the living than of the dead, of having played her these tricks. The Princess informed Napoleon of her mother's losses, as well as of her own innocence, and asked him to apply to the police to find out the thief, who no doubt was one of the pious rogues who almost devoured their mother.

On the next day Napoleon invited Madame Letitia to dinner, and Fouché had orders to make a strict search, during her absence, among the persons composing her household. Though he, on this occasion, did not find what he was looking for, he made a discovery which very much mortified Madame Letitia.

Her first chambermaid, Rosina Gaglini, possessed both her esteem and confidence, and had been sent for purposely from Ajaccio, in Corsica, on account of her general renown for great piety, and a report that she was an exclusive favourite with the Virgin Mary, by whose interference she had even performed, it was said, some miracles: such as restoring stolen goods, runaway cattle, lost children, and procuring prizes in the lottery. Rosina was as relic-mad as her mistress; and as she had no means to procure them otherwise, she determined to partake of her lady's by cutting off a small part of each relic of Madame Letitia's principal saints. These precious morceaux she placed in a box upon which she kneeled to say her prayers during the day; and which, for a mortification, served her as a pillow during the night. Upon each of the sacred bits she had affixed a label with the name of the saint it belonged to, which occasioned the disclosure.

When Madame Letitia heard of this pious theft, she insisted on having the culprit immediately and severely punished; and though the Princess Borghese, as the innocent cause of poor Rosina's misfortune, interfered, and Rosina herself promised never more to plunder saints, she was without mercy turned away, and even denied money sufficient to carry her back to Corsica. Had she made free with Madame Letitia's plate or wardrobe, there is no doubt but that she had been forgiven; but to presume to share with her those sacred supports on her way to Paradise was a more unpardonable act with a devotee than to steal from a lover the portrait of an adored mistress.

In the meantime the police were upon the alert to discover the person whom they suspected of having stolen the relics for the diamonds, and not the diamonds for the relics. Among our fashionable and new saints, surprising as you may think it, Madame de Genlis holds a distinguished place; and she, too, is an *amateur* and collector of relics in proportion to her means; and with her were found those missed by Madame Letitia. Being asked to give up the name of him from whom she had purchased them, she mentioned Abbé Saladin, the pretended priest from Jerusalem. He, in his turn, was questioned, and by his answers gave rise to suspicion that he himself was the thief. The person of whom he pretended to have bought them was not to be found, nor was anyone of such a description remembered to have been seen anywhere. On being carried to prison, he claimed the protection of Madame Letitia, and produced a letter in which this lady had promised him a bishopric either in France or in Italy.

When she was informed of his situation, she applied to her son Napoleon for his liberty; urging that a priest who from Jerusalem had brought with him to Europe such an extraordinary relic as the shoulder of St. John, could not be culpable.

Abbé Saladin had been examined by Real, who concluded, from the accent and perfection with which he spoke the French language, that he was some French adventurer who had imposed on the credulity and superstition of Madame Letitia; and, therefore, threatened him with the rack if he did not confess the truth. He continued, however, in his story, and was going to be released upon an order from the Emperor, when a gendarme recognized him as a person who, eight years before, had, under the name of Lanoue, been condemned for theft and forgery to the galleys, from whence he had made his escape. Finding himself discovered, he avowed everything. He said he had served in Egypt, in the guides of Bonaparte, but· deserted to the Turks and turned Mussulman, but afterwards returned to the bosom of the Church at Jerusalem. There he persuaded the friars that he had been a priest, and obtained the certificates which introduced him to the Pope and to the Emperor's mother; from whom he had received twelve thousand livres—£500—for part of the jaw-bone of a whale, which he had sold her for the shoulder-bone of a saint. As the police believe the certificates he has produced to be also forged, he is detained in prison until an answer arrives from our consul in Syria.

Madame Letitia did not resign without tears the relic he had sold her; and there is reason to believe that many other pieces of her collections, worshipped by her as remains of saints, are equally genuine as this shoulder-bone of St. John.

LETTER XXI

PARIS, *August*, 1805.

MY LORD,—That the population of this capital has, since the Revolution, decreased near two hundred thousand souls, is not to be lamented. This focus of corruption and profligacy is still too populous, though the inhabitants do not amount to six hundred thousand; for I am well persuaded that more crimes and excesses of every description are committed here in one year, than are perpetrated in the same period of time in all other European capitals put together. From not reading in our newspapers, as we do in yours, of the robberies, murders and frauds discovered and punished, you may, perhaps, be inclined to suppose my assertion erroneous or exaggerated; but it is the policy of our present Government *to labour as much as possible in the dark;* that is to say, to prevent, where it can be done, all publicity of anything directly or indirectly tending to inculpate it of oppression, tyranny, or even negligence; and to conceal the immorality of the people so nearly connected with its own immoral power. It is true that many vices and crimes here, as well as everywhere else, are unavoidable, and the natural consequences of corruption and might be promulgated, therefore, without attaching any reproach to our rulers; but they are so accustomed to the mystery adherent to tyranny, that even the most unimportant lawsuit, uninteresting intrigue, elopement, or divorce, are never allowed to be mentioned in our journals, without a previous permission from the prefect of police, who very seldom grants it.

Most of the enormities now deplored in this country, are the consequence of moral and religious licentiousness, that have succeeded to political anarchy, or rather were produced by it, and survive it. Add to this the numerous examples of the impunity of guilt, prosperity of infamy, misery of honesty and sufferings of virtue, and you will not think it surprising that, notwithstanding half-a-million of spies, our roads and streets are covered with robbers and assassins, and our scaffolds with victims.

The undeniable TRUTH that this city alone is watched by one hundred thousand spies (so that, when in company with six persons, one has reason to dread the presence of one spy), proclaims at once the morality of the governors and that of the governed: were the former just, and the latter good, this mass of vileness would never be employed, or, if employed, wickedness would expire for want of fuel, and the hydra of tyranny perish by its own pestilential breath.

According to the official registers published by Manuel in 1792, the number of spies all over France during the reign of Louis XVI. were nineteen thousand three hundred (five thousand less than under Louis XV.), and of this number six thousand were distributed in Paris, and in a circle of four leagues around it, including Versailles. You will undoubtedly ask me, even allowing for our extension of territory, what can be the cause of this disproportionate increase of mistrust and depravity? I will explain it as far as my abilities admit, according to the opinions of others compared with my own remarks.

When factions usurped the supremacy of the kings, vigilance augmented with insecurity; and almost everybody who was not an opposer, who refused being an accomplice, or feared to be a victim, was obliged to serve as an informer and vilify himself by becoming a spy. The rapidity with which parties followed and destroyed each other made the criminals as numerous as the sufferings of honour and loyalty innumerable; and I am sorry to say few persons exist in my degraded country, whose firmness and constancy were proof against repeated torments and trials, and who, to preserve their lives, did not renounce their principles and probity.

Under the reign of Robespierre and of the Committee of Public Safety, every member of Government, of the clubs, of the tribunals, and of the communes, had his private spies; but no regular register was kept of their exact number. Under the Directory a police minister was nominated, and a police office established. According to the declaration of the police minister, Cochon, in 1797, the spies, who were then regularly paid, amounted to one hundred and fifty thousand; and of these, thirty thousand did duty in this capital. How many they were in 1799, when Fouché, for the first time, was appointed a chief of the department of police, is not known, but suppose them doubled within two years; their increase since is nevertheless immense, considering that France has enjoyed upwards of four years' uninterrupted Continental peace, and has not been exposed to any internal convulsions during the same period.

You may, perhaps, object that France is not rich enough to keep up as numerous an army of spies as of soldiers; because the expense of the former must be triple the amount of the latter. Were all these spies, now called police agents, or agents of the secret police, paid regular salaries, your objection would stand, but most of them have no other reward than the protection of the police; being employed in gambling-houses, in coffee-houses, in taverns, at the theatres, in the public gardens, in the hotels, in lottery offices, at pawnbrokers', in brothels, and in bathing-houses, where the proprietors or masters of these establishments pay them. They receive nothing from the police, but when they are enabled to make any great discoveries, those who have been robbed or defrauded, and to whom they have been serviceable, are, indeed, obliged to present them with some douceur, fixed by the police at the rate of the value recovered; but such occurrences are merely accidental. To these are to be added all individuals of either sex who by the law are obliged to obtain from the police licences to exercise their trade, as pedlars, tinkers. masters of puppet-shows, wild beasts, &c. These, on receiving their passes, inscribe themselves, and take the oaths as spies; and are forced to send in their regular reports of what they hear or see. Prostitutes, who, all over this country, are under the necessity of paying for regular licences, are obliged also to give information, from time to time, to the nearest police commissary of what they observe or what they know respecting their visitors, neighbours, &c. The number of unfortunate women of this description who had taken out licences during the year 12, or from September, 1803, to September, 1804, is officially known to have amounted to two hundred and twenty thousand, of whom *forty thousand were employed by the armies.*

It is no secret that Napoleon Bonaparte has his secret spies upon his wife, his brothers, his sisters, his ministers, senators, and other public functionaries, and also upon his public spies. These are all under his own immediate control and that of Duroc, who does the duty of his private police minister, and in whom he confides more than even in the members of his own family. In imitation of their master, each of the other Bonapartes, and each of the ministers, have their individual spies, and are watched in their turn by the spies of their secretaries, clerks, &c. This infamous custom of espionage goes *ad infinitum*, and appertains almost to the establishment and to the suite of each man in place, who does not think himself secure a moment if he remains in ignorance of the transactions of his rivals, as well as of those of his equals and superiors.

Fouché and Talleyrand are reported to have disagreed before Bonaparte on some subject or other, which is frequently the case. The former, offended at some doubts thrown out about his intelligence, said to the latter, " I am so well served that I can tell you the name of every man or woman you have conversed with, both yesterday and to-day; where you saw them, and how long you remained with them or they with you." — " If such commonplace espionage evinces any merit," retorted Talleyrand, " I am even here your superior; because I know not only what has already passed with you and in your house, but what is to pass hereafter. I can inform you of every dish you had for your dinners this week, who provided these dinners, and who is expected to provide your meats to-morrow and the day after. I can whisper you, *in confidence*, who slept with Madame Fouché last night, and who has an appointment with her to-night." Here Bonaparte interrupted them, in his usual dignified language: "Hold both your tongues; you are both great rogues, but I am at a loss to decide which is the greatest." Without uttering a single syllable, Talleyrand made a profound reverence to Fouché. Bonaparte smiled, and advised them to live upon good terms if they were desirous of keeping their places.

A man of the name of Ducroux, who, under Robespierre, had from a barber been made a general, and afterwards broken for his ignorance, was engaged by Bonaparte as a private spy upon Fouché, who employed him in the same capacity upon Bonaparte. His reports were always written, and delivered in person into the hands both of the Emperor and of his minister. One morning he, by mistake, gave to Bonaparte the report of him instead of that intended for him. Bonaparte began to read: "Yesterday, at nine o'clock, the Emperor acted the complete part of a madman; he swore, stamped, kicked, foamed, roared"—here poor Ducroux threw himself at Bonaparte's feet, and called for mercy for the terrible blunder he had committed. "For whom," asked Bonaparte, "did you intend this treasonable correspondence? I suppose it is composed for some English or Russian agent, for Pitt or for Marcofl. How long have you conspired with my enemies, and where are your accomplices?"—"For God's sake, hear me, Sire," prayed Ducroux. "Your Majesty's enemies have always been mine. The report is for one of your best friends; but were I to mention his name, he will ruin me."—"Speak out, or you die!" vociferated Bonaparte.—"Well, Sire, it is for Fouché—for nobody else but Fouché." Bonaparte then rang the bell for Duroc, whom he ordered to see Ducroux shut up in a dungeon, and afterwards to send for Fouché. The minister denied all knowledge of Ducroux, who, after undergoing several tortures, expiated his blunder upon the rack.

LETTER XXII

Paris, *August*, 1805.

My Lord,—The Pope, during his stay here, rose regularly every morning at five o'clock, and went to bed every night before ten. The first hours of the day he passed in prayers, breakfasted after the Mass was over, transacted business till one, and dined at two. Between three and four he took his *siesta*, or nap; afterwards he attended the vespers, and when they were over, he passed an hour with the Bonapartes, or admitted to his presence some members of the clergy. The day was concluded, as it was begun, with some hours of devotion.

Had Pius VII. possessed the character of a Pius VI., he would never have crossed the Alps; or had he been gifted with the spirit and talents of Sextus V. or Leo X., he would never have entered France to crown Bonaparte, without previously stipulating for himself that he should be put into possession of the sovereignty of Italy. You can form no idea what great stress was laid on this act of his Holiness by the Bonaparte family, and what sacrifices were destined to be made had any serious and obstinate resistance been apprehended. Threats were, indeed, employed personally against the Pope, and bribes distributed to the refractory members of the Sacred College ; but it was no secret, either here or at Milan, that Cardinal Fesch had *carte blanche* with regard to the restoration of all provinces seized, since the war, from the Holy See, or full territorial indemnities in their place, at the expense of Naples and Tuscany ; and, indeed, whatever the Roman Pontiff has lost in Italy has been taken from him by Bonaparte alone, and the apparent generosity which policy and ambition required, would, therefore, have merely been an act of justice. Confiding foolishly in the *honour* and *rectitude* of Napoleon, without any other security than the assertion of Fesch, Pius VII., within a fortnight's stay in France, found the great difference between the promises held out to him when residing as a Sovereign at Rome, and their accomplishment when he had so far forgotten himself and his sacred dignity as to inhabit as a guest the castle of the Tuileries.

Pius VII. mentioned, the day after his arrival at Fontainebleau, that it would be a gratification to his own subjects were he enabled to communicate to them the restoration of the former ecclesiastical domains, as a *free gift* of the Emperor of the French, at their first conference, as they would then be as well convinced of Napoleon's *good faith* as he was himself. In answer, his Holiness was informed that the Emperor was unprepared then to discuss political subjects, being totally occupied with the thoughts how to entertain worthily his high visitor, and to acknowledge becomingly the great honour done and the great happiness conferred on him by such a visit. As soon as the ceremony of the coronation was over, everything, *he hoped*, would be arranged to the reciprocal satisfaction of both parties.

About the middle of last December, Bonaparte was again asked to fix a day when the points of negotiation between him and the Pope could be discussed and settled. Cardinal Caprara, who made this demand, was referred to Talleyrand, who denied having yet any instructions, though in daily expectation of them. Thus the time went on until February, when Bonaparte informed the Pope of his determination to assume the crown of Italy, and of some new changes necessary in consequence on the other side of the Alps.

Either seduced by caresses, or blinded by his unaccountable partiality for Bonaparte, Pius VII., if left to himself, would not only have renounced all his former claims, but probably have made new sacrifices to this idol of his infatuation. Fortunately, his counsellors were wiser and less deluded, otherwise the remaining patrimony of

St. Peter might now have constituted a part of Napoleon's *inheritance* in Italy. "Am I not, Holy Father!" exclaimed the Emperor frequently, "your son, the work of your hand? And if the pages of history assign me any glory, must it not be shared with you — or rather, do you not share it with me? Anything that impedes my successes, or makes the continuance of my power uncertain or hazardous, reflects on you and is dangerous to you. With me you will shine or be obscured, rise or fall. Could you, therefore, hesitate (were I to demonstrate to you the necessity of such a measure) to remove the Papal See to Avignon, where it formerly was and continued for centuries, and to enlarge the limits of my kingdom of Italy with the Ecclesiastical States? Can you believe my throne at Milan safe as long as it is not the SOLE throne of Italy? Do you expect to govern at Rome when I cease to reign at Milan? No, Holy Father! the Pontiff who placed the crown on my head, should it be shaken, will fall to rise no more." If what Cardinal Caprara said can be depended upon, Bonaparte frequently used to intimidate or flatter the Pope in this manner.

The representations of Cardinal Caprara changed Napoleon's first intention of being again crowned by the Pope as a King of Italy. His crafty Eminence observed that, according to the Emperor's own declaration, it was not intended that the crowns of France and Italy should continue united. But were he to cede one supremacy confirmed by the sacred hands of a Pontiff, the partisans of the Bourbons, or the factions in France, would then take advantage to diminish in the opinion of the people his right and the sacredness of his Holiness, and perhaps make even the crown of the French empire unstable. He did not deny that Charlemagne was crowned by a Pontiff in Italy, but this ceremony was performed at Rome, where that Prince was proclaimed an Emperor of the Holy Roman and German empires, as well as a King of Lombardy and Italy. Might not circumstances turn out so favourably for Napoleon the First that he also might be inaugurated an Emperor of the Germans as well as of the French? This last compliment, or *prophecy*, as Bonaparte's courtiers call it (what a prophet a Caprara!) had the desired effect, as it flattered equally Napoleon's ambition and vanity. For fear, however, of Talleyrand and other anti-Catholic counsellors, who wanted him to consider the Pope merely as his first almoner, and to treat him as all other persons of his household, his Eminence sent his Holiness as soon as possible packing for Rome. Though I am neither a Cardinal nor a prophet, should you and I live twenty years longer, and the other Continental Sovereigns not alter their present incomprehensible conduct, I can, without any risk, predict that we shall see Rome salute the second Charlemagne an Emperor of the Holy Roman Empire, if before that time death does not put a period to his encroachments and gigantic plans.

LETTER XXIII

PARIS, *August*, 1805.

MY LORD,—No sovereigns have, since the Revolution, displayed more grandeur of soul, and evinced more firmness of character, than the present King and Queen of Naples. Encompassed by a revolutionary volcano more dangerous than the physical one, though disturbed at home and defeated abroad, they have neither been disgraced nor dishonoured. They have, indeed, with all other Italian princes, suffered territorial and pecuniary losses; but these were not yielded through cowardice or treachery, but enforced by an absolute necessity, the consequence of the desertion or inefficacy of allies.

But their Sicilian Majesties have been careful, as much as they were able, to exclude from their councils both German Illuminati and Italian philosophers. Their principal minister, Chevalier Acton, has proved himself worthy of the confidence with which his Sovereigns have honoured him, and of the hatred with which he has been honoured by all revolutionists—the natural and irreconcilable enemies of all legitimate sovereignty.

Chevalier Acton is the son of an Irish physician, who first was established at Besançon in France, and afterwards at Leghorn in Italy. He is indebted for his present elevation to his own merit and to the penetration of the Queen of Sardinia, who discovered in him, when young, those qualities which have since distinguished him as a faithful counsellor and an able minister. As loyal as wise, he was, from 1789, an enemy to the French Revolution. He easily foresaw that the specious promise of regeneration held out by impostors or fools to delude the ignorant, the credulous and the weak, would end in that universal corruption and general overthrow which we since have witnessed, and the effects ot which our grandchildren will mourn.

When our Republic, in April, 1792, declared war against Austria, and when in the September following, the dominions of his Sardinian Majesty were invaded by our troops, the neutrality of Naples continued, and was acknowledged by our Government. On the 16th of December following, our fleet from Toulon, however, cast anchor in the Bay of Naples, and a grenadier of the name of Belleville was landed as an ambassador of the French Republic, and threatened a bombardment in case the demands he presented in a note were not acceded to within twenty-four hours. Being attacked in time of peace, and taken by surprise, the Court of Naples was unable to make any resistance, and Chevalier Acton informed our grenadier ambassador that this note had been laid before his Sovereign, who had ordered him to sign an agreement in consequence.

When in February, 1793, the King of Naples was obliged, for his own safety, to join the league against France, Acton concluded a treaty with your country, and informed the Sublime Porte of the machinations of our Committee of Public Safety in sending De Semonville as an ambassador to Constantinople, which, perhaps, prevented the Divan from attacking Austria, and occasioned the capture and imprisonment of our emissary.

Whenever our Government has, by the success of our arms, been enabled to dictate to Naples, the removal of Acton has been insisted upon; out though he has ceased to transact business ostensibly as a minister, his influence has always, and deservedly, continued unimpaired, and he still enjoys the just confidence and esteem of his Prince.

But is his Sicilian Majesty equally well represented at the Cabinet of St. Cloud as served in his own capital? I have told you before that Bonaparte is extremely particular in his acceptance of foreign diplomatic agents, and admits none near his person whom he does not believe to be well inclined to him.

Marquis de Gallo, the ambassador of the King of the Two Sicilies to the Emperor of the French, is no novice in the diplomatic career. His Sovereign has employed him for these fifteen years in the most delicate negotiations, and nominated him in May, 1795, a minister of the Foreign Department, and a successor of Chevalier Acton, an honour which he declined. In the summer and autumn, 1797, Marquis de Gallo assisted at the conferences at Udine, and signed, with the Austrian plenipotentiaries, the Peace of Campo Formio, on the 17th of October, 1797.

During 1798, 1799 and 1800 he resided as Neapolitan ambassador at Vienna, and was again entrusted by his Sovereign with several important transactions with Austria and Russia. After a peace had been agreed to between France and the Two Sicilies, in March, 1801, and the Court of Naples had every reason to fear, and of course to please, the Court of St. Cloud, he obtained his present appointment, and is one of the few foreign ambassadors here who has escaped both Bonaparte's *private* admonitions in the diplomatic circle and public lectures in Madame Bonaparte's drawing-room.

This escape is so much the more fortunate and singular as our Government is far from being content with the *mutinous* spirit (as Bonaparte calls it) of the Government of Naples, which, considering its precarious and enfeebled state, with a French army in the heart of the kingdom, has resisted our attempts and insults with a courage and dignity that demand our admiration.

It is said that the Marquis de Gallo is not entirely free from some taints of modern philosophy, and that he, therefore, does not consider the consequences of our innovations so fatal as most loyal men judge them; nor thinks a *sans-culotte* Emperor more dangerous to civilized society than a *sans-culotte* sovereign people.

It is evident from the names and rank of its partisans that the Revolution of Naples in 1799 was different in many respects from that of every other country in Europe; for, although the political convulsions seem to have originated among the middle classes of the community, the extremes of society were everywhere else made to act against each other; the rabble being the first to triumph, and the nobles to succumb. But here, on the contrary, the *lazzaroni*, composed of the lowest portion of the population of a luxurious capital, appear to have been the most strenuous, and, indeed, almost the only supporters of royalty; while the great families, instead of being indignant at novelties which levelled them, in point of political rights, with the meanest subject, eagerly embraced the opportunity of altering that form of government which alone made them great. It is, however, but justice to say that, though Marquis de Gallo gained the good graces of Bonaparte and of France in 1797, he was never, directly or indirectly, inculpated in the revolutionary transactions of his countrymen in 1799, when he resided at Vienna; and indeed, after all, it is not improbable that he disguises his real sentiments the better to serve his country, and by that means has imposed on Bonaparte and acquired his favour.

The address and manners of a courtier are allowed Marquis de Gallo by all who know him, though few admit that he possesses any talents as a statesman. He is said to have read a great deal, to possess a good memory and no bad judgment · but that, notwithstanding this, all his knowledge is superficial, *aliquid in omnibus et nihil in toto.*

LETTER XXIV

PARIS, *August*, 1805

MY LORD,—You have perhaps heard that Napoleon Bonaparte, with all his brothers and sisters, was last Christmas *married* by the Pope according to the Roman Catholic rite, being previously only *united* according to the municipal laws of the French Republic, which consider marriage only as a civil contract. During the two last months of his Holiness's residence here, hardly a day passed that he was not petitioned to perform the same ceremony for our *conscientious* grand functionaries and courtiers, which he, however, according to the Emperor's *desire*, declined But his Cardinals were not under the same restrictions, and to an attentive observer who has watched the progress of the Revolution and not lost sight of its actors, nothing could appear more ridiculous, nothing could inspire more contempt of our versatility and inconsistency, than to remark among the foremost to demand the nuptial benediction, a Talleyrand, a Fouché, a Real, an Augereau, a Chaptal, a Reubel, a Lasnes, a Bessieres, a Thuriot, a Treilhard, a Merlin, with a hundred other equally notorious revolutionists, who were, twelve or fifteen years ago, not only the first to declaim against religious ceremonies as ridiculous, but against religion itself as useless, whose motives produced, and whose votes sanctioned, those decrees of the legislature which proscribed the worship, together with its priests and sectaries. But then the fashion of barefaced infidelity was as much the order of the day as that of external sanctity is at present. I leave to casuists the decision: whether to the morals of the people, naked atheism, exposed with all its deformities, is more or less hurtful than concealed atheism, covered with the garb of piety; but for my part I think the noon-day murderer less guilty and much less detestable than the midnight assassin who stabs in the dark.

A hundred anecdotes are daily related of our new saints and fashionable devotees. They would be laughable were they not scandalous, and contemptible did they not add duplicity to our other vices.

Bonaparte and his wife go now every morning to hear Mass, and on every Sunday or holiday they regularly attend at vespers, when, of course, all those who wish to be distinguished for their piety or rewarded for their flattery never neglect to be present. In the evening of last Christmas Day, the imperial chapel was, as usual, early crowded in expectation of Their Majesties, when the chamberlain, Salmatoris, entered, and said to the captain of the guard, loud enough to be heard by the audience, "The Emperor and the Empress have just resolved not to come here to-night, His Majesty being engaged by some unexpected business, and the Empress not wishing to come without her consort." In ten minutes the chapel was emptied of every person but the guards, the priests, and three old women who had nowhere else to pass an hour. At the arrival of our Sovereigns, they were astonished at the unusual vacancy, and indignantly regarded each other. After vespers were over, one of Bonaparte's spies informed him of the cause, when, instead of punishing the despicable and hypocritical courtiers, or showing them any signs of his displeasure, he ordered Salmatoris under arrest, who would have experienced a complete disgrace had not his friend Duroc interfered and made his peace.

At another time, on a Sunday, Fouché entered the chapel in the midst of the service, and whispered to Bonaparte, who immediately beckoned to his lord-in-waiting and to Duroc. These both left the imperial chapel, and returning in a few minutes at the head of five grenadiers, entered the grand gallery, generally frequented by the most scrupulous devotees, and seized every book. The cause of this domiciliary visit was an anonymous communication received by the minister of police, stating, that libels against the imperial family, bound in the form of Prayer-Books, had been placed there. No such libels were, however, found; but of one hundred and sixty pretended breviaries, twenty-eight were volumes or novels, sixteen of poems, and eleven of indecent books. It is not necessary to add that the proprietors of these *edifying* works never reclaimed them. The opinions are divided here, whether this curious discovery originated in the malice of Fouché, or whether Talleyrand took this method of duping his rival, and at the same time of gratifying his own malignity. Certain it is, that Fouché was severely reprimanded for the transaction, and that Bonaparte was highly offended at the disclosure.

The common people, and the middle classes, are neither so ostentatiously devout, nor so basely perverse. They go to church as to the play, to gape at others, or to be stared at themselves · to pass the time, and to admire the show: and they do not conceal that such is the object of their attendance. Their indifference about futurity equals their ignorance of religious duties. Our revolutionary charlatans have as much brutalized their understanding as corrupted their hearts. They heard the Grand Mass said by the Pope with the same feelings as they formerly heard Robespierre proclaim himself a high priest of a Supreme Being, and they looked at the imperial processions with the same insensibility as they once saw the daily caravans of victims passing for execution.

Even in Bonaparte's own guard, and among the officers of his household troops, several examples of rigour were necessary before they would go to any place of worship, or suffer in their corps any almoners: but now, after being drilled into a belief of Christianity, they march to the Mass as to a parade or to a review With any other people, Bonaparte would not so easily have changed in two years the customs of twelve, and forced military men to kneel before priests, whom they but the other day were encouraged to hunt and massacre like wild beasts.

On the day of the Assumption of the Holy Virgin, a company of gendarmes d'Élite, headed by their officers, received publicly, and *by orders*, the sacrament: when the Abbé Frelaud approached Lieutenant Ledoux, he fell into convulsions, and was carried into the sacristy. After being a little recovered, he looked round him, as if afraid that some one would injure him, and said to the Grand Vicar Clauset, who enquired the cause of his accident and terror: "Good God! that man who gave me, on the 2nd of September, 1792, in the convent of the Carenes, the five wounds from which I still suffer, is now an officer, and was about to receive the sacrament from my hands." When this occurrence was reported to

Bonaparte, Ledoux was dismissed ; but Abbé Frelaud was transported, and the Grand Vicar Clauset sent to the Temple, for the scandal their indiscretion had caused. This act was certainly as unjust towards him who was bayoneted at the altar, as towards those who served the altar under the protection of the bayonets.

LETTER XXV

Paris, *August*, 1805.

My Lord,—Although the seizure of Sir George Rumbold might in your country, as well as everywhere else, inspire indignation, it could nowhere justly excite surprise. We had crossed the Rhine seven months before to seize the Duke of Enghien; and when any prey invited, the passing of the Elbe was only a natural consequence of the former outrage, of audacity on our part, and of endurance or indifference on the part of other Continental States. Talleyrand's note at Aix-la-Chapelle had also informed Europe that we had adopted a new and military diplomacy, and, in confounding power with right, would respect no privileges at variance with our ambition, interest or *suspicions*, or any independence it was thought useful or convenient for us to invade.

It was reported here, at the time, that Bonaparte was much offended with General Frère, who commanded this political expedition, for permitting Sir George's servant to accompany his master, as Fouché and Real had already tortures prepared and racks waiting, and after forcing your agent *to speak out*, would have announced his sudden death, either by his own hands or by a *coup-de-sang*, before any Prussian note could require his release. The known *morality* of our Government must have removed all doubts of the veracity of this assertion; a man might, besides, from the fatigues of a long journey, or from other causes, expire suddenly; but the exit of two, in the same circumstances, would have been thought at least extraordinary, even by our friends, and suspicious by our enemies.

The official declaration of Rheinhard (our minister to the Circle of Lower Saxony) to the Senate at Hamburg, in which he disavowed all knowledge on the subject of the capture of Sir George Rumbold, occasioned his disgrace. This man, a subject of the Elector of Würtemberg by birth, is one of the negative accomplices of the criminals of France, who, since the Revolution, have desolated Europe. He began in 1792 his diplomatic career, under Chauvelin and Talleyrand, in London, and has since been the tool of every faction in power. In 1796 he was appointed a minister to the Hanse Towns, and, without knowing why, was hailed as the point of rally to all the *philosophers, philanthropists*, Illuminati and other revolutionary amateurs, with which the North of Germany, Poland, Denmark and Sweden then abounded. A citizen of Hamburg — or rather, *of the world* — of the name of Seveking, bestowed on him the hand of a sister; and though he is not accused of avarice, some of the contributions extorted by our Government from the neutral Hanse Towns are said to have been left behind in his coffers instead of being forwarded to this capital. Either on this account, or for some other reason, he was recalled from Hamburg in January, 1797, and remained unemployed until the latter part of 1798, when he was sent as minister to Tuscany.

When, in the summer of 1799, Talleyrand was forced by the Jacobins to resign his place as a minister of the Foreign Department, he had the adroitness to procure Rheinhard to be nominated his successor, so that, though no longer nominally the minister, he still continued to influence the decisions of our Government as much as if still in office, because, though not without parts, Rheinhard has neither energy of character nor consistency of conduct. He is so much accustomed, and wants so much to be governed, that in 1796, at Hamburg, even the then emigrants, Madame de Genlis and General Valence, directed him when he was not ruled or dictated to by his wife or brother-in-law.

In 1800, Bonaparte sent him as a representative to the Helvetian Republic, and in 1802, again to Hamburg, where he was last winter superseded by Bourrienne, and ordered to an inferior station at the Electoral Court at Dresden. Rheinhard will never become one of those daring diplomatic banditti whom revolutionary governments always employ in preference. He has some moral principles, and, though not religious, is rather scrupulous. He would certainly sooner resign than undertake to remove by poison or by the steel of a bravo, a rival of his own or a person obnoxious to his employers. He would never, indeed, betray the secrets of his Government if he understood they intended to rob a despatch or to stop a messenger; but no allurements whatever would induce him to head the parties perpetrating these acts of our modern diplomacy.

Our present minister at Hamburg (Bourrienne) is far from being so nice. A revolutionist from the beginning of the Revolution, he shared, with the partisans of La Fayette, imprisonment under Robespierre, and escaped death only by emigration. Recalled afterwards by his friend, the late Director (Barras), he acted as a kind of secretary to him until 1796, when Bonaparte demanded him, having known him at the military college. During all Bonaparte's campaigns in Italy, Egypt, and Syria, he was his sole and confidential secretary—a situation which he lost in 1802, when Talleyrand denounced his corruption and cupidity because he had rivalled him in speculating in the funds and profiting by the information which his place afforded him. He was then made a counsellor of staté, but in 1803 he was involved in the fraudulent bankruptcy of one of our principal houses to the amount of a million of livres —£42,000—and, from his correspondence with it, some reasons appeared to suspect that he frequently had committed a breach of confidence against his master, who, after erasing his name from among the counsellors of state, had him conveyed a prisoner to the Temple, where he remained six months. A small volume, called *Le Livre Rouge* of the Consular Court, made its appearance about that time, and contained some articles which gave Bonaparte reason to suppose that Bourrienne was its author. On being questioned by the grand judge Regnier and the minister Fouché, before whom he was carried, he avowed that he had written it, but denied that he had any intention of making it public. As to its having found its way to the press during his confinement, that could only be ascribed to the ill-will or treachery of those police agents who inspected his papers and put their seals upon them. "Tell Bonaparte," said he, "that, had I been inclined to injure him in the public opinion, I should not have stooped to such trifles as *Le Livre Rouge*, while I have deposited with a friend his *original* orders, letters, and other curious documents as materials for an edifying history of our military hospitals during the campaigns of Italy and Syria—all authentic testimonies of his humanity and tenderness for the wounded and dying French soldiers."

After the answers of this interrogatory had been laid before Bonaparte, his brother Joseph was sent to the Temple to negotiate with Bourrienne, who was offered his liberty and a prefecture if he would give up all the original papers that, as a private secretary, he had had opportunity to collect. "These papers," answered Bourrienne, "are my only security against your brother's wrath and his assassins. Were I weak enough to deliver them up to-day, to-morrow probably I should no longer be counted among the living; but I have now taken my measures so effectually that, were I murdered to-day, these originals would be printed to-morrow. If Napoleon does not confide in my word of honour, he may trust to an assurance of discretion, with which my own interest is nearly connected. If he suspects me of having wronged him, he is convinced also of the eminent services I have rendered him, sufficient surely to outweigh his present suspicion. Let him again employ me in any post worthy of him and of me, and he shall soon see how much I will endeavour to regain his confidence."

Shortly afterwards Bourrienne was released, and a pension, equal to the salary of a counsellor of state, was granted him until some suitable place became vacant. On Champagny's being appointed a minister of the Home De partment, the embassy at Vienna was demanded by Bourrienne, but refused, as previously promised to La Rochefoucauld, our late minister at Dresden. When Rheinhard, in a kind of disgrace, was transferred to that relatively insignificant post, Bourrienne was ordered, with *extensive* instructions, to Hamburg. The Senate soon found the difference between a timid and honest minister, and an unprincipled and crafty intriguer. New loans were immediately required from Hanover; but hardly were these acquitted, than fresh extortions were insisted on. In some secret conferences Bourrienne is, however, said to have *hinted* that some douceurs were expected for alleviating the rigour of his instructions. This hint has, no doubt, been taken, because he suddenly altered his conduct, and instead of hunting the purses of the Germans, pursued the persons of his emigrated countrymen; and, in a memorial, demanded the expulsion of all Frenchmen who were not registered and protected by him, under pretence that every one of them who declined the honour of being a subject of Bonaparte, must be a traitor against the French Government and his country.

Bourrienne is now stated to have connected himself with several stock-jobbers, both in Germany, Holland and England; and already to have pocketed considerable sums by such connections. It is, however, not to be forgotten that several houses have been ruined in this capital by the *profits* allowed him, who always refused to share their losses; but, whatever were the consequences, enforced to its full amount the payment of that value which he chose to set on his communications.

A place in France would, no doubt, have been preferable to Bourrienne, particularly one near the person of Bonaparte. But if nothing else prevented the accomplishment of his wishes, his long familiarity with all the Bonapartes, whom he always treated as equals, and even now (with the exception of Napoleon) does not think his superiors, will long remain an insurmountable barrier.

I cannot comprehend how Bonaparte (who is certainly no bad judge of men) could so long confide in Bourrienne, who, with the usual presumption of my countrymen, is continually boasting to a degree that borders on indiscretion; and, by an artful questioner, may easily be led to overstep those bounds. Most of the particulars of his quarrel with Napoleon I heard him relate himself, as a proof of his great consequence, in a company of forty individuals, many of whom were unknown to him.

On the first discovery which Bonaparte made of Bourrienne's infidelity, Talleyrand complimented him upon not having suffered more from it. "Do you not see," answered Bonaparte, "it is also one of the extraordinary gifts of my extraordinary good fortune? Even traitors are unable to betray me. Plots respect me as much as bullets." I need not tell you that Fortune is the sole divinity sincerely worshipped by Napoleon.

LETTER XXVI

PARIS, *August*, 1805.

MY LORD, — Joseph Bonaparte leads a much more retired life, and sees less company, than any of his brothers or sisters. Except the members of his own family, he but seldom invites any guests, nor has Madame Joseph those regular assemblies and circles which Madame Napoleon and Madame Louis Bonaparte have. His hospitality is, however, greater at his country seat Morfontaine, than at his hotel here. Those whom he likes, or does not mistrust (who, by-the-bye, are very few), may visit him without much formality in the country, and prolong their stay according to their own inclination or discretion; but they must come without their servants, or send them away on their arrival.

As soon as an agreeable visitor presents himself, it is the etiquette of the house to consider him as an inmate; but to allow him at the same time a perfect liberty to dispose of his hours and his person as suits his convenience or caprice. In this extensive and superb mansion a suite of apartments is assigned him with a valet-de-

THE FINAL EPISODE IN THE CHÂTEAU MORFONTAINE

After the painting by ...

LETTER XXVI

PARIS, *August* 1805.

MY LORD,—Joseph Bonaparte leads a much more retired life, and sees less company, than any of his brothers or sisters. Except the members of his own family, he but seldom invites any guests, nor has Madame Joseph those regular assemblies and parties which Madame Napoleon and Madame Louis Bonaparte have. His hospitality is, however, greater at his country seat Morfontaine, than at his household. Persons whom he admits or invites are welcome there, by the same, an easy feet, may stay there without much formality in the manor and pursuing their day according to their own inclination or convenience; but they must come without their servants, or send them away on their arrival.

As soon as an agreeable visitor presents himself, it is the etiquette of the house to consider him as an inmate; but to allow him at the same time a perfect liberty to dispose of his hours and his person as suits his convenience or caprice. In this extensive and superb mansion a suite of apartments is assigned him with a valet-de-

LETTER XXVI

Paris, August, 1805

My Lord,—Joseph Bonaparte leads a much more retired life, and sees less company, than any of his brothers or sisters. Except the members of his own family, he but seldom invites any guests, nor has Madame Joseph those regular assemblies and circles which Madame Napoleon and Madame Louis Bonaparte have. His hospitality is, however, greater at his country seat Morfontaine, than at his town house. Those who visit him there are not under the necessity of being at any great expense, nor need they trouble themselves to procure a new carriage and attending suite, or anything of that kind; to and from the place they must come without those services to send them away on their arrival.

As soon as an agreeable visitor presents himself, it is the etiquette of the house to consider him as an inmate; but to allow him at the same time a perfect liberty to dispose of his hours and his person as suits his convenience or caprice. In this extensive and superb mansion a suite of apartments is assigned him with a valet-de-

chambre, a lackey, a coachman, a groom, and a jockey, all under his own exclusive command. He has allotted him a chariot, a gig, and riding horses, if he prefers such an exercise. A catalogue is given him of the library of the château; and every morning he is informed what persons compose the company at breakfast, dinner, and supper, and of the hours of these different repasts. A bill ot fare is at the same time presented to him, and he is asked to point out those dishes to which he gives the preference, and to declare whether he chooses to join the company or to be served in his own rooms.

During the summer season, players from the different theatres of Paris are paid to perform three times in the week; and each guest, according to the period of his arrival, is asked in his turn, to command either a comedy or a tragedy, a farce or a ballet. Twice in the week concerts are executed by the first performers of the opéra-bouffe; and twice in the week invitations to tea-parties are sent to some of the neighbours, or accepted from them.

Besides four billiard-tables, there are other gambling-tables for Rouge et Noir, Trente et Quarante, Faro, La Roulette, Birribi, and other games of hazard. The bankers are young men from Corsica, to whom Joseph, who advances the money, allows all the gain, while he alone suffers the loss. Those who are inclined may play from morning till night, and from night till morning, without interruption, as no one interferes. Should Joseph hear that any person has been too severely treated by Fortune, or suspects that he has not much cash remaining, some *rouleaux* of napoléons d'or are placed on the table of his dressing-room, which he may use or leave untouched, as he judges proper.

The hours of Joseph Bonaparte are neither so late as yours in England, nor so early as they were formerly in France. Breakfast is ready served at ten o'clock, dinner at four, and supper at nine. Before midnight he retires to bed with his family, but visitors do as they like and follow their own usual hours, and their servants are obliged to wait for them.

When any business calls Joseph away, either to preside in the Senate here, or to travel in the provinces, he notices it to the visitors, telling them at the same time not to displace themselves on account of his absence, but wait till his return, as they would not observe any difference in the economy of his house, of which Madame Joseph always does the honours, or, in her absence, some lady appointed by her.

Last year, when Joseph first assumed a military rank, he passed nearly four months with the army of England on the coast or in Brabant. On his return, all his visitors were gone, except a young poet of the name of Montaigne, who does not want genius, but who is rather too fond of the bottle. Joseph is considered the best *gourmet* or connoisseur in liquors and wines of this capital, and Montaigne found his champagne and burgundy so excellent that he never once went to bed, that he was not heartily intoxicated. But the best of the story is that he employed his mornings in composing a poem holding out to abhorrence the disgusting vice of drunkenness, and presented it to Joseph, requesting permission to dedicate it to him when published. To those who have read it, or only seen extracts from it, the compilation appears far from being contemptible, but Joseph still keeps the copy, though he has made the author a present of one hundred napoléons d'or, and procured him a place of an amanuensis in the chancellory of the Senate, having resolved never to accept any dedication, but wishing also not to hurt the feelings of the author by a refusal.

In a château where so many visitors of licentious and depraved morals meet, of both sexes, and where such an unlimited liberty reigns, intrigues must occur, and have of course not seldom furnished materials for the scandalous chronicle. Even Madame Joseph herself has either been gallant or calumniated. Report says that to the nocturnal assiduities of Eugenius de Beauharnais and of Colonel la

Fond-Blaniac she is exclusively indebted for the honour of maternity, and that these two rivals even fought a duel concerning the right of paternity. Eugenius de Beauharnais never was a great favourite with Joseph Bonaparte, whose reserved manners and prudence form too great a contrast to his noisy and blundering way to accord with each other. Before he set out for Italy, it was well known in our fashionable circles that he had been interdicted the house of his uncle, and that no reconciliation took place, notwithstanding the endeavours of Madame Napoleon. To humble him so much the more, Joseph even nominated la Fond-Blaniac an equerry to his wife, who therefore easily consoled herself for the departure of her *dear* nephew.

The husband of Madame Miot (one of Madame Joseph's ladies-in-waiting) was not so patient, nor such a philosopher as Joseph Bonaparte. Some charitable person having reported in the company of a *bonne amie* of Miot, that his wife did not pass her nights in solitude, but that she sought consolation among the many gallants and disengaged visitors at Morfontaine, he determined to surprise her. It was past eleven o'clock at night when his arrival was announced to Joseph, who had just retired to his closet. Madame Miot had been in bed ever since nine, ill of a *migraine*, and her husband was too *affectionate* not to be the first to inform her of his presence, without permitting anybody previously to disturb her. With great reluctance, Madame Miot's maid delivered the key of her rooms, while she accompanied him with a light. In the antechamber he found a hat and a great-coat, and in the closet adjoining the bed-room, a coat, a waistcoat, and a pair of breeches, with drawers, stockings, and slippers. Though the maid kept coughing all the time, Madame Miot and her gallant did not awake from their slumber, till the enraged husband began to use the bludgeon of the lover, which had also been left in the closet. A battle then ensued, in which the lover retaliated so vigorously, that the husband called out "Murder! murder!" with all his might. The château was instantly in an uproar, and the apartments crowded with half dressed and half naked lovers. Joseph Bonaparte alone was able to separate the combatants; and enquiring the cause of the riot, assured them that he would suffer no scandal and no intrigues in his house, without seriously resenting it. An explanation being made, Madame Miot was looked for but in vain; and the maid declared that, being warned by a letter from Paris of her husband's jealousy and determination to surprise her, her mistress had reposed herself in her room; while, to punish the ungenerous suspicions of her husband, she had persuaded Captain d'Hortcuil to occupy her place in her own bed. The maid had no sooner finished her deposition, than her mistress made her appearance and upbraided her husband severely, in which she was cordially joined by the spectators. She enquired if, on seeing the dress of a gentleman, he had also discovered the attire of a female and she appealed to Captain d'Horteuil whether he had not the two preceding nights also slept in her bed. To this he, of course, assented; adding that, had M. Miot attacked him the first night, he would not then perhaps have been so roughly handled as now; for then he was prepared for a visit, which this night was rather unexpected This connubial farce ended by Miot begging pardon of his wife and her gallant; the former of whom, after much entreaty by Joseph, at last consented to share with him her bed. But being disfigured with two black eyes and suffering from several bruises, and also ashamed of his unfashionable behaviour, he continued *invisible* for ten days afterwards, and returned to this city as he had left it, by stealth.

This Miot was a spy under Robespierre, and is a counsellor of state under Bonaparte. Without bread, as well as without a home, he was, from the beginning of the Revolution, one of the most ardent *patriots*, and the first Republican minister in Tuscany. After the Sovereign of that country had, in 1793, joined the League, Miot returned to France, and was, for his want of address to negotiate as a minister, shut up to perform the part of a spy in the Luxembourg; then transformed into a prison for suspected persons. Thanks to his *patriotism*, upwards of two hundred individuals of both sexes were denounced, transferred to the Conciergerie prison, and afterwards guillotined. After that, until 1799, he continued so despised that no faction would accept him for an accomplice; but in the November of that year, after Bonaparte had declared himself a First Consul, Miot was appointed a tribune, an office from which he was advanced, in 1802, to be a counsellor of state. As Miot squanders away his salary with harlots and in gambling-houses, and is pursued by creditors he neither will nor can pay, it was merely from charity that his wife was received among the other ladies of Madame Joseph Bonaparte's household.

LETTER XXVII

PARIS, *August*, 1805.

MY LORD,—Notwithstanding the ties of consanguinity, honour, duty, interest and gratitude, which bound the Spanish Bourbons to the cause of the Bourbons of France, no monarch has rendered more service to the cause of rebellion, and done more harm to the cause of royalty, than the King of Spain.

But here, again, you must understand me. When I speak of princes whose talents are known not to be brilliant, whose intellects are known to be feeble, and whose good intentions are rendered null by a want of firmness of character or consistency of conduct; while I deplore their weakness and the consequent misfortunes of their contemporaries, I lay all the blame on their wicked or ignorant counsellors; because if no ministers were fools or traitors, no sovereigns would tremble on their thrones, and no subjects dare to shake their foundation. Had Providence blessed Charles IV. of Spain with that judgment in selecting his ministers, and that constancy of persevering in his choice, as your George III.; had the helm of Spain been in the firm and able hands of a Grenville, a Windham, and a Pitt, the Cabinet of Madrid would never have been oppressed by the yoke of the Cabinet of St. Cloud, nor paid a heavy tribute for its bondage, degrading as well as ruinous.

"This is the age of upstarts," said Talleyrand to his cousin, Prince de Chalais, who reproached him for an unbecoming servility to low and vile personages; "and I prefer bowing to them to being trampled upon and crushed by them." Indeed, as far as I remember, nowhere in history are hitherto recorded so many low persons who, from obscurity and meanness, have suddenly and at once attained rank and notoriety. Where do we read of such a numerous crew of upstart emperors, kings, grand pensionaries, directors, imperial highnesses, princes, field-marshals, generals, senators, ministers, governors, cardinals, &c., as we now witness figuring upon the theatre of Europe, and who chiefly decide on the destiny of nations? Among these, several are certainly to be found whose superior parts have made them worthy to pierce the crowd and to shake off their native mud; but others again, and by far the greatest number of these *novi homines*, owe their present elevation to shameless intrigues or atrocious crimes.

The prime minister — or rather, the viceroy of Spain,

the Prince of Peace — belongs to the latter class. From a man in the ranks of the guards he was promoted to a general-in-chief, and from a harp-player in ante-chambers to a president of the councils of a prince; and that within the short period of six years. Such a fortune is not common; but to be absolutely without capacity as well as virtue, genius as well as good breeding, and, nevertheless, to continue in an elevation so little merited, and in a place formerly so subject to changes and so unstable, is a fortune that no upstart ever before experienced in Spain.

An intrigue of his elder brother with the present Queen, then Princess of Asturia, which was discovered by the late King, introduced him first at Court as a harp-player, and, when his brother was exiled, he was entrusted with the correspondence of the Princess with her gallant. After she had ascended the throne, he thought it more profitable to be the lover than the messenger, and contrived therefore to supplant his brother in the royal favour. Promotions and riches were consequently heaped upon him, and, what is surprising, the more undisguised the partiality of the Queen was, the greater the attachment of the King displayed itself; and it has ever since been an emulation between the royal couple who should the most forget and vilify birth and supremacy by associating this man not only in the courtly pleasures, but in the functions of sovereignty.

Had he been gifted with sound understanding, or possessed any share of delicacy, generosity, or discretion, he would, while he profited by their imprudent condescension, have prevented them from exposing their weaknesses and frailties to a discussion and ridicule among courtiers, and from becoming objects of humiliation and scandal among the people. He would have warned them of the danger which at all times attends the publicity of the foibles and vices of princes, but particularly in the present times of trouble and innovations. He would have told them: "Make me great and wealthy, but not at the expense of your own grandeur or of the loyalty of your people. Do not treat a humble subject as an equal, nor suffer your Majesties, whom Providence destined to govern a high-spirited nation, to be openly ruled by one born to obey. I am too dutiful not to lay aside my private vanity when the happiness of my King and the tranquillity of my fellow-subjects are at stake. I am already too high. In descending a little, I shall not only rise in the eyes of my contemporaries, but in the opinion of posterity. Every step I am advancing undermines your throne. In retreating a little, if I do not strengthen, I can never injure it." But I beg your pardon for this digression, and for putting the language of dignified reason into the mouth of a man as corrupt as he is imbecile.

Do not suppose because the Prince of Peace is no

friend of my nation that I am his enemy. No! Had he shown himself a true patriot, a friend of his own country, and of his too liberal Prince, or even of monarchy in general, or of anybody else but himself—although I might have disapproved of his policy, if he has any—I would never have lashed the individual for the acts of the minister. But you must have observed with me, that never before his administration was the Cabinet of Madrid worse conducted at home or more despised abroad; the Spanish Monarch more humbled or Spanish subjects more wretched; the Spanish power more dishonoured or the Spanish resources worse employed. Never before the treaty with France of 1796, concluded by this wiseacre (which made him a Prince of Peace, and our Government the Sovereign of Spain), was the Spanish monarchy reduced to such a lamentable dilemma as to be forced into an expensive war without a cause, and into a disgraceful peace—not only unprofitable, but absolutely disadvantageous. Never before were its treasures distributed among its oppressors to support their tyranny, nor its military and naval forces employed to fight the battles of rebellion. The loyal subjects of Spain have only one hope left. The delicate state of his present Majesty's health does not promise a much longer continuance of his reign, and the Prince of Asturia is too well informed to endure the guidance of the most ignorant minister that ever was admitted into the cabinet and confidence of a sovereign. It is more than probable that under a new reign the misfortunes of the Prince of Peace will inspire as much compassion as his rapid advancement has excited astonishment and indignation.

A cabinet thus badly directed cannot be expected to have representatives abroad either of abilities or patriotism. The Admiral and General Gravina, who but lately left this capital as an ambassador from the Court of Spain to assume the command of a Spanish fleet, is more valiant than wise, and more an enemy of your country than a friend of his own. He is a profound admirer of Bonaparte's *virtues* and successes, and was, during his residence, one of the most ostentatiously awkward courtiers of Napoleon the First. It is said that he has the modesty and loyalty to wish to become a Spanish Bonaparte, and that he promises to restore by his genius and exploits the lost lustre of the Spanish monarchy. When this was reported to Talleyrand, he smiled with contempt; but when it was told to Bonaparte, he stamped with rage at the impudence of the Spaniard in daring to associate his name of acquired and established greatness with his own impertinent schemes of absurdities and impossibilities.

In the summer of 1793, Gravina commanded a division of the Spanish fleet in the Mediterranean, of which Admiral

Langara was the commander-in-chief. At the capitulation of Toulon, after the combined English and Spanish forces had taken possession of it, when Rear-Admiral Goodall was declared governor, Gravina was made the commandant of the troops. At the head of these he often fought bravely in different sorties, and on the 1st of October was wounded at the re-capture of Fort Pharon. He complains still of having suffered insults or neglect from the English, and even of having been exposed unnecessarily to the fire and sword of the enemy merely because he was a *patriot* as well as an envied or suspected ally. His inveteracy against your country takes its date, no doubt, from the siege of Toulon, or perhaps from its evacuation.

When in May, 1794, our troops were advancing towards Collioure, he was sent with a squadron to bring it succours, but he arrived too late, and could not save that important place. He was not more successful at the beginning of the campaign of 1795 at Rosa, where he had only time to carry away the artillery before the enemy entered. In August that year, during the absence of Admiral Massaredo, he assumed *ad interim* the command of the Spanish fleet in the Mediterranean; but in the December following he was disgraced, arrested, and shut up as a state prisoner.

During the embassy of Lucien Bonaparte to the Court

of Madrid, in the autumn of 1800, Gravina was by his influence restored to favour; and after the death of the late Spanish Ambassador to the Cabinet of St. Cloud, Chevalier d'Azara, by the special desire of Napoleon, was nominated both his successor and a representative of the King of Etruria. Among the members of our diplomatic corps, he was considered somewhat of a Spanish gasconader and a bully. He more frequently boasted of his wounds and battles than of his negotiations or conferences, though he pretended, indeed, to shine as much in the cabinet as in the field.

In his suite were two Spanish women, one about forty, and the other about twenty years of age. Nobody knew what to make of them, as they were neither treated as wives, mistresses, nor servants; and they avowed themselves to be no relations. After a residence here of some weeks, he was, by *superior orders*, waylaid one night at the opera, by a young and beautiful dancing girl of the name of Barrois, who engaged him to take her into keeping. He hesitated, indeed, for some time; at last, however, love got the better of his scruples, and he furnished for her an elegant apartment on the new Boulevard. On the day he carried her there, he was accompanied by the chaplain of the Spanish Legation; and told her that, previous to any further intimacy, she must be married to him, as his religious prin-

ciples did not permit him to cohabit with a woman who
was not his wife. At the same time he laid before her an
agreement to sign, by which she bound herself never to
claim him as a husband before her turn—that is to say,
until sixteen other women, to whom he had been previously
married, were dead. She made no opposition, either to
the marriage or to the conditions annexed to it. This girl
had a sweetheart of the name of Valere, an actor at one
of the little theatres on the Boulevards, to whom she communicated her adventure. He advised her to be scrupulous
in her turn, and to ask a copy of the agreement. After
some difficulty this was obtained. In it no mention was
made of her maintenance, nor in what manner her children
were to be regarded, should she have any. Valere had,
therefore, another agreement drawn up, in which all these
points were arranged according to his own interested views.
Gravina refused to subscribe to what he plainly perceived
were only extortions; and the girl, in her turn, not only
declined any further connexion with him, but threatened to
publish the act of polygamy. Before they had done discussing this subject, the door was suddenly opened and the
two Spanish ladies presented themselves. After severely
upbraiding Gravina, who was struck mute by surprise, they
announced to the girl that whatever promise or contract of
marriage she had obtained from him was of no value, as

before they came with him to France he had bound himself, before a public notary at Madrid, not to form any new connexions, nor to marry any other woman without their written consent. One of these ladies declared that she had been married to Gravina twenty-two years, and was his oldest wife but one; the other said that she had been married to him six years. They insisted upon his following them, which he did, after putting a purse of gold into Barrois' hand.

When Valere heard from his mistress this occurrence, he advised her to make the most money she could of the Spaniard's curious *scruples*. A letter was therefore written to him, demanding one hundred thousand livres—£4,000— as the price of secrecy and withholding the particulars of this business from the knowledge of the tribunals and the police; and an answer was required within twenty-four hours. The same night Gravina offered one thousand louis, which were accepted, and the papers returned; but the next day Valere went to his hotel, Rue de Provence, where he presented himself as a brother of Barrois. He stated that he still possessed authenticated copies of the papers returned, and that he must have either the full sum first asked by his sister, or an annuity of twelve thousand livres settled upon her. Instead of an answer, Gravina ordered him to be turned out of the house. An attorney then waited on his Excellency, on the part of the brother and the sister, and repeated their threats and their demands, adding that he would write a memorial both to the Emperor of the French and to the King of Spain, were justice refused to his principals any longer.

Gravina was well aware that this affair, though more laughable than criminal, would hurt both his character and credit if it were known in France; he therefore consented to pay seventy-six thousand livres more, upon a formal renunciation by the party of all future claims. Not having money sufficient by him, he went to borrow it from a banker, whose clerk was one of Talleyrand's secret agents. Our minister, therefore, ordered every step of Gravina to be watched; but he soon discovered that instead of wanting this money for a political intrigue, it was necessary to extricate him out of an amorous scrape. Hearing, however, in what a scandalous manner the ambassador had been duped and imposed upon, he reported it to Bonaparte, who gave Fouché orders to have both Valere, Barrois and the attorney immediately transported to Cayenne, and to restore Gravina his money. The former part of this order the minister of police executed so much the more willingly, as it was according to his plan that Barrois had pitched upon Gravina for a lover. She had been intended by him as a spy on his Excellency, but had deceived him by her reports — a *crime* for which transportation was a usual punishment

Notwithstanding the care of our Government to conceal and bury this affair in oblivion, it furnished matter both for conversation in our fashionable circles, and subjects for our caricaturists. But these artists were soon seized by the police, who found it more easy to chastise genius than to silence tongues. The declaration of war by Spain against your country was a lucky opportunity for Gravina to quit with *honour* a Court where he was an object of ridicule, to assume the command of a fleet which might one day make him an object of terror. When he took leave of Bonaparte, he was told to return to France victorious, or never to return any more; and Talleyrand warned him as a friend, "whenever he returned to his post in France, to leave his marriage mania behind him in Spain. Here," said he, "you may, without ridicule, intrigue with a hundred women, but you run a great risk by marrying even one."

I have been in company with Gravina, and after what I heard him say, so far from judging him superstitious, I thought him really impious. But infidelity and bigotry are frequently next-door neighbours.

LETTER XXVIII

Paris, *August*, 1805.

My Lord,—It cannot have escaped the observation of the most superficial traveller of rank, that, at the Court of St. Cloud, want of morals is not atoned for by good breeding or good manners. The hideousness of vice; the pretensions of ambition; the vanity of rank; the pride of favour, and the shame of venality, do not wear here that delicate veil, that gloss of virtue, which, in other Courts, lessens the deformity of corruption and the scandal of depravity. Duplicity and hypocrisy are here very common indeed, more so than dissimulation anywhere else; but barefaced knaves and impostors must always make indifferent courtiers. Here the minister tells you, I must have such a sum for a place; and the chamberlain tells you, Count down so much for my protection. The princess requires a necklace of such a value for interesting herself for your advancement ; and the lady-in-waiting demands a diamond of such worth on the day of your promotion. This tariff of favours and of infamy descends *ad infinitum*. The secretary for signing, and the clerk for writing your commissions; the cashier for delivering it, and the messenger for informing you of it, have all their fixed prices. Have you a lawsuit, the judge announces to you that so much has been offered by your opponent, and so much is expected from you if you desire to win your cause. When you are the defendant against the Crown, the attorney- or solicitor-general lets you know that such a douceur is requisite to procure such an issue. Even in criminal proceedings, not only honour, but life may be saved by pecuniary sacrifices.

A man of the name of Martin, by profession a stock-jobber, killed, in 1803, his own wife; and for twelve thousand livres—£500—he was acquitted, and recovered his liberty. In November last year, in a quarrel with his own brother, he stabbed him through the heart, and for another sum of twelve thousand livres he was acquitted, and released before last Christmas. This wretch is now in prison again, on suspicion of having poisoned his own daughter, with whom he had an incestuous intercourse, and he boasts publicly of the certainty of soon being liberated.

Another person, Louis de Saurac, the younger son of Baron de Saurac, who together with his eldest son had emigrated, forged a will in the name of his parent, whom he pretended to be dead, which left him the sole heir of all the disposable property, to the exclusion of two sisters. After the nation had shared its part as heir of all emigrants, Louis took possession of the remainder. In 1802, both his father and brother accepted of the general amnesty, and returned to France. To their great surprise, they heard that this Louis had, by his ill-treatment, forced his sisters into servitude, refusing them even the common necessaries of life. After upbraiding him for his want of duty, the father desired, according to the law, the restitution of the unsold part of his estates. On the day fixed for settling the accounts and entering into his right, Baron de Saurac was arrested as a conspirator and imprisoned in the Temple. He had been denounced as having served in the army of Condé, and as being a secret agent of Louis XVIII. To disprove the first part of the charge, he produced certificates from America, where he had passed the time of his emigration, and even upon the rack he denied the latter. During his arrest, the eldest son discovered that Louis had become the owner of their possessions, by means of the will he had forged in the name of his father; and that it was he who had been unnatural enough to denounce the author of his days. With the wreck of their fortune in St. Domingo, he procured his father's release; who, being acquainted with the perversity of his younger son, addressed himself to the department to be reinstated in his property. This was opposed by Louis, who defended his title to the estate by the revolutionary maxim which had passed into a law, enacting that all emigrants should be considered as politically dead. Hitherto Baron de Saurac had, from affection, declined to mention the forged will; but shocked by his son's obduracy, and being reduced to distress, his counsellor produced this document, which not only went to deprive Louis of his property, but exposed him to a criminal prosecution.

This unnatural son, who was not yet twenty-five, had imbibed all the revolutionary morals of his contemporaries, and was well acquainted with the *moral* characters of his revolutionary countrymen. He addressed himself, therefore, to Merlin of Douai, Bonaparte's Imperial attorney-general and commander of his Legion of Honour; who, for a bribe of fifty thousand livres—£2,100—obtained for him, after he had been defeated in every other court, a judgment in his favour, in the tribunal of cassation, under the sophistical conclusion that all emigrants, being according to law considered as politically dead, a will in the name of any one of them was merely a pious fraud to preserve the property in the family.

This Merlin is the son of a labourer of Anchin, and was a servant of the Abbey of the same name. One of the monks, observing in him some application, charitably sent him to be educated at Douai, after having bestowed on him some previous education. Not satisfied with this generous act, he engaged the other monks, as well as the chapter of Cambray, to subscribe for his expenses of admission as an attorney by the parliament of Douai, in which situation the Revolution found him. By his dissimulation and assumed modesty, he continued to dupe his benefactors; who, by their influence, obtained for him the nomination as a representative of the people to our First National Assembly. They soon, however, had reason to repent of their generosity. He joined the Orleans faction and became one of the most persevering, violent and cruel persecutors of the privileged classes, particularly of the clergy, to whom he was indebted for everything. In 1792 he was elected a member of the National Convention, where he voted for the death of his King. It was he who proposed a law (justly called, by Prudhomme, the production of the deliberate homicide Merlin) against *suspected* persons; which was decreed on the 17th of September, 1793, and caused the imprisonment or proscription of two hundred thousand families. This decree procured him the appellation of *Merlin Suspects* and of *Merlin Potence*. In 1795 he was first appointed a minister of police, and soon afterwards a minister of justice. After the revolution in favour of the Jacobins of the 4th of

September, 1797, he was made a director; a place which he was obliged by the same Jacobins to resign in June, 1799. Bonaparte expressed at first the most sovereign contempt for this Merlin; but on account of one of his sons, who was his aide-de-camp, he was appointed by him, when First Consul, his attorney-general.

As nothing paints better the true features of a government than the *morality* or *vices* of its functionaries, I will finish this man's portrait with the following characteristic touches.

Merlin de Douai has been successively the counsel of the late Duke of Orleans, the friend of Danton, of Chabot and of Hébert, the admirer of Marat, and the servant of Robespierre. An accomplice of Rewbell, Barras and la Reveillière, an author of the law of suspected persons, an advocate of the Septembrizers, and an ardent apostle of the St. Guillotine. Cunning as a fox and ferocious as a tiger, he has outlived all the factions with which he has been connected. It has been his policy to keep in continual fermentation rivalships, jealousies, inquietudes, revenge and all other odious passions; establishing by such means his influence on the terror of some, the ambition of others, and the credulity of them all. Had I, when Merlin proposed his law concerning suspected persons, in the name of *liberty* and *equality*, been *free* and his *equal*,

I should have said to him, "Monster, this, your atrocious law, is your sentence of death; it has brought thousands of innocent persons to an untimely end—you shall die by my hands as a victim, if the tribunals do not condemn you to the scaffold as an executioner or as a criminal."

Merlin has bought national property to the amount of fifteen millions of livres—£625,000—and he is supposed to possess money nearly to the same amount, in your or our funds. For a man born a beggar, and educated by charity, this fortune, together with the liberal salaries he enjoys, might seem sufficient without selling justice, protecting guilt, and oppressing or persecuting innocence.

LETTER XXIX

PARIS, *August*, 1805.

MY LORD,—The household troops of Napoleon the First are by thousands more numerous than those even of Louis XIV. were. Grenadiers on foot and on horseback, riflemen on foot and on horseback, heavy and light artillery, dragoons and hussars, mamelukes and sailors, artificers and pontoneers, gendarmes, gendarmes d'Élite, Velites and veterans, with Italian grenadiers, riflemen, dragoons, &c., &c., compose all together a not inconsiderable army.

Though it frequently happens that the pay of the other troops is in arrears, those appertaining to Bonaparte's household are as regularly paid as his senators, counsellors of state, and other public functionaries. All the men are picked, and all the officers as much as possible of birth, or at least of education. In the midst of this voluptuous and seductive capital, they are kept very strict, and the least negligence or infraction of military discipline is more severely punished than if committed in garrison or in an encampment. They are both better clothed, accoutred, and paid, than the troops of the line, and have everywhere the precedency of them. All the officers, and many of the soldiers, are members of Bonaparte's Legion of Honour, and carry arms of honour distributed to them by imperial favour, or for military exploits. None of them are quartered upon the citizens; each corps has its own spacious barracks, hospitals, drilling-ground, riding or fencing-houses, gardens, bathing-houses, billiard-table, and even libraries. A chapel has lately been constructed near each barrack, and almoners are already appointed. In the meantime, they attend regularly at Mass, either in the Imperial Chapel or in the parish churches. Bonaparte discourages much all marriages among the military in general, but particularly among those of his household troops. That they may not, however, be entirely deprived of the society of women, he allows five to each company, with the same salaries as the men, under the name of washerwomen.

With a vain and fickle people, fond of shows and innovations, nothing in a military despotism has a greater political utility, gives greater satisfaction, and leaves behind a more useful terror and awe, than Bonaparte's grand military reviews. In the beginning of his consulate, they regularly occurred three times in the month; after his victory of Marengo, they were reduced to once in a fortnight, and since he has been proclaimed Emperor, to once only in the month. This ostentatious exhibition of usurped power is always closed with a diplomatic review of the representatives of lawful Princes, who introduce on those occasions their fellow-subjects to another subject, who successfully has seized, and continues to usurp the authority of his own Sovereign. What an example for ambition! what a lesson to treachery!

Besides the household troops, this capital and its vicinity have, for these three years past, never contained less than from fifteen to twenty thousand men of the regiments of the line, belonging to what is called the first military division of the Army of the Interior. These troops are selected from among the brigades that served under Bonaparte in Italy and Egypt with the greatest *éclat*, and constitute a kind of dépôt for recruiting his household troops with tried and trusty men. They are also regularly paid, and generally better accoutred than their comrades encamped on the coast, or quartered in Italy or Holland.

But a standing army, upon which all revolutionary rulers can depend, and that always will continue their faithful support, unique in its sort and composition, exists in the bosom as well as in the extremities of this country. I mean, one hundred and twenty thousand invalids, mostly young men under thirty, forced by conscription against their will into the field, quartered and taken care of by our Government, and all possessed with the absurd prejudice that, as they have been maimed in fighting the battles of rebellion, the restoration of legitimate sovereignty would to them be an epoch of destruction, or at least of misery and want; and this prejudice is kept alive by emissaries employed on purpose to mislead them. Of these, eight thousand are lodged and provided for in this city; ten thousand at Versailles, and the remainder in Piedmont, Brabant, and in the conquered departments on the left bank of the Rhine; countries where the inhabitants are discontented and disaffected, and require therefore to be watched, and to have a better spirit infused.

Those whose wounds permit it are also employed to do garrison duty in fortified places not exposed to an attack by enemies, and to assist in the different arsenals and laboratories, foundries and dépôts of military or naval stores. Others are attached to the police offices, and some as gendarmes, to arrest suspected or guilty individuals; or as *garnissaires*, to enforce the payment of contributions from the unwilling or distressed. When the period for the payment of taxes is expired, two of these *garnissaires* present themselves at the house of the persons in arrears, with a billet signed by the director of the contributions and countersigned by the police commissary. If the money is not immediately paid, with half-a-crown to each of them besides, they remain quartered in the house, where they are to be boarded and to receive half-a-crown a day each until an order from those who sent them informs them that what was due to the State has been acquitted. After their entrance into a house, and during their stay, no furniture or effects whatever can be removed or disposed of, nor can the master or mistress go out-of-doors without being accompanied by one of them.

In the houses appropriated to our invalids, the inmates are very well treated, and Government takes great care to make them satisfied with their lot. The officers have large halls, billiards, and reading-room to meet in ; and the common men are admitted into apartments adjoining libraries, from which they can borrow what books they contain, and read them at leisure. This is certainly a very good and even a humane institution, though these libraries chiefly contain military histories or novels.

As to the morals of these young invalids, they may be well conceived when you remember the *morality* of our Revolution ; and that they, without any religious notions or restraints, were not only permitted, but *encouraged* to partake of the debauchery and licentiousness which were carried to such an extreme in our armies and encampments. In an age when the passions are strongest, and often blind reason and silence conscience, they have not the means nor the permission to marry; in their vicinity it is, therefore, more difficult to discover one honest woman or a dutiful wife, than hundreds of harlots and of adulteresses. Notwithstanding that many of them have been accused before the tribunals of seductions, rape and violence against the sex, not one has been punished for what the *morality* of our government consider merely as *bagatelles*. Even in cases where husbands, brothers and lovers have been killed by them while defending or avenging the honour of their wives, sisters and mistresses, our tribunals have been ordered by our grand judge, according to the commands of the Emperor, *not to proceed*. As most of them have no occupation, the vice of idleness augments the mass of their corruption; for men of their principles, when they have nothing to do, never do anything good.

I do not know if my countrywomen feel themselves honoured by or obliged to Bonaparte, for leaving their virtue and honour unprotected, except by their own prudence and strength; but of this I am certain, that all our other troops, as well as the invalids, may live on free quarters with the sex without fearing the consequences; provided they keep at a distance from the females of our

Imperial Family, and of those of our grand officers of state and principal functionaries. The wives and the daughters of the latter have, however, sometimes declined the *advantage* of these exclusive privileges.

A horse grenadier of Bonaparte's imperial guard, of the name of Rabais, notorious for his amours and debauchery, was accused before the imperial judge Thuriot, at one and the same time by several husbands and fathers, of having seduced the affections of their wives and of their daughters. As usual, Thuriot refused to listen to their complaints; at the same time insultingly advising them to retake their wives and children, and for the future to be more careful of them. Triumphing, as it were, in his injustice, he inconsiderately mentioned the circumstance to his own wife, observing that he never knew so many charges of the same sort exhibited against one man.

Madame Thuriot, who had been a servant-maid to her husband before he made her his wife, instead of being disgusted at the recital, secretly determined to see this Rabais. An intrigue was then begun, and carried on for four months, if not with discretion, at least without discovery; but the lady's own imprudence at last betrayed her: or I should say rather, her jealousy. But for this, she might still have been admired among our modest women, and Thuriot among fortunate husbands and happy fathers;

for the lady, for the first time since her marriage, proved, to the great joy and pride of her husband, in the family way. Suspecting, however, the fidelity of her paramour, she watched his motions so closely that she discovered an intrigue between him and the chaste spouse of a rich banker; but the consequence of this discovery was the detection of her own crime.

On the discovery of his disgrace, Thuriot obtained an audience of Bonaparte, in which he exposed his misfortune, and demanded punishment on his wife's gallant. As, however, he also acknowledged that his own indiscretion was an indirect cause of their connection, he received the same advice which he had given to other unfortunate husbands: to retake, and for the future guard better, his dear *moiety*.

Thuriot had, however, an early opportunity of wreaking his vengeance on the gallant Rabais. It seems his prowess had reached the ears of Madame Baciocchi, the eldest sister of Bonaparte. This lady has a children mania, which is very troublesome to her husband, disagreeable to her relations and injurious to herself. She never beholds any lady, particularly any of her family, in the way which women wish to be who love their lords, but she is absolutely frantic. Now, Thuriot's worthy friend Fouché had discovered, by his spies, that Rabais paid frequent and secret visits to the hotel Baciocchi, and that Madame Baciocchi was the object of these visits. Thuriot, on this discovery, instantly denounced him to Bonaparte.

Had Rabais ruined all the women of this capital, he would not only have been forgiven, but applauded by Napoleon, and his counsellors and courtiers; but to dare to approach, or only to cast his eyes on one of our Imperial Highnesses, was a crime nothing could extenuate or avenge, but the most exemplary punishment. He was therefore arrested, sent to the Temple, and has never since been heard of; so that his female friends are still in the cruel uncertainty whether he has died on the rack, been buried alive in the *oubliettes*, or is wandering an exile in the wilds of Cayenne.

In examining his trunk, among the curious effects discovered by the police were eighteen portraits and one hundred *billets-doux*, with medallions, rings, bracelets, tresses of hair, &c., as numerous. Two of the portraits occasioned much scandal, and more gossiping. They were those of two of our most devout and most *respectable* Court ladies, maids-of-honour to our Empress, Madame Ney and Madame Lasnes; who never miss an opportunity of going to church, who have received the private blessing of the Pope, and who regularly confess to some bishop or other once in a fortnight. Madame Napoleon *cleared* them, however, of all *suspicion*, by declaring publicly in her drawing-room that these portraits had come into the possession of Rabais by the infidelity of their maids; who had confessed their faults, and therefore had been charitably pardoned. Whether the opinions of Generals Ney and Lasnes coincide with Madame Napoleon's assertion is uncertain; but Lasnes has been often heard to say that, from the instant his wife began to confess, he was convinced she was inclined to dishonour him; so that nothing surprised him.

One of the medallions in Rabais' collection contained on one side the portrait of Thuriot, and on the other that of his wife; both set with diamonds, and presented to her by him on their last wedding-day. For the supposed theft of this medallion, two of Thuriot's servants were in prison, when the arrest of Rabais explained the manner in which it had been lost. This so enraged him that he beat and kicked his wife so heartily that for some time even her life was in danger, and Thuriot lost all hopes of being a father.

Before the Revolution, Thuriot had been, for fraud and forgery, struck off the roll as an advocate, and therefore joined it as a *patriot*. In 1791, he was chosen a deputy to the National Assembly, and in 1792 to the National Convention. He always showed himself one of the most ungenerous enemies of the clergy, of monarchy, and of his King, for whose death he voted. On the 25th of May,

1792, in declaiming against Christianity and priesthood, he wished them both, *for the welfare of mankind*, at the bottom of the sea; and on the 18th of December the same year, he declared in the Jacobin Club that, if the National Convention evinced any signs of clemency towards Louis XVI., he would go himself to the Temple and *blow out the brains* of this unfortunate King. He defended in the tribune the massacres of the prisoners, affirming that the tree of liberty could never flourish *without being inundated with the blood* of aristocrats and other enemies of the Revolution. He has been convicted by rival factions of the most shameful robberies, and his infamy and depravity were so notorious that neither Marat, Brissot, Robespierre, nor the Directory would or could employ him. After the Revolution of the 9th of November, 1799, Bonaparte gave him the office of judge of the criminal tribunal, and in 1804 made him a Commander of his Legion of Honour. He is now one of our Emperor's most faithful subjects and *most sincere* Christians. Such is now his tender conscientiousness, that he was among those who were the first to be married again by some Cardinal to their present wives, to whom they had formerly been united only by the municipality. This new marriage, however, took place before Madame Thuriot had introduced herself to the acquaintance of the Imperial Grenadier Rabais.

LETTER XXX

Paris, *August*, 1805.

My Lord,—Being considered as a connoisseur, though I have no pretensions but that of being an amateur, Lucien Bonaparte, shortly before his disgrace, invited me to pass some days with him in the country, and to assist him in arranging his very valuable collection of pictures—next our public ones, the most curious and most valuable in Europe, and of course in the world. I found here, as at Joseph Bonaparte's, the same splendour, the same etiquette, and the same liberty, which latter was much enhanced by the really engaging and unassuming manners and conversation of the host. At Joseph's, even in the midst of abundance and of liberty, in seeing the person or meditating on the character of the host, you feel both your inferiority of fortune and the humiliation of dependence, and that you visit a master instead of a friend, who indirectly tells you, "Eat, drink, and rejoice as long and as much as you like; but remember that, if you are happy, it is to my generosity you are indebted, and if unhappy, that I do not care a pin about you." With Lucien it is the very reverse. His conduct seems to indicate that by your company you confer an obligation on him, and he is studious to remove on all occasions that distance which fortune has placed between him and his guests; and as he cannot compliment them upon being wealthier than himself, he seizes with delicacy every opportunity to shew that he acknowledges their superiority in talents and in genius as more than an equivalent for the absence of riches.

He is, nevertheless, himself a young man of uncommon parts, and, as far as I could judge from my short intercourse with the reserved Joseph and with the haughty Napoleon, he is abler and better informed than either, and much more open and sincere. His manners are also more elegant, and his language more polished, which is the more creditable to him when it is remembered how much his education has been neglected, how vitiated the Revolution made him, and that but lately his principal associates were, like himself, from among the vilest and most vulgar of the rabble. It is not necessary to be a keen observer to remark in Napoleon the upstart soldier, and in Joseph the former low member of the law; but I defy the most refined courtier to see in Lucien anything indicating a *ci-devant sans-culotte*. He has, besides, other qualities (and those more estimable) which will place him much above his elder brothers in the opinion of posterity. He is extremely compassionate and liberal to the truly distressed, serviceable to those whom he knows are not his friends, and forgiving and obliging even to those who have proved and avowed themselves his enemies. These are virtues commonly very scarce, and hitherto never displayed by any other member of the Bonaparte family.

An acquaintance of yours, and a friend of mine, Count de T——, at his return here from emigration, found of his whole former fortune, producing once eighty thousand livres —£3,300—in the year, only four farms unsold; and these were advertised for sale. A man who had once been his servant, but was then a groom to Lucien, offered to present a memorial for him to his master, to prevent the disposal of the only support which remained to subsist himself, with a wife and four children. Lucien asked Napoleon to prohibit the sale, and to restore the Count the farms, and obtained his consent; but Fouché, whose cousin wanted them, having purchased other national property in the neighbourhood, prevailed upon Napoleon to forget his promise, and the farms were sold. As soon as Lucien heard of it, he sent for the Count, delivered into his hands an annuity of six thousand livres—£250—for the life of himself, his wife, and his children, *as an indemnity for the inefficacy of his endeavours to serve him*, as he expressed himself. Had the Count recovered the farms, they would not have given him a clear profit of half the amount, all taxes paid.

A young author of the name of Gauvan, irritated by the loss of parents and fortune by the Revolution, attacked, during 1799, in the public prints, as well as in pamphlets, every Revolutionist who had obtained notoriety or popularity. He was particularly vehement against Lucien, and laid before the public all his crimes and all his errors, and asserted as facts atrocities which were either calumnies or merely rumours. When, after Napoleon's assumption of the Consulate, Lucien was appointed a Minister of the Interior, he sent for Gauvan, and said to him, "Great misfortunes have early made you wretched and unjust, and you have frequently revenged yourself on those who could not prevent them, among whom I am one. You do not want capacity, nor, I believe, probity. Here is a commission which makes you a Director of Contributions in the departments of the Rhine and Moselle, an office with a salary of twelve thousand livres—£500—but producing double that sum. If you meet with any difficulties, write to me; I am your friend. Take those one hundred louis d'or for the expenses of your journey. Adieu!" This anecdote I have read in Gauvan's own handwriting, in a letter to his sister. He died in 1802; but Mademoiselle Gauvan, who is not yet fifteen, has a pension of three thousand livres a year— £125—from Lucien, who has never seen her.

Lucien Bonaparte has another good quality; he is consistent in his political principles. Either from conviction or delusion he is still a Republican, and does not conceal that, had he suspected Napoleon of any intent to re-establish monarchy, much less tyranny, he would have joined those deputies who, on the 9th of November, 1799, in the sitting at St. Cloud, demanded a decree of outlawry against him. If the present quarrel between these two brothers were sifted to the bottom, perhaps it would be found to originate more from Lucien's Republicanism than from his marriage.

I know, with all France and Europe, that Lucien's youth has been very culpable; that he has committed many indiscretions, much injustice, many imprudences, many errors, and, I fear, even some crimes. I know that he has been the most profligate among the profligate, the most debauched among libertines, the most merciless among the plunderers, and the most perverse among rebels. I know that he is accused of being a Septembrizer; of having murdered one wife and poisoned another; of having been a spy, a denouncer, a persecutor of innocent persons in the Reign of Terror. I know that he is accused of having fought his brothers-in-law; of having ill-used his mother, and of an incestuous commerce with his own sisters. I have read and heard of these and other enormous accusations, and far be it from me to defend, extenuate, or even deny them. But suppose all this infamy to be real, to be proved, to be authenticated, which it never has been, and, to its whole extent, I am persuaded, never can be—what are the cruel and depraved acts of which Lucien has been *accused* to the enormities and barbarities of which Napoleon is convicted? Is the poisoning a wife more criminal than the poisoning a whole hospital of wounded soldiers; or the assisting to kill some confined persons, suspected of being enemies, more atrocious than the massacre in cold blood of thousands of disarmed prisoners? Is incest with a sister more shocking to humanity than the well-known unnatural pathic—— but I will not continue the disgusting comparison. As long as Napoleon is unable to acquit himself of such barbarities and monstrous crimes, he has no right to pronounce Lucien unworthy to be called his brother; nor have Frenchmen, as long as they obey the former as a Sovereign, or the Continent as long as it salutes him as such, any reason to despise the latter for crimes which lose their enormity when compared to the horrid perpetrations of his imperial brother.

An elderly lady, a relation of Lucien's wife, and a person in whose veracity and morality I have the greatest confidence, and for whom he always had evinced more regard than even for his own mother, has repeated to me many of their conversations. She assures me that Lucien deplores frequently the want of a good and religious education, and the tempting examples of perversity he met with almost at his entrance upon the revolutionary scene. He says that he determined to get rich *per fas aut nefas*, because he observed that money was everything, and that most persons plotted and laboured for power merely to be enabled to gather treasure, though, after they had obtained both, much above their desert and expectation, instead of being satiated or even satisfied, they bustled and intrigued for more, until success made them unguarded and prosperity indiscreet, and they became with their wealth the easy prey of rival factions. Such was the case of Danton, of Fabre d'Eglantine, of Chabot, of Chaumette, of Stebert, and other contemptible wretches, butchered by Robespierre and his partisans—victims in their turn to men as unjust and sanguinary as themselves. He had, therefore, laid out a different plan of conduct for himself. He had fixed upon fifty millions of livres—£2,100,000—as the maximum he should wish for, and when that sum was in his possession, he resolved to resign all pretensions to rank and employment, and to enjoy *otium cum dignitate*. He had kept to his determination, and so regulated his income that, with the expenses, pomp, and retinue of a prince, he is enabled to make more persons happy and comfortable than his extortions have ruined or even embarrassed. He now lives like a *philosopher*, and endeavours to forget the past, to delight in the present, and to be *indifferent* about futurity. He chose, therefore, for a wife, a lady whom he loved and esteemed, in preference to one whose birth would have been a continual reproach to the meanness of his own origin.

You must, with me, admire the *modesty* of a citizen *sans-culotte*, who, without a shilling in the world, fixes upon fifty millions as a reward for his revolutionary achievements, and with which he would be satisfied to sit down and begin his singular course of singular philosophy. But his success is more extraordinary that his pretensions were extravagant. This immense sum was amassed by him in the short period of four years, chiefly by bribes from foreign Courts, and by selling his protections in France.

But most of the other Bonapartes have made as great and as rapid fortunes as Lucien, and yet, instead of being generous, contented, or even *philosophers*, they are still profiting by every occasion to increase their ill-gotten treasures, and no distress was ever relieved, no talents encouraged, or virtues recompensed by them. The mind of their garrets lodges with them in their palaces, while Lucien seems to ascend as near as possible to a level with his circumstances. Without being ostentatious, I have myself found him beneficent.

Among his numerous pictures, I observed four that had formerly belonged to my father's, and afterwards to my own cabinet. I enquired how much he had paid for them, without giving the least hint that they had been my property, and were plundered from me by the nation. He had, indeed, paid their full value. In a fortnight after I had quitted him, these, with six other pictures, were deposited in my room, with a very polite note, begging my acceptance of them, and assuring me that he had but the day before heard from his picture-dealer that they had belonged to me. He added that he would never retake them, unless he received an assurance from me that I parted with them without reluctance, and at the same time affixed their price. I returned them, as I knew they were desired by him for his collection, but he continued obstinate. I told him, therefore, that, as I was acquainted with his inclination to perform a generous action, I would, instead of payment for the pictures, indicate a person deserving his assistance. I mentioned the old Duchess de ——, who is seventy-four years of age and blind; and, after possessing in her youth an income of eight hundred thousand livres—£33,000—is now in her old age almost destitute. He did for this worthy lady more than I expected; but happening, in his visits to relieve my friend, to cast his eye on the daughter of the landlady where she lodged, he found means to prevail on the simplicity of the poor girl, and seduced her. So much do I know personally of Lucien Bonaparte, who certainly is a composition of good and bad qualities, but which of them predominate I will not take upon me to decide. This I can affirm—*Lucien is not the worst member of the Bonaparte family.*

LETTER XXXI

PARIS, *August*, 1805.

MY LORD,—As long as Austria ranks among independent nations, Bonaparte will take care not to offend or alarm the ambition and interest of Prussia by incorporating the Batavian Republic with the other provinces of his empire. Until that period, the Dutch must continue (as they have been these last ten years) under the appellation of allies, oppressed like subjects and plundered like foes. Their mock sovereignty will continue to weigh heavier on them than real servitude does on their Belgic and Flemish neighbours, because Frederick the Great pointed out to his successors the Elbe and the Texel as the *natural* borders of the Prussian monarchy, whenever the right bank of the Rhine should form the *natural* frontiers of the kingdom of France.

That during the present summer a project for a partition treaty of Holland has by the Cabinet of St. Cloud been laid before the Cabinet of Berlin is a fact, though disseminated only as a rumour by the secret agents of Talleyrand. Their object was on this, as on all previous occasions when any names, rights or liberties of people were intended to be erased from among the annals of independence, to sound the ground, and to prepare by such rumours the mind of the public for another outrage and another overthrow. But Prussia, as well as France, knows the value of a military and commercial navy, and that to obtain it good harbours and navigable rivers are necessary, and therefore, as well as from principles of justice, perhaps, declined the acceptance of a plunder, which, though tempting, was contrary to the policy of the House of Brandenburg.

According to a copy circulated among the members of our diplomatic corps, this partition treaty excluded Prussia from all the Batavian seaports except Delfzijl, and those of the river Ems, but gave her extensive territories on the side of Guelderland, and a rich country in Friesland. Had it been acceded to by the Court of Berlin, with the annexed condition of a defensive and offensive alliance with the Court of St. Cloud, the Prussian monarchy would, within half-a-century, have been swallowed up in the same gulf with the Batavian Commonwealth and the Republic of Poland; and by some future scheme of some future Bonaparte or Talleyrand, be divided in its turn, and serve as a pledge of reconciliation or inducement of connection between some future rulers of the French and Russian empires.

Talleyrand must, indeed, have a very mean opinion of

the capacity of the Prussian ministers, or a high notion of his own influence over them, if he was serious in this overture. For my part, I am rather inclined to think that it was merely thrown out to discover whether Frederick William III. had entered into any engagement contrary to the interest of Napoleon the First; or to allure his Prussian Majesty into a negotiation which would suspend, or at least interfere with, those supposed to be then on the carpet with Austria, Russia, or perhaps even with England.

The late Batavian Government had, ever since the beginning of the present war with England, incurrred the displeasure of Bonaparte. When it apprehended a rupture from the turn which the discussion respecting the occupation of Malta assumed, the Dutch ambassadors at St. Petersburg and Berlin were ordered to demand the interference of these two Cabinets for the preservation of the neutrality of Holland, which your country had promised to acknowledge if respected by France. No sooner was Bonaparte informed of this step, than he marched troops into the heart of the Batavian Republic, and occupied its principal forts, ports and arsenals. When, some time afterwards, Count de Markoff received instructions from his Court, according to the desire of the Batavian Directory, and demanded, in consequence, an audience from Bonaparte, a map was laid before him, indicating the position of the

French troops in Holland, and plans of the intended encampment of our army of England on the coast of Flanders and France; and he was asked whether he thought it probable that our Government would assent to a neutrality so injurious to its *offensive* operations against Great Britain. "But," said the Russian ambassador, "the independence of Holland has been admitted by you in formal treaties."—"So has the cession of Malta by England," interrupted Bonaparte, with impatience.—"True," replied Markoff, "but you are now at war with England for this point; while Holland, against which you have no complaint, has not only been invaded by your troops, but, contrary both to its inclination and interest, involved in a war with you, by which it has much to lose and nothing to gain."—"I have no account to render to anybody for my transactions, and I desire to hear nothing more on this subject," said Bonaparte, retiring furious, and leaving Markoff to meditate on our Sovereign's singular principles of political justice and of *jus gentium*.

From that period Bonaparte resolved on another change of the executive power of the Batavian Republic. But it was more easy to displace one set of men for another than to find proper ones to occupy a situation in which, if they do their duty as patriots, they must offend France; and if they are our tools, instead of the independent governors of their country, they must excite a discontent among their fellow-citizens, disgracing themselves as individuals, and exposing themselves as chief magistrates to the fate of the De Witts, should ever fortune forsake our arms or desert Bonaparte.

No country has of late been less productive of great men than Holland. The Van Tromps, the Russel, and the William III. all died without leaving any posterity behind them; and the race of Batavian heroes seems to have expired with them, as that of patriots with the De Witts and Barneveldt. Since the beginning of the last century we read, indeed, of some able statesmen, as most, if not all, the former grand pensionaries have been; but the name of no warrior of any great eminence is recorded. This scarcity of native genius and valour has not a little contributed to the present humbled, disgraced and oppressed state of wretched Batavia.

Admiral de Winter certainly neither wants courage nor genius, but his private character has a great resemblance to that of General Moreau. Nature has destined him to obey, and not to govern. He may direct as ably and as valiantly the manœuvres of a fleet as Moreau does those of an army, but neither the one nor the other at the head of his nation would long render himself respected, his country flourishing, or his countrymen happy and tranquil.

Destined from his youth for the navy, Admiral de Winter entered into the naval service of his country before he was fourteen, and was a second lieutenant when the Batavian *patriots*, in rebellion against the Stadtholder, were in 1787 reduced to submission by the Duke of Brunswick, the commander of the Prussian army that invaded Holland. His parents and family being of the anti-Orange party, he emigrated to France, where he was made an officer in the legion of Batavian refugees. During the campaign of 1793 and 1794, he so much distinguished himself under that competent judge of merit, Pichegru, that this commander obtained for him the commission of a general of brigade in the service of the French; which, after the conquest of Holland in January, 1795, was exchanged for the rank of a vice-admiral of the Batavian Republic. His exploits as commander of the Dutch fleet, during the battle of the 11th of October, 1797, with your fleet, under Lord Duncan, I have heard applauded even in your presence, when in your country. Too honest to be seduced, and too brave to be intimidated, he is said to have incurred Bonaparte's hatred by resisting both his offers and threats, and declining to sell his own liberty as well as to betray the liberty of his fellow-subjects. When, in 1800, Bonaparte proposed to him the presidency and consulate of the United States for life, on condition that he should sign a treaty, which made him a vassal of France, he refused with dignity and with firmness, and preferred retirement to a supremacy so dishonestly acquired, and so dishonourably occupied.

General Daendels, another Batavian revolutionist of some notoriety, from an attorney became a lieutenant-colonel, and served as a spy under Dumouriez in the winter of 1792 and in the spring of 1793. Under Pichegru he was made a general, and exhibited those talents in the field which are said to have before been displayed in the forum. In June, 1795, he was made a lieutenant-general of the Batavian Republic, and he was the commander-in-chief of the Dutch troops combating in 1799 your army under the Duke of York. In this place he did not much distinguish himself, and the issue of the contest was entirely owing to our troops and to our generals.

After the Peace of Amiens, observing that Bonaparte intended to annihilate instead of establishing universal liberty, Daendels gave in his resignation and retired to obscurity, not wishing to be an instrument of tyranny, after having so long fought for freedom. Had he possessed the patriotism of a Brutus or a Cato, he would have bled or died for his cause and country sooner than have deserted them both; or had the ambition and love of glory of a Caesar held a place in his bosom, he would have attempted to be the chief of his country, and by generosity and clemency atone, if possible, for the loss of liberty. Upon the line of baseness, the deserter is placed next to the traitor.

Dumonceau, another Batavian general of some publicity, is not by birth a citizen of the United States, but was born at Brussels in 1758, and was by profession a stonemason when in 1789 he joined, as a volunteer, the Belgian insurgents. After their dispersion in 1790 he took refuge and served in France, and was made an officer in the corps of Belgians, formed after the declaration of war against Austria in 1792. Here he frequently distinguished himself, and was, therefore, advanced to the rank of a general; but the Dutch general officers being better paid than those of the French Republic, he was, with the permission of our Directory received, in 1795, as a lieutenant-general of the Batavian Republic. He has often evinced bravery, but seldom great capacity. His natural talents are considered as but indifferent, and his education is worse.

These are the only three military characters who might, with any prospect of success, have tried to play the part of a Napoleon Bonaparte in Holland.

LETTER XXXII

Paris, *August*, 1805.

My Lord,—Not to give umbrage to the Cabinet of Berlin, Bonaparte communicated to it the *necessity* he was under of altering the form of government in Holland, and, if report be true, even condescended to ask *advice* concerning a chief magistrate for that country. The young Prince of Orange, brother-in-law of his Prussian Majesty, naturally presented himself; but, after some time, Talleyrand's agents discovered that great pecuniary sacrifices could not be expected from that quarter, and perhaps less submission to France experienced than from the former governors. An eye was then cast on the Elector of Bavaria, whose past *patriotism*, as well as that of his ministers, was a full guarantee for future obedience. Had he consented to such an arrangement, Austria might have aggrandized herself on the Inn, Prussia in Franconia, and France in Italy; and the present bone of contest would have been chiefly removed.

This intrigue, for it was nothing else, was carried on by the Cabinet of St. Cloud in March, 1804, about the time that Germany was invaded and the Duke of Enghien seized.

JÉRÔME BONAPARTE, KING OF
WESTPHALIA, AND HIS WIFE

Painting by F. Kinson

LETTER XXXII

Paris, *August*, 1805.

My Lord,—Not to give umbrage to the Cabinet of Berlin, Bonaparte communicated to it the *necessity* he was under of altering the form of government in Holland, and, if report be true, even condescended to ask *advice* concerning a chief magistrate for that country. The young Prince of Orange, brother-in-law of His Prussian Majesty, naturally presented himself; but, after some time, Talleyrand's agents discovered that great pecuniary sacrifices could not be expected from that quarter, and perhaps less subjection to France experienced than from the former government. An eye was then cast on the Elector of Bavaria, whose past *patriotism*, as well as that of his ministers, was a full guarantee for future obedience. Had he consented to such an arrangement, Austria might have aggrandized herself on the Inn, Prussia in Franconia, and France in Italy; and the present bone of contest would have been chiefly removed.

This intrigue, for it was nothing else, was carried on by the Cabinet of St. Cloud in March, 1804, about the time that Germany was invaded and the Duke of Enghien seized.

This explains to you the reason why the Russian note, delivered to the Diet of Ratisbon on the 8th of the following May, was left without any support, except the ineffectual one from the King of Sweden. How any cabinet could be dupe enough to think Bonaparte serious, or the Elector of Bavaria so weak as to enter into his schemes, is difficult to be conceived, had not Europe witnessed still greater credulity on one side, and still greater effrontery on the other.

In the meantime Bonaparte grew every day more discontented with the Batavian Directory, and more irritated against the members who composed it. Against his regulations for excluding the commerce and productions of your country, they resented with spirit instead of obeying them without murmur as was required. He is said to have discovered, after his own soldiers had forced the customhouse officers to obey his orders, that, while in their proclamations the directors publicly prohibited the introduction of British goods, some of them were secret insurers of this forbidden merchandise, introduced by fraud and by smuggling; and that while they officially wished for the success of the French arms and destruction of England, they withdrew by stealth what property they had in the French funds, to place it in the English. This refractory and, as Bonaparte called it, mercantile spirit so enraged him, that he had already signed an order for arresting and transferring *en masse* his high allies, the Batavian directors, to his Temple, when the representations of Talleyrand moderated his fury, and caused the order to be recalled, which Fouché was ready to execute.

Had Jerome Bonaparte not offended his brother by his *transatlantic* marriage, he would long ago have been the Prince Stadtholder of Holland; but his disobedience was so far useful to the Cabinet of St. Cloud as it gave it an opportunity of intriguing with, or deluding, other cabinets that might have any pretensions to interfere in the regulation of the Batavian Government. By the choice finally made, you may judge how difficult it was to find a suitable *subject* to represent it, and that this representation is intended only to be temporary.

Schimmelpenninck, the present grand pensionary of the Batavian Republic, was destined by his education for the bar, but by his natural parts to await in quiet obscurity the end of a dull existence. With some property, little information, and a tolerably good share of common sense, he might have lived and died respected, and even regretted, without any pretension, or perhaps even ambition, to shine. The anti-Orange faction, to which his parents and family appertained, pushed him forward, and elected him, in 1795, a member of the first Batavian National Convention, where, according to the spirit of the times, his speeches were rather those of a demagogue than those of a Republican. Liberty, Equality and Fraternity were the constant themes of his political declamations, infidelity his religious profession, and the examples of immorality his social lessons; so rapid and dangerous are the strides with which seduction frequently advances on weak minds.

In 1800 he was appointed an ambassador to Napoleon Bonaparte and Charles Maurice Talleyrand. The latter used him as a stockbroker, and the former for anything he thought proper; and he was the humble and submissive valet of both. More ignorant than malicious, and a greater fool than a rogue, he was more laughed at and despised than trusted or abused. His patience being equal to his phlegm, nothing either moved or confounded him; and he was, as Talleyrand remarked, "A model of an ambassador, according to which he and Bonaparte wished that all other independent princes and states would choose their representatives to the French Government."

When our minister and his Sovereign were discussing the *difficulty of properly filling up* the vacancy of the Dutch Government, judged necessary by both, the former mentioned Schimmelpenninck with a smile; and serious as Bonaparte commonly is, he could not help laughing. "I should have been less astonished," said he, "had you proposed my

Mameluke, Rostan." This rebuke did not deter Talleyrand (who had settled his terms with Schimmelpenninck) from continuing to point out the advantage which France would derive from this nomination. "Because no man could easier be directed when in office, and no man easier turned out of office when disagreeable or unnecessary. Both as Batavian plenipotentiary at Amiens, and as Batavian ambassador in England, he had proved himself as obedient and submissive to France as when in the same capacity at Paris."

By returning often to the charge, with these and other remarks, Talleyrand at last accustomed Bonaparte to the idea, which had once appeared so humiliating, of writing to a man so much inferior in everything, "*Great and dear Friend!*" and therefore said to the minister, "Well! let us then make him a grand pensionary and a *locum tenens for five years;* or until Jerome, when he repents, returns to his duty, and is pardoned."—"Is he, then, not to be a grand pensionary for life?" asked Talleyrand; "whether for one month or for life, he would be equally obedient to resign when commanded; but the latter would be more popular in Holland, where they were tired of so many changes."— "Let them complain, if they dare," replied Bonaparte. "Schimmelpenninck is their chief magistrate only for five years, if so long; but you may add that they may re-elect him."

It was not before Talleyrand had compared the pecuniary proposal made to his agents by foreign princes with those of Schimmelpenninck to himself, that the latter obtained the preference. The exact amount of the purchase-money for the supreme magistracy in Holland is not well known to any but the contracting parties. Some pretended that the whole was paid down beforehand, being advanced by a society of merchants at Amsterdam, the friends or relatives of the grand pensionary; others, that it is to be paid by annual instalments of two millions of livres—£84,000—for a certain number of years. Certain it is, that this high office was sold and bought; and that, had it been given for life, its value would have been proportionately enhanced; which was the reason that Talleyrand endeavoured to have it thus established.

Talleyrand well knew the precarious state of Schimmelpenninck's grandeur; that it not only depended upon the whim of Napoleon, but had long been intended as an hereditary sovereignty for Jerome. Another Dutchman asked him not to ruin his friend and his family for what he was well aware could never be called a sinecure place, and was so precarious in its tenure. "Foolish vanity," answered the minister, "can never pay enough for the gratification of its desires. All the Schimmelpennincks in the world do not possess property enough to recompense me for the sovereign honours which I have procured for one of their name and family, were he even deposed within twenty-four hours. What treasures can indemnify me for connecting such a name and such a personage with the great name of the First Emperor of the French?"

I have only twice in my life been in Schimmelpenninck's company, and I thought him both timid and reserved; but from what little he said, I could not possibly judge of his character and capacity. His portrait and its accompaniments have been presented to me, such as delivered to you by one of his countrymen, a Mr. M—— (formerly an ambassador also), who was both his schoolfellow and his comrade at the university. I shall add the following traits in his own words as near as possible: "More vain than ambitious, Schimmelpenninck from his youth, and particularly from his entrance into public life, tried every means to make a noise, but found none to make a reputation. He caressed in succession all the systems of the French Revolution, without adopting one for himself. All the kings of faction received in their turns his homage and felicitations. It was impossible to mention to him a man of any notoriety, of whom he did not become immediately a partisan. The virtues or the vices, the merit or defects, of the individual were of no consideration; according to his judgment it was sufficient to be famous. Yet with all the extravagances of a head filled with paradoxes, and of a heart spoiled by modern philosophy, added to a habit of licentiousness, he had no idea of becoming an instrument for the destruction of liberty in his own country, much less of becoming its tyrant, in submitting to be the slave of France. It was but lately that he took the fancy, after so long admiring all other *great* men of our age, to be at any rate one of their number, and of being admired as a *great* man in his turn. On this account many accuse him of hypocrisy, but no one deserves that appellation less, his vanity and exaltation never permitting him to dissimulate; and no presumption, therefore, was less disguised than his, to those who studied the man. Without acquired ability, without natural genius or political capacity, destitute of discretion and address, as confident and obstinate as ignorant, he is only elevated to fall and to rise no more."

Madame Schimmelpenninck, I was informed, is as amiable and accomplished as her husband is awkward and deficient; though well acquainted with his infidelities and profligacy, she is too virtuous to listen to revenge, and too generous not to forgive. She is, besides, said to be a lady of uncommon abilities, and of greater information than she chooses to display. She has never been the worshipper of Bonaparte, or the friend of Talleyrand; she loved her country, and detested its tyrants. Had *she* been created a grand pensionary, she would certainly have swayed with more *glory* than her husband; and been hailed by contemporaries, as well as posterity, if not a heroine, at least a patriot—a title which in our times, though often prostituted, so few have any claim to, and therefore so much the more valuable.

When it was known at Paris that Schimmelpenninck had set out for his new sovereignty, no less than sixteen girls of the Palais Royal demanded passes for Holland. Being questioned by Fouché as to their business in that country, they answered that they intended to visit their friend, the grand pensionary, in his new dominions. Fouché communicated to Talleyrand both their demands and their business, and asked his advice. He replied, "Send two, and those of whose vigilance and intelligence you are sure. Refuse by all means the other fourteen. Schimmelpenninck's time is precious, and were they at the Hague, he would neglect everything for them. If they are fond of travelling, and are handsome and adroit, advise them to set out for London or for St. Petersburg; and if they consent, order them to my office, and they shall be supplied, if approved of, both with instructions, and with their travelling expenses."—Fouché answered his colleague, "That they were in every respect the very reverse of his description; that they seemed to have passed their lives in the lowest stage of infamy, and that they could neither read nor write." You have, therefore, no reason to fear that these belles will be sent to disseminate corruption in your happy island.

LETTER XXXIII

PARIS, *August*, 1805.

MY LORD,—The Italian subjects of Napoleon the First were far from displaying the same zeal and the same *gratitude* for his paternal care and kindness in taking upon himself the trouble of governing them, as we *good* Parisians have done. Notwithstanding that a brigade of our police agents and spies, drilled for years to applaud and to excite enthusiasm, proceeded as his advanced guard to raise the public spirit, the reception at Milan was cold and everything else but cordial and pleasing. This absence of *duty* did not escape his observation and resentment. Convinced, in his own mind, of the great blessing, prosperity and liberty his victories and sovereignty have conferred on the inhabitants of the other side of the Alps, he ascribed their present passive or mutinous behaviour to the effect of foreign emissaries from Courts envious of his glory and jealous of his authority.

He suspected particularly England and Russia of having selected this occasion of a solemnity that would complete his grandeur to humble his just pride. He had also some idea within himself that even Austria might indirectly have dared to influence the sentiments and conduct of her *ci-devant* subjects of Lombardy; but his own high opinion of the awe which his very name inspired at Vienna dispersed these thoughts, and his wrath fell entirely on the audacity of Pitt and Markoff. Strict orders were therefore issued to the prefects and commissaries of police to watch vigilantly all foreigners and strangers who might have arrived, or who should arrive, to witness the ceremony of the coronation, and to arrest instantly anyone who should give the least reason to suppose that he was an enemy instead of an admirer of His Imperial and Royal Majesty. He also commanded the prefects of his palace not to permit any persons to approach his sacred person, of whose morality and politics they had not previously obtained a good account.

These great measures of security were not entirely unnecessary. Individual vengeance and individual patriotism sharpened their daggers, and, to use Senator Rœderer's language, "were near transforming the most *glorious* day of rejoicing into a day of *universal* mourning."

All our writers on the Revolution agree that in France, within the first twelve years after we had reconquered our lost *liberty*, more conspiracies have been denounced than during the six centuries of the most brilliant epoch of ancient and free Rome. These facts and avowals are speaking evidences of the internal *tranquillity* of our unfortunate country, of our *affection* to our rulers, and of the *unanimity* with which all the changes of government have been, notwithstanding *our printed votes*, received and approved.

The frequency of conspiracies not only shows the discontent of the governed, but the insecurity and instability of the governors. This truth has not escaped Napoleon, who has therefore ordered an expeditious and secret *justice* to despatch instantly the conspirators, and to bury the conspiracy in oblivion, except when any *grand coup d'état* is to be struck; or, to excite the passions of hatred, any proofs can be found, or must be fabricated, involving an inimical or rival foreign Government in an odious plot. Since the farce which Mehée de la Touche exhibited, you have, therefore, not read in the *Moniteur* either of the danger our Emperor has incurred several times since from the machinations of implacable or fanatical foes, or of the alarm these have caused his partisans. They have, indeed, been hinted at in some speeches of our public functionaries, and in some paragraphs of our public prints, but their particulars will remain concealed from historians, unless someone of those composing our Court, our fashionable or our political circles, has taken the trouble of noting them down; but even to these they are but imperfectly or incorrectly known.

Could the veracity of a Fouché, a Real, a Talleyrand, or a Duroc (the only members of this new *secret* and *invisible* tribunal for expediting conspirators) be depended upon, they would be the most authentic annalists of these and other interesting *secret* occurrences

What I intend relating to you on this subject are circumstances such as they have been reported in our best informed societies by our most inquisitive companions. Truth is certainly the foundation of these anecdotes; but their parts may be extenuated, diminished, altered, or exaggerated. Defective or incomplete as they are, I hope you will not judge them unworthy of a page in a letter, considering the grand personage they concern, and the mystery with which he and his Government encompass themselves, or in which they wrap up everything not agreeable concerning them.

A woman is said to have been at the head of the first plot against Napoleon since his proclamation as an Emperor of the French. She called herself Charlotte Encore; but her real name is not known. In 1803 she lived and had furnished a house at Abbéville, where she passed for a young widow of property, subsisting on her rents. About the same time several other strangers settled there; but though she visited the principal inhabitants, she never publicly had any connection with the newcomers.

In the summer of 1803, a girl at Amiens — some say a real enthusiast of Bonaparte's, but, according to others, engaged by Madame Bonaparte to perform the part she did — demanded, upon her knees, in a kind of paroxysm of joy, the happiness of embracing him, in doing which she fainted, or pretended to faint away, and a pension of three thousand livres — £125 — was settled on her for her affection.

Madame Encore, at Abbéville, to judge of her discourse and conversation, was also an ardent friend and well-wisher of the Emperor; and when in July, 1804, he passed through Abbéville, on his journey to the coast, she also threw herself at his feet, and declared that she would die content if allowed the honour of embracing him. To this he was going to assent, when Duroc stepped between them, seized her by the arm, and dragged her to an adjoining room, whither Bonaparte, near fainting from the sudden alarm his friend's interference had occasioned, followed him, trembling. In the right sleeve of Madame Encore's gown was found a stiletto, the point of which was poisoned. She was the same day transported to this capital, under the inspection of Duroc, and imprisoned in the Temple. In her examination she denied having any accomplices, and she expired on the rack without telling even her name. The sub-prefect at Abbéville, the once famous André Dumont, was ordered to disseminate a report that she was shut up as insane in a madhouse.

In the strict search made by the police in the house occupied by her, no papers or any other indications were discovered that involved other persons, or disclosed who she was, or what induced her to attempt such a rash action. Before the secret tribunal she is reported to have said, "that being convinced of Bonaparte's being one of the greatest criminals that ever breathed upon the earth, she took upon herself the office of a volunteer executioner; having, with every other good or loyal person, a right to punish him whom the law could not, or dared not, reach." When, however, some repairs were made in the house at Abbéville by a new tenant, a bundle of papers was found, which proved that a M. Franquonville, and about thirty other individuals (many of whom were the late newcomers there), had for six months been watching an opportunity to seize Bonaparte in his journeys between Abbéville and Montreuil, and to carry him to some part of the coast, where a vessel was ready to sail for England with him. Had he, however, made resistance, he would have been shot in France, and his assassins have saved themselves in the vessel.

The numerous escort that always, since he was an Emperor, accompanied him, and particularly his concealment of the days of his journeys, prevented the execution of this plot; and Madame Encore, therefore, took upon her to sacrifice herself for what she thought the welfare of her country. How Duroc suspected or discovered her intent is not known; some say that an anonymous letter informed him of it, while others assert that, in throwing herself at Bonaparte's feet, this prefect observed the steel through the sleeve of her muslin gown. Most of her associates were secretly executed; some, however, were carried to Boulogne and shot at the head of the army of England as English spies.

LETTER XXXIV

Paris, *August*, 1805.

My Lord,—After the discovery of Charlotte Encore's attempt, Bonaparte, who hitherto had flattered himself that he possessed the good wishes, if not the affection, of his female subjects, made a regulation according to which no women who had not previously given in their names to the prefects of his palaces, and obtained previous permission, can approach his person or throw themselves at his feet, without incurring his displeasure, and even arrest. Of this imperial decree, ladies, both of the capital and of the provinces, when he travels, are officially informed. Notwithstanding this precaution, he was a second time last spring, at Lyons, near falling the victim of the vengeance or malice of a female.

In his journey to be crowned King of Italy, he occupied his uncle's episcopal palace at Lyons during the forty-eight hours he remained there. Most of the persons of both sexes composing the household of Cardinal Fesch were from his own country, Corsica; among these was one of the name of Pauline Riotti, who inspected the economy of the kitchens. It is Bonaparte's custom to take a dish of chocolate in the forenoon, which she, on the morning of his departure, against her custom, but under pretence of knowing the taste of the family, desired to prepare. One of the cooks observed that she mixed it with something from her pocket, but, without saying a word to her that indicated suspicion, he warned Bonaparte, in a note delivered to a page, to be upon his guard. When the chamberlain carried in the chocolate, Napoleon ordered the person who had prepared it to be brought before him. This being told Pauline, she fainted away, after having first drunk the remaining contents of the chocolate pot. Her convulsions soon indicated that she was poisoned, and, notwithstanding the endeavours of Bonaparte's physician, Corvisart, she expired within an hour; protesting that her crime was an act of revenge against Napoleon, who had seduced her when young, under a promise of marriage; but who, since his elevation, had not only neglected her, but reduced her to despair by refusing an honest support for herself and her child, sufficient to preserve her from the degradation of servitude. Cardinal Fesch received a severe reprimand for admitting among his domestics individuals with whose former lives he was not better acquainted, and the same day he dismissed every Corsican in his service. The cook was, with the reward of a pension, made a member of the Legion of Honour, and it was given out by Corvisart that Pauline died insane.

Within three weeks after this occurrence, Bonaparte was, at Milan, again exposed to an imminent danger. According to his commands, the vigilance of the police had been very strict, and even severe. All strangers who could not give the most satisfactory account of themselves, had either been sent out of the country, or were imprisoned. He never went out unless strongly attended, and during his audiences the most trusty officers always surrounded him; these precautions increased in proportion as the day of his coronation approached. On the morning of that day, about nine o'clock, when full dressed in his imperial and royal robes, and all the grand officers of state by his side, a paper was delivered to him by his chamberlain, Talleyrand, a nephew of the minister. The instant he had read it, he flew into the arms of Berthier, exclaiming, "My friend, I am betrayed; are you among the number of conspirators? Jourdan, Lasnes, Mortier, Bessieres, St. Cyr, are you also forsaking your friend and benefactor?" They all instantly encompassed him, begging that he would calm himself; that they all were what they always had been, dutiful and faithful subjects. "But read this paper from my prefect, Salmatoris; he says that if I move a step I may cease to live, as the assassins are near me, as well as before me."

The commander of his guard then entered with fifty grenadiers, their bayonets fixed, carrying with them a prisoner, who pointed out four individuals not far from Bonaparte's person, two of whom were Italian officers of the Royal Italian Guard, and two were dressed in Swiss uniforms. They were all immediately seized, and at their feet were found three daggers. One of those in Swiss regimentals, exclaimed, before he was taken, "Tremble, tyrant of my country! Thousands of the descendants of William Tell have, with me, sworn your destruction. You escape this day, but the just vengeance of outraged humanity follows you like your shade. Depend upon it an untimely end is irremediably reserved you." So saying he pierced his heart and fell a corpse into the arms of the grenadiers who came to arrest him.

This incident suspended the procession to the cathedral for an hour, when Berthier announced that the conspirators were punished. Bonaparte evinced on this occasion the same absence of mind and of courage as on the 9th of November, 1799, when Arena and other deputies drew their daggers against him at St. Cloud. As this scene did not redound much to the honour of the Emperor and King, all mention of the conspiracy was severely prohibited, and the deputations ready to congratulate him on his escape were dispersed to attend their other duties.

The conspirators are stated to have been four young men who had lost their parents and fortunes by the Revolutions effected by Bonaparte in Italy and Switzerland, and who had sworn fidelity to each other, and to avenge their individual wrongs with the injuries of their countries at the same time. They were all prepared and resigned to die, expecting to be cut to pieces the moment Bonaparte fell by their hands; but one of the Italians, rather superstitious, had, before he went to the drawing-room, confessed and received absolution from a priest, whom he knew to be an enemy of Bonaparte: but the priest, in hope of reward, disclosed the conspiracy to the master of ceremonies, Salmatoris. The three surviving conspirators are said to have been literally torn to pieces by the engines of torture, and the priest was shot for having given absolution to an assassin, and for having concealed his knowledge of the plot an hour after he was acquainted with it. Even Salmatoris had some difficulty to avoid being disgraced for having written a terrifying note which had exposed the Emperor's weakness, and shown that his life was dearer to him at the head of empires than when only at the head of armies.

My narrative of this event I have from an officer present, whose veracity I can guarantee. He also informed me that in consequence of it, all the officers of the Swiss brigades in the French service that were quartered or encamped in Italy were, to the number of near fifty, dismissed at once. Of the Italian guards, every officer who was known to have suffered any losses by the new order of things in his country, was ordered to resign, if he would not enter into the regiments of the line.

Whatever the police agents did to prevent it, and in spite of some unjust and cruel chastisement, Bonaparte continued, during his stay in Italy, an object of ridicule in conversation, as well as in pamphlets and caricatures. One of these represented him in the ragged garb of a *sans-culotte*, pale and trembling on his knees, with bewildered looks and his hair standing upright on his head like pointed horns, tearing the map of the world to pieces, and, to save his life, offering each of his generals a slice, who in return regarded him with looks of contempt mixed with pity.

I have just heard of a new plot, or rather a league against Bonaparte's ambition. At its head the generals Jourdan, Macdonald, Le Courbe and Dessolles are placed, though many less victorious generals and officers, civil as well as military, are reported to be its members. Their object is not to remove or displace Bonaparte as an Emperor of the French; on the contrary, they offer their lives to strengthen his authority and to resist his enemies;

but they ask and advise him to renounce for himself, for his relations, and for France, all possessions on the Italian side of the Alps as the only means to establish a permanent peace, and to avoid a war with other States, whose safety is endangered by our great encroachments. A mutinous kind of address to this effect has been sent to the camp of Boulogne and to all other encampments of our troops, that those generals and other military persons there who chose, might both see the object and the intent of the associates. It is reported that Bonaparte ordered it to be burnt by the hands of the common executioner at Boulogne; that sixteen officers there who had subscribed their names in approbation of the address were broken, and dismissed with disgrace; that Jourdan is deprived of his command in Italy, and ordered to render an account of his conduct to the Emperor. Dessolles is also said to be dismissed, and with Macdonald, Le Courbe, and eighty-four others of His Majesty's subjects, whose names appeared under the remonstrance (or petition, as some call it), exiled to different departments of this country, where they are to expect their Sovereign's further determination, and in the meantime remain under the inspection and responsibility of his constituted authorities and commissaries of police.

As it is as dangerous to enquire as to converse on

this and other subjects, which the mysterious policy of our Government condemns to silence or oblivion, I have not yet been able to gather any more or better information concerning this league, or unconstitutional opposition to the executive power; but as I am intimate with one of the actors, should he have an opportunity, he will certainly write to me at full length, and be very explicit.

LETTER XXXV

PARIS, *August*, 1805.

MY LORD, — I believe I have before remarked that, under the government of Bonaparte, causes relatively the most insignificant have frequently produced effects of the greatest consequence. A capricious or whimsical character, swaying with unlimited power, is certainly the most dangerous guardian of the prerogatives of sovereignty, as well as of the rights and liberties of the people. That Bonaparte is as vain and fickle as a coquette, as obstinate as a mule, and equally audacious and unrelenting, everyone who has witnessed his actions or meditated on his transactions must be convinced. The least opposition irritates his pride, and he determines and commands, in a moment of impatience or vivacity, what may cause the misery of millions for ages, and, perhaps, his own repentance for years.

When Bonaparte was officially informed by his ambassador at Vienna, the young La Rochefoucauld, that the Emperor of Germany had declined being one of his grand officers of the Legion of Honour, he flew into a rage, and used against this Prince the most gross, vulgar and unbecoming language. I have heard it said that he went so far as to say, "Well, Francis II. is tired of reigning. I hope to have strength enough to carry a third crown. He who dares refuse to be and continue my equal, shall soon, as a vassal, think himself honoured with the regard which, as a master, I may condescend from compassion to bestow on him." Though forty-eight hours had elapsed after this furious sally before he met with the Austrian ambassador, Count de Cobentzel, his passion was still so furious, that, from his grossness and violence, all the members of the diplomatic corps trembled, both for this their respected member, and for the honour of our nation thus represented.

When the diplomatic audience was over, he said to Talleyrand, in a commanding and harsh tone of voice, in the presence of all his aides-de-camp and generals, "Write this afternoon, by an extraordinary courier, to my minister at Genoa, Salicetti, to prepare the Doge and the people for the immediate incorporation of the Ligurian Republic with my empire. Should Austria dare to murmur, I shall, within three months, also incorporate the *ci-devant* Republic of Venice with my Kingdom of Italy!"—" But—but—Sire!" uttered the minister, trembling.—"There exists no 'but,' and I will listen to no 'but,'" interrupted His Majesty. "Obey my orders without further discussions. Should Austria dare to arm, I shall, before next Christmas, make Vienna the headquarters of a fiftieth military division. In an hour I expect you with the despatches ready for Salicetti."

This Salicetti is a Corsican of a respectable family, born at Bastia, in 1758, and it was he who, during the siege of Toulon in 1793, introduced his countryman, Napoleon Bonaparte, his present Sovereign, to the acquaintance of Barras, an occurrence which has since produced consequences so terribly notorious.

Before the Revolution an advocate of the superior council of Corsica, he was elected a member to the First National Assembly, where, on the 30th of November, 1789, he pressed the decree which declared the Island of Corsica an integral part of the French monarchy. In 1792, he was sent by his fellow-citizens as a deputy to the National Convention, where he joined the terrorist faction, and voted for the death of his King. In May, 1793, he was in Corsica, and violently opposed the partisans of General Paoli. Obliged to make his escape in August from that island, to save himself, he joined the army of General Carteaux, then marching against the Marseilles insurgents, whence he was sent by the National Convention with Barras, Gasparin, Robespierre the younger, and Ricrod, as a representative of the people to the army before Toulon, where, as well as at Marseilles, he shared in all the atrocities committed by his colleagues and by Bonaparte; for which, after the death of the Robespierres, he was arrested with him as a terrorist.

He had not known Bonaparte much in Corsica, but, finding him and his family in great distress, with all other Corsican refugees, and observing his adroitness as a captain of artillery, he recommended him to Barras, and upon their representation to the Committee of Public Safety, he was promoted to a *chef de brigade*, or colonel. In 1796, when Barras gave Bonaparte the command of the army of Italy, Salicetti was appointed a commissary of government to the same army, and in that capacity behaved with the greatest insolence towards all the princes of Italy, and most so towards the Duke of Modena, with whom he and Bonaparte signed a treaty of neutrality, for which they received a large sum in ready money; but shortly afterwards the duchy was again invaded, and an attempt made to surprise and seize the Duke. In 1797 he was chosen a member of the Council of Five Hundred, where he always continued a supporter of violent measures.

When, in 1799, his former protégé, Bonaparte, was proclaimed a First Consul, Salicetti desired to be placed in the *Conservative* Senate; but his familiarity displeased Napoleon, who made him first a commercial agent, and afterwards a minister to the Ligurian Republic so as to keep him at a distance. During his several missions, he has amassed a fortune, calculated at the lowest, of six millions of livres—£250,000.

The order Salicetti received to prepare the incorporation of Genoa with France, would not, without the presence of our troops, have been very easy to execute, particularly as he, six months before, had prevailed on the Doge and the senate to resign all sovereignty to Lucien Bonaparte, under the title of a Grand Duke of Genoa.

The cause of Napoleon's change of opinion with regard to his brother Lucien, was that the latter would not separate from a wife he loved, but preferred domestic happiness to external splendour frequently accompanied with internal misery. So that this act of incorporation of the Ligurian Republic, in fact, originated, notwithstanding the great and deep calculations of our profound politicians and political schemers, in nothing else but in the keeping of a wife, and in the refusal of a riband.

That corruption, seduction and menaces seconded the intrigues and bayonets which *convinced* the Ligurian Government of the *honour* and *advantage* of becoming subjects of Bonaparte, I have not the least doubt; but that the Doge, Jerome Durazzo, and the Senators Morchio, Maglione, Travega, Maghella, Roggieri, Taddei, Balby and Langlade sold the independence of their country for ten millions of livres—£430,000—though, it has been positively asserted, I can hardly believe; and, indeed, money was as little necessary, as resistance would have been unavailing, all the forts and strong positions being in the occupation of our troops. A general officer present when the Doge of Genoa, at the head of the Ligurian deputation, offered Bonaparte their homage at Milan, and exchanged liberty for bondage, assured me that this *ci-devant* chief magistrate spoke with a faltering voice and with tears in his eyes, and that indignation was read on the countenance of every member of the deputation thus forced to prostitute their rights as citizens, and to vilify their sentiments as patriots.

When Salicetti, with his secretary, Milhaud, had arranged this honourable affair, they set out from Genoa to announce to Bonaparte, at Milan, their success. Not above a league from the former city their carriage was stopped, their persons stripped, and their papers and effects seized by a gang, called in the country the gang of PATRIOTIC ROBBERS, commanded by Mulieno. This chief is a descendant of a good Genoese family, proscribed by France, and the men under him are all above the common class of people. They never commit any murders, nor do they rob any but Frenchmen, or Italians known to be adherents of the French party. Their spoils they distribute among those of their countrymen who, like themselves, have suffered from the revolutions in Italy within these last nine years. They usually send the amount destined to relieve these persons to the curates of the several parishes, signifying in what manner it is to be employed. Their conduct has procured them many friends among the low and the poor, and though frequently pursued by our gendarmes, they have hitherto always escaped. The papers captured by them on this occasion from Salicetti are said to be of a most curious nature, and throw great light on Bonaparte's future views on Italy. The original act of consent of the Ligurian Government to the incorporation with France was also in this number. It is reported that they were deposited with the Austrian minister at Genoa, who found means to forward them to his Court; and it is supposed that their contents did not a little to hasten the present movements of the Emperor of Germany.

Another gang, known under the appellation of the PATRIOTIC AVENGERS, also desolates the Ligurian Republic. They never rob, but always murder those whom they consider as enemies of their country. Many of our officers, and even our sentries on duty, have been wounded or killed by them; and after dark, therefore, no Frenchman dares walk out unattended. Their chief is supposed to be a *ci-devant* abbé, Sagati, considered a political as well as a religious fanatic. In consequence of the deeds of these patriotic avengers, Bonaparte's first act, as a Sovereign of

Liguria, was the establishment of special military commissions, and a law prohibiting, under pain of death, every person from carrying arms who could not show a written permission of our commissary of police. Robbers and assassins are unfortunately common to all nations, and all people of all ages; but those of the above description are only the production and progeny of revolutionary and troublesome times. They pride themselves, instead of violating the laws, on supplying their inefficacy and counteracting their partiality.

LETTER XXXVI

PARIS, *September*, 1805.

MY LORD, — Bonaparte is now the knight of more royal Orders than any sovereign in Europe, and were he to put them on all at once, their ribands would form stuff enough for a light summer coat of as many different colours as the rainbow. The Kings of Spain, of Naples, of Prussia, of Portugal, and of Etruria have admitted him a knight-companion, as well as the Electors of Bavaria, Hesse and Baden, and the Pope of Rome. In return he has appointed these Princes his grand officers of HIS Legion of Honour, the highest rank of his newly instituted imperial order. It is even said that some of these Sovereigns have been honoured by him with the grand star and broad riband of the Order of HIS Iron Crown of the Kingdom of Italy.

Before Napoleon's departure for Milan last spring, Talleyrand intimated to the members of the foreign diplomatic corps here, that their presence would be agreeable to the Emperor of the French at his coronation at Milan as a King of Italy. In the preceding summer a similar *hint*, or *order*, had been given by him for a diplomatic trip to Aix-la-Chapelle, and all their excellencies set a-packing instantly; but some legitimate Sovereigns, having since discovered that it was indecent for their representatives to be crowding the suite of an insolently and proudly-travelling usurper, under different pretences declined the *honour* of the invitation and journey to Italy. It would, besides, have been pleasant enough to have witnessed the ambassadors of Austria and Prussia, whose Sovereigns had not acknowledged Bonaparte's right to his assumed title of King of Italy, indirectly approving it by figuring at the solemnity which inaugurated him as such. Of this inconsistency and impropriety Talleyrand was well aware; but audacity on one side, and endurance and submission on the other, had so often disregarded these considerations before, that he saw no indelicacy or impertinence in the proposal. His master had, however, the gratification to see at his levée, and in his wife's drawing-room, the ambassadors of Spain, Naples, Portugal and Bavaria, who laid at the imperial and royal feet the Order decorations of their own Princes, to the no little entertainment of His Imperial and Royal Majesty, and to the great edification of his dutiful subjects on the other side of the Alps.

The expenses of Bonaparte's journey to Milan, and his coronation there (including also those of his attendants from France), amounted to no less a sum than fifteen millions of livres—£625,000—of which one hundred and fifty thousand livres—£6,000—was laid out in fireworks, double that sum in decorations of the royal palace and the cathedral, and three millions of livres—£125,000—in presents to different generals, grand officers, deputations, &c. The poor also shared his bounty; medals to the value of fifty thousand livres — £2,100 — were thrown out among them on the day of the ceremony, besides an equal sum given by Madame Napoleon to the hospitals and orphan-houses. These last have a kind of hereditary or family claim on the purse of our Sovereign; their parents were the victims of the Emperor's first step towards *glory* and *grandeur*.

Another three millions of livres was expended for the march of troops from France to form *pleasure* camps in Italy, and four millions more was requisite for the forming and support of these encampments during two months, and the Emperor distributed among the officers and men composing them two million livres' worth of rings, watches, snuff-boxes, portraits set with diamonds, stars, and other trinkets, as evidences of His Majesty's satisfaction with their behaviour, presence and performances.

These troops were under the command of Bonaparte's field-marshal, Jourdan, a general often mentioned in the military annals of our revolutionary war. During the latter part of the American war, he served under General Rochambeau as a common soldier, and obtained in 1783, after the peace, his discharge. He then turned a pedlar, in which situation the Revolution found him. He had also married for her fortune a lame daughter of a tailor, who brought him a *fortune* of two thousand livres—£84—from whom he has since been divorced, leaving her to shift for herself as she can, in a small milliner's shop at Limoges, where her husband was born in 1763.

Jourdan was among the first members and pillars ot the Jacobin club organized in his native town, which procured him rapid promotion in the National Guards, of whom, in 1792, he was already a colonel. His known love of liberty and equality induced the Committee of Public Safety in 1793 to appoint him to the chief command of the armies of Ardennes and of the North, instead of Lamarche and Houchard. On the 17th ot October the same year, he gained the victory of Wattignies, which obliged the united forces of Austria, Prussia and Germany to raise the siege ot Maubeuge. The jealous Republican Government, in reward, deposed him and appointed Pichegru his successor, which was the origin ot that enmity and malignity with which Jourdan pursued this unfortunate general even to his grave. He never forgave Pichegru the acceptance of a command which he could not decline without risking his life; and when he should have avenged his disgrace on the real causes of it, he chose to resent it on him who, like himself, was merely an instrument, or a slave, in the hands and under the whip of a tyrannical power.

After the imprisonment of General Hoche in March, 1794, Jourdan succeeded him as chief of the army of the Moselle. In June he joined, with thirty thousand men, the right wing of the army of the North, forming a new one, under the name of the army of the Sambre and Meuse. On the 16th of the same month, he gained a complete victory over the Prince of Coburg, who tried to raise the siege of Charleroy. This battle, which was fought near Trasegnies, is nevertheless commonly called the battle of Fleurus. After Charleroy had surrendered on the 25th, Jourdan and his army were ordered to act under the direction of General Pichegru, who had drawn the plan of that brilliant campaign. Always envious of this general, Jourdan did everything to retard his progress; and at last intrigued so well that the army of the Sambre and the Meuse was separated from that of the North.

With the former of these armies Jourdan pursued the retreating confederates, and after driving them from different stands and positions, he repulsed them to the banks of the Rhine, which river they were obliged to pass. Here ended his successes this year, successes that were not obtained without great loss on our side.

Jourdan began the campaigns of 1795 and 1796 with equal brilliancy, and ended them with equal disgrace. After penetrating into Germany with troops as numerous as well-disciplined, he was defeated at the end of them by Archduke Charles, and retreated always with such precipitation, and in such confusion, that it looked more like the flight of a disorderly rabble than the retreat of regular troops; and had not Moreau, in 1796, kept the enemy in awe, few of Jourdan's officers or men would again have seen France; for the inhabitants of Franconia rose on these marauders, and cut them to pieces, wherever they could surprise or waylay them.

In 1797, as a member of the Council of Five Hundred, he headed the Jacobin faction against the moderate party, of which Pichegru was a chief; and he had the cowardly vengeance of base rivalry to pride himself upon having procured the transportation of that patriotic general to Cayenne. In 1799, he again assumed the command of the army of Alsace and of Switzerland; but he crossed the Rhine and penetrated into Suabia only to be again routed by the Archduke Charles, and to repass this river in disorder. Under the necessity of resigning as a general-in-chief, he returned to the Council of Five Hundred more violent than ever, and provoked there the most oppressive measures against his fellow-citizens. Previous to the revolution effected by Bonaparte in November of that year, he had entered with Garreau and Santerre into a conspiracy, the object of which was to restore the Reign of Terror, and to prevent which Bonaparte said he made those changes which placed him at the head of government. It was even printed in the papers of that period, which Bonaparte on the 10th of November addressed to the then deputy of Mayenne, Prevost: "If the plot entered into by Jourdan and others, and of which they have not blushed to propose to me the execution, had not been defeated, they would have surrounded the place of your sitting, and to crush all future opposition, ordered a number of deputies to be massacred. That done, they were to establish the sanguinary despotism of the Reign of Terror." But whether such was Jourdan's project, or whether it was merely given out to be such by the consular faction, to extenuate their own usurpation, he certainly had connected himself with the most guilty and contemptible of the former terrorists, and drew upon himself by such conduct the hatred and blame even of those whose opinion had long been suspended on his account.

General Jourdan was among those terrorists whom the Consular Government condemned to transportation; but after several interviews with Bonaparte he was not only pardoned, but made a counsellor of state of the military section; and afterwards, in 1801, an administrator-general of Piedmont, where he was replaced by General Menou in 1803, being himself entrusted with the command in Italy This place he has preserved until last month, when he was ordered to resign it to Massena, with whom he had a quarrel, and would have fought him in a duel, had not the Viceroy, Eugenius de Beauharnais, put him under arrest and ordered him back hither, where he is daily expected. If Massena's report to Bonaparte be true, the army of Italy was very far from being as orderly and numerous as Jourdan's assertions would have induced us to believe. But this accusation of a rival must be listened to with caution; because, should Massena meet with repulse, he will no doubt make use of it as an apology; and should he be victorious, hold it out as a claim for more honour and praise.

The same doubts which still continue of Jourdan's political opinions remain also with regard to his military capacity. But the unanimous declaration of those who have served under his orders as a general must silence both his blind admirers and unjust slanderers. They all allow him some military ability; he combines and prepares in the cabinet a plan of defence and attack with method and intelligence, but he does not possess the quick *coup d'œil*, and that promptitude which perceives, and rectifies accordingly, an error on the field of battle. If, on the day of action, some accident, or some manœuvre, occurs which has not been foreseen by him, his dull and heavy genius does not enable him to alter instantly his dispositions, or to remedy errors, misfortunes or improvidences. This kind of talent, and this kind of absence of talent, explain equally the causes of his advantages, as well as the origin of his frequent disasters. Nobody denies him courage, but, with most of our other republican generals, he has never been careful of the lives of the troops under him. I have heard an officer of superior talents and rank assert, in the presence of Carnot, that the number of wounded and killed under Jourdan when victorious, frequently surpassed the number of enemies he had defeated. I fear it is too true that we are as much, if not more, indebted for our successes to the superior number as to the superior valour of our troops.

Jourdan is, with regard to fortune, one of our poorest republican generals who have headed armies. He has not, during all his campaigns, collected more than a capital of eight millions of livres—£333,000—a mere trifle compared to the fifty millions of Massena, the sixty millions of Le Clerc, the forty millions of Murat, and the thirty-six millions of Augereau; not to mention the hundred millions of Bonaparte. It is also true that Jourdan is a gambler and a debauchee, fond of cards, dice and women; and that in Italy, except two hours in twenty-four allotted to business, he passed the remainder of his time either at the gaming-tables, or in the boudoirs of his seraglio—I say seraglio, because he kept in the extensive house joining his palace as governor and commander, ten women—three French, three Italians, two Germans, and two Irish or English girls. He supported them all in style; but they were his slaves and he was their sultan, whose official mutes (his aides-de-camp) both watched them, and, if necessary, chastised them.

LETTER XXXVII

PARIS, *September*, 1805.

MY LORD,—I can truly defy the world to produce a corps of such a heterogeneous composition as our Conservative Senate, when I except the members composing Bonaparte's Legion of Honour. Some of our senators have been tailors, apothecaries, merchants, chemists, quacks, physicians, barbers, bankers, soldiers, drummers, dukes, shopkeepers, mountebanks, abbés, generals, savants, friars, ambassadors, counsellors, or presidents of parliament, admirals, barristers, bishops, sailors, attorneys, authors, barons, spies, painters, professors, ministers, *sans-culottes*, atheists, stonemasons, robbers, mathematicians, philosophers, regicides, and a long *et cetera*. Any person reading through the official list of the members of the senate, and who is acquainted with their former situations in life, may be convinced of this truth. Should he even be ignorant of them, let him but enquire, with the list in his hand, in any of our fashionable or political circles; he will meet with but few persons who are not able or willing to remove his doubts, or to gratify his curiosity. There are not many of them whom it is possible to elevate, but those are still more numerous whom it is impossible to degrade. Their past lives, vices, errors, or crimes, have settled their characters and reputation; and they must live and die in *statu quo*, either as fools or as knaves, and perhaps as both.

I do not mean to say that they are all criminals, or all equally criminal, if insurrection against lawful authority and obedience to usurped tyranny, are not to be considered as crimes; but there are few indeed who can lay their hands on their bosoms and say, *vitam expendere vero*. Some of them, as a Lagrange, Berthollet, Chaptal, Laplace, François de Neuf-Château, Tronchet, Monge, Lacépede and Bougainville, are certainly men of talents; but others, as a Porcher, Resnier, Vimar, Auber, Peré, Sers, Vernier, Vien, Villetard, Tascher, Rigal, Baciocchi, Bevière, Beauharnais, de Luynes (a *ci-devant* duke, known under the name of *Le Gros Cochon*), nature never destined but to figure among those half-idiots and half-imbeciles who are, as it were, intermedial between the brute and human creation.

Siéyes, Cabanis, Garran Coulon, Lecouteul, Canteleu, Lenoin Laroche, Volney, Grégoire, Emmery, Joucourt, Boissy d'Anglas, Fouché and Rœderer form another class. Some of them regicides, others assassins and plunderers, but all intriguers whose machinations date from the beginning of the Revolution. They are all men of parts, of more or less knowledge, and of great presumption. As to their morality, it is on a level with their religion and loyalty. They betrayed their king, and had denied their God already in 1789.

After these come some others, who again have neither talents to boast of nor crimes of which they have to be ashamed. They have but little pretension to genius, none to consistency, and their honesty equals their capacity. They joined our political revolution as they might have done a religious procession. *It was at that time a fashion;* and they applauded our revolutionary innovations as they would have done the introduction of a new opera, of a new tragedy, of a new comedy, or of a new farce. To this fraternity appertain a *ci-dèvant* Count de Stult-Tracy, Dubois—Dubay, Kellerman, Lambrechts, Lemercier, Pleville — Le Pelley, Clément de Ris, Pérégeaux, Berthélemy, Vaubois, Perignon, d'Agier, Abrial, de Belloy, Delannoy, Aboville, and St. Martin La Motte.

Such are the characteristics of men whose *senatus consultum* bestows an emperor on France, a king on Italy, makes of principalities departments of a republic, and transforms republics into provinces or principalities. To show the absurdly fickle and ridiculously absurd appellations of our shamefully perverted institutions, this senate was called the Conservative Senate; that is to say, it was to preserve the republican consular constitution in its integrity, both against the encroachments of the executive and legislative power, both against the manœuvres of the factions, the plots of the royalists or monarchists, and the clamours of a populace of levellers. But during the five years that these honest wiseacres have been preserving, everything has perished — the republic, the consuls, free discussions, free election, the political liberty, and the liberty of the Press; all — all are found nowhere but in old, useless and rejected codes. They have, however, in a truly *patriotic* manner taken care of their own dear selves. Their salaries are more than doubled since 1799.

Besides mock senators, mock praetors, mock quaestors, other *nomina libertatis* are revived, so as to make the loss of the reality so much the more galling. We have also two curious commissions; one called "the Senatorial Commission of Personal Liberty," and the other "the Senatorial Commission of the Liberty of the Press." The imprisonment without cause, and transportation without trial, of thousands of persons of both sexes weekly, show the grand advantages which arise from the former of these commissions; and the contents of our new books and daily prints evince the utility and liberality of the latter.

But from the past conduct of these *our* senators,

members of these commissions, one may easily conclude what is to be expected in future from their justice and patriotism. Lenoin Laroche, at the head of the one, was formerly an advocate of some practice, but attended more to politics than to the business of his clients, and was, therefore, at the end of the session of the first assembly (of which he was a member), forced, for subsistence, to become the editor of an insignificant journal. Here he preached licentiousness, under the name of Liberty, and the agrarian law in recommending Equality. A prudent courtier of all systems in fashion, and of all factions in power, he escaped proscription, though not accusation of having shared in the national robberies. A short time in the summer of 1797, after the dismissal of Cochon, he acted as a minister of police; and in 1798 the Jacobins elected him a member of the Council of Ancients, where he, with other deputies, sold himself to Bonaparte, and was, in return, rewarded with a place in the senate. Under monarchy he was a republican, and under a republic he extolled monarchical institutions. He wished to be singular, and to be rich. Among so many shocking originals, however, he was not distinguished; and among so many philosophical marauders, he had no opportunity to pillage above two millions of livres—£84,000. This friend of liberty is now one of the most despotic senators, and this lover of equality never answers when spoken to, if not addressed as "his Excellency," or "Monseigneur."

Boissy d'Anglas, another member of this commission, was before the Revolution a steward to Louis XVIII. when Monsieur; and, in 1789, was chosen a deputy of the first assembly, where he joined the factions, and in his speeches and writings defended all the enormities that dishonoured the beginning as well as the end of the Revolution. A member afterwards of the National Convention, he was sent in mission to Lyons, where, instead of healing the wounds of the inhabitants, he inflicted new ones. When, on the 15th of March, 1796, in the Council of Five Hundred, he pronounced the oath of hatred to royalty, he added, that *this oath was in his heart*, otherwise no power upon earth could have forced him to take it; and he is now a sworn subject of Napoleon the First! He pronounced the panegyric of Robespierre, and the apotheosis of Marat. "The soul," said he, "was moved and elevated in hearing Robespierre speak of the Supreme Being with philosophical ideas, embellished by eloquence"; and he signed the removal of the ashes of Marat to the temple consecrated *to humanity!* In September, 1797, he was, as a *royalist*, condemned to transportation by the Directory; but, in 1799, Bonaparte recalled him, made him first a tribune and afterwards a senator.

Boissy d'Anglas, though an apologist of robbers and assassins, has neither murdered nor plundered; but, though he has not enriched himself, he has assisted in ruining all his former protectors, benefactors and friends.

Sers, a third member of this commission, was before the Revolution a bankrupt merchant at Bordeaux, but in 1791 was a municipal officer of the same city, and sent as a deputy to the National Assembly, where he attempted to rise from the clouds that encompassed his heavy genius by a motion for pulling down all the statues of kings all over France. He seconded another motion of Bonaparte's prefect, Jean Debrie, to decree a corps of tyrannicides, destined to murder all emperors, kings and princes. At the club of the Jacobins, at Bordeaux, he prided himself on having caused the arrest and death of three hundred aristocrats; and boasted that he never went out without a dagger to despatch, by a *summary justice*, those who had escaped the laws. After meeting with well-merited contempt, and living for some time in the greatest obscurity, by a handsome present to Madame Bonaparte, in 1799, he obtained the favour of Napoleon, who dragged him forward to be placed among other ornaments of his senate. Sers has just cunning enough to be taken for a man of sense when with fools; when with men of sense, he reassumes the place allotted him by Nature. Without education, as well as without parts, he for a long time confounded brutal scurrility with oratory, and thought himself eloquent when he was only insolent or impertinent. His ideas of liberty are such that, when he was a municipal officer, he signed a mandate of arrest against sixty-four individuals of both sexes, who were at a ball, because they had refused to invite to it one of his nieces.

Abrial, Emmery, Vernier and Lemercier are the other four members of that commission; of these, two are old intriguers, two are nullities, and all four are slaves.

Of the seven members of the senatorial commission for preserving the liberty of the Press, Garat and Rœderer are the principal. The former is a pedant, while pretending to be a philosopher; and he signed the sentence of his good King's death, while declaring himself a royalist. A mere valet to Robespierre, his fawning procured him opportunities to enrich himself with the spoil of those whom his calumnies and plots caused to be massacred or guillotined. When, as a minister of justice, he informed Louis XVI. of his condemnation, he did it with such an affected and atrocious indifference that he even shocked his accomplices, whose nature had not much of tenderness. As a member of the first assembly, as a minister under the convention, and as a deputy of the Council of Five Hundred, he always opposed the liberty of the Press. "The laws, you say" (exclaimed he in the council) "punish libellers; so they do thieves and housebreakers; but would you, therefore, leave your doors unbolted? Is not the character, the honour, and the tranquillity of a citizen preferable to his treasures? and, by the liberty of the Press, you leave them at the mercy of every scribbler who can write or think. The wound inflicted may heal, but the scar will always remain. Were you, therefore, determined to decree the motion for this dangerous and impolitic liberty, I make this amendment, *that conviction of having written a libel carries with it capital punishment*, and that a label be fastened on the breast of the libeller, when carried to execution, with this inscription: *A social murderer*, or *A murderer of characters!*"

Rœderer has belonged to all religious or anti-religious sects, and to all political or anti-social factions, these last twenty years; but, after approving, applauding and serving them, he has deserted them, sold them, or betrayed them. Before the Revolution, a counsellor of parliament at Metz, he was a spy of the Court on his colleagues; and, since the Revolution, he served the Jacobins as a spy on the Court. Immoral and unprincipled to the highest degree, his profligacy and duplicity are only equalled by his perversity and cruelty. It was he who, on the 10th of August, 1792, betrayed the King and the royal family into the hands of their assassins, and who himself made a merit of this infamous act. After being repulsed by all, even by the most sanguinary of our parties and partisans, by a Brissot, a Marat, a Robespierre, a Tallien, and a Barras, Bonaparte adopted him first as a counsellor of state, and afterwards as a senator. His own and only daughter died in a miscarriage, the consequence of an incestuous commerce with her unnatural parent; and his only son is disinherited by him for resenting his father's baseness in debauching a young girl whom the son had engaged to marry.

With the usual consistency of my revolutionary countrymen, he has, at one period, asserted that the liberty of the Press was necessary for the preservation both of men and things, for the protection of governors as well as of the governed, and that it was the best support of a constitutional government. At another time he wrote that, as it was impossible to fix the limits between the liberty and the licentiousness of the Press, the latter destroyed the benefits of the former; that the liberty of the Press was only useful against a Government which one wished to overturn, but dangerous to a Government which one wished to preserve. To show his indifference about his own character, as well as about the opinion of the public, these opposite declarations were inserted in one of our daily papers, and *both* were signed "Rœderer."

In 1789 he was indebted above one million two hundred thousand livres — £50,000 — and he now possesses national property purchased for seven millions of livres — £292,000 — and he avows himself to be worth three millions more in money placed in our public funds. He often says, laughingly, that he is under great obligations to Robespierre, whose guillotine acquitted in one day all his debts. All his creditors, after being denounced for their *aristocracy*, were murdered *en masse* by this instrument of death.

Of all the old beaux and superannuated libertines whose company I have had the misfortune of not being able to avoid, Rœderer is the most affected, silly and disgusting. His wrinkled face, and effeminate and childish air; his assiduities about every woman of beauty or fashion; his confidence in his own merit, and his presumption in his own power, wear such a curious contrast with his trembling hands, running eyes, and enervated person, that I have frequently been ready to laugh at him in his face, had not indignation silenced all other feeling. A light-coloured wig covers a bald head; his cheeks and eyelids are painted, and his teeth false; and I have seen a woman faint away from the effect of his breath, notwithstanding that he infects with his musk and perfumes a whole house only with his presence. When on the ground floor, you may smell him in the attic.

LETTER XXXVIII

Paris, *September*, 1805.

My Lord,—The reciprocal jealousy and even interest of Austria, France and Russia have hitherto prevented the tottering Turkish empire from being partitioned like Poland, or seized like Italy; to serve as indemnities, like the German empire; or to be shared, as reward to the allies, like the empire of Mysore.

When we consider the anarchy that prevails, both in the Government and among the subjects, as well in the capital as in the provinces of the Ottoman Porte; when we reflect on the mutiny and cowardice of its armies and navy, the ignorance and incapacity of its officers and military and naval commanders, it is surprising indeed, as I have heard Talleyrand often declare, that more foreign political intrigues should be carried on at Constantinople alone than in all other capitals of Europe taken together. These intrigues, however, instead of doing honour to the sagacity and patriotism of the members of the Divan, expose only their corruption and imbecility; and instead of indicating a dread of the strength of the Sublime

Sultan, show a knowledge of his weakness, of which the gold of the most wealthy, and the craft of the most subtle, by turns are striving to profit.

Beyond a doubt the enmity of the Ottoman Porte can do more mischief than its friendship can do service. Its neutrality is always useful, while its alliance becomes frequently a burden, and its support of no advantage. It is, therefore, more from a view of preventing evils than from expectation of profit, that all other Powers plot, cabal and bribe. The map of the Turkish empire explains what may be thought absurd or nugatory in this assertion.

As soon as a war with Austria was resolved on by the Brissot faction, in 1792, emissaries were despatched to Constantinople to engage the Divan to invade the provinces of Austria and Russia, thereby to create a diversion in favour of this country. Our ambassador in Turkey at that time, Count de Choiseul-Gouffier, though an admirer of the Revolution, was not a republican, and therefore secretly counteracted what he officially seemed to wish to effect. The Imperial Court succeeded, therefore, in establishing the neutrality of the Ottoman Porte, but Count de Choiseul was proscribed by the Convention. As *academician* he was, however, at St. Petersburg, liberally recompensed by Catherine II. for the services the ambassador had performed at Constantinople.

In May, 1793, the Committee of Public Safety determined to expedite another embassy to the Grand Seignior, at the head of which was the famous intriguer, De Semonville, whose revolutionary diplomacy had, within three years, alarmed the Courts of Madrid, Naples and Turin, as well as the Republican Government of Genoa. His career towards Turkey was stopped in the Grisons Republic on the 25th of July following, where he, with sixteen other persons of his suite, was arrested, and sent a prisoner, first to Milan, and afterwards to Mantua. He carried with him presents of immense value, which were all seized by the Austrians. Among them were four superb coaches, highly finished, varnished and gilt; what is iron or brass in common carriages was here gold or silver-gilt. Two large chests were filled with stuff of gold brocade, India gold muslins and shawls, and laces of very great value. Eighty thousand louis d'or—£80,000—in ready money; a service of gold plate of twenty covers, which formerly belonged to the kings of France; two small boxes full of diamonds and brilliants, the intrinsic worth of which was estimated at forty-eight millions of livres—£2,000,000—and a great number of jewels; among others, the crown diamond, called here the Regents', and in your country the Pitt Diamond, fell, with other riches, into the hands of the captors. Notwithstanding this loss and this disappointment, we contrived in vain to purchase the hostility of the Turks against our enemies, though with the sacrifice of no less a sum (according to the report of St. Just in June, 1794) than seventy millions of livres— £3,000,000. These official statements prove the means which our so often extolled *economical* and *moral* republican governments have employed in their negotiations.

After the invasion of Egypt, in time of peace, by Bonaparte, the Sultan became at last convinced of the *sincerity* of our professions of friendship, which he returned with a declaration of war. The preliminaries of peace with your country, in October, 1801, were, however, soon followed with a renewal of our former *friendly* intercourse with the Ottoman Porte. The voyage of Sebastiani into Egypt and Syria, in the autumn of 1802, showed that our *tenderness* for the inhabitants of these countries had not diminished, and that we soon intended to confer on them new hugs of fraternity. Your pretensions to Malta impeded our prospects in the East, and your obstinacy obliged us to postpone our so well-planned schemes of encroachments. It was then that Bonaparte first selected for his representative to the Grand Seignior, General Brune, commonly called by Moreau, Macdonald, and other competent judges of military merit, *an intriguer at the head of armies, and a warrior in time of peace when seated in the council chamber.*

This Brune was, before the Revolution, a journeyman

printer, and married to a washerwoman, whose industry and labour alone prevented him from starving, for he was as vicious as idle The money he gained when he chose to work was generally squandered away in brothels among prostitutes. To supply his excesses he had even recourse to dishonest means, and was shut up in the prison of Bicêtre, for robbing his master of types and of paper.

In the beginning of the Revolution, his very crimes made him an acceptable associate of Marat, who, with the money advanced by the Orleans faction, bought him a printing-office, and he printed the so dreadfully well-known journal, called *L'Amie du Peuple*. From the principles of this atrocious paper, and from those of his sanguinary patron, he formed his own political creed. He distinguished himself frequently at the clubs of the Cordeliers, and of the Jacobins, by his extravagant motions, and by provoking laws of proscription against a wealth he did not possess, and against a rank he would have dishonoured, but did not see without envy. On the 30th of June, 1791, he said, in the former of these clubs: "We hear everywhere complaints of poverty; were not our eyes so often disgusted with the sight of unnatural riches, our hearts would not so often be shocked at the unnatural sufferings of humanity. The *blessings* of our Revolution will never be felt by the world, until we in France are on a level, with regard to rank as well as to fortune. I, for my part, know too well the dignity of human nature ever to bow to a superior; but, brothers and friends, it is not enough that we are all politically equal, we must also be all equally rich or equally poor—we must either all strive to become men of property, or reduce men of property to become *sans-culottes*. Believe me, the aristocracy of property is more dangerous than the aristocracy of prerogative or fanaticism, because it is more common. Here is a list sent to *L'Amie du Peuple*, but of which prudence yet prohibits the publication. It contains the names of all the men of property of Paris, and of the Department of the Seine, the amount of their fortunes, and a proposal how to reduce and divide it among our patriots. Of its great utility in the moment when we have been striking our grand blows, nobody dares doubt; I therefore move that a brotherly letter be sent to every society of our brothers and friends in the provinces, inviting each of them to compose one of similar contents and of similar tendency in their own districts, with what remarks they think proper to affix, and to forward them to us, to be deposited in the mother club, after taking copies of them for the archives of their own society." His motion was decreed.

Two days afterwards, he again ascended the tribune. "You approved," said he, "of the measures I lately proposed against the aristocracy of property; I will now tell you of another aristocracy which we must also crush—I mean that of religion, and of the clergy. Their supports are folly, cowardice and ignorance. All priests are to be proscribed, and punished as criminals, and despised as impostors or idiots; and all altars must be reduced to dust as unnecessary. To prepare the public mind for such events, we must enlighten it; which can only be done by disseminating extracts from *L'Amie du Peuple*, and other *philosophical* publications. I have here some ballads of my own composition, which have been sung in my quarter; where all superstitious persons have already trembled, and all fanatics are raving. If you think proper, I will, for a mere trifle, print twenty thousand copies of them, to be distributed and disseminated gratis all over France." After some discussion, the treasurer of the club was ordered to advance Citizen Brune the sum required, and the secretary to transmit the ballads to the fraternal societies in the provinces.

Brune put on his first regimentals as an aide-de-camp to General Santerre in December, 1792, after having given proofs of his military prowess the preceding September, in the massacre of the prisoners in the Abbey. In 1793 he was appointed a colonel in the revolutionary army, which, during the Reign of Terror, laid waste the departments of the Gironde, where he was often seen commanding his corps, with a human head fixed on his sword. On the day when he entered Bordeaux with his troops, a new-born child occupied the same place, to the great horror of the inhabitants. During this brilliant expedition he laid the first foundation of his present fortune, having pillaged in a most unmerciful manner, and arrested or shot every suspected person who could not, or would not, exchange property for life. On his return to Paris, his *patriotism* was recompensed with a commission of a general of brigade. On the death of Robespierre, he was arrested as a terrorist, but, after some months' imprisonment, again released.

In October, 1795, he assisted Napoleon Bonaparte in the massacre of the Parisians, and obtained for it, from the director Barras, the rank of a general of division. Though occupying in time of war such a high military rank, he had hitherto never seen an enemy, or witnessed an engagement.

After Bonaparte had planned the invasion and pillage of Switzerland, Brune was charged to execute this unjust outrage against the law of nations. His capacity to intrigue procured him this distinction, and he did honour to the choice of his employers. You have no doubt read that, after lulling the Government of Berne into security by repeated proposals of accommodation, he attacked the Swiss and Bernese troops during a truce, and obtained by treachery successes which his valour did not promise him. The pillage, robberies and devastations in Helvetia added several more millions to his previously great riches.

It was after his campaign in Holland, during the autumn of 1799, that he first began to claim some military glory. He owed, however, his successes to the superior number of his troops, and to the talents of the generals and officers serving under him. Being made a counsellor of state by Bonaparte, he was entrusted with the command of the army against the Chouans. Here again he seduced by his promises, and duped by his intrigues, acted infamously—but was successful.

LETTER XXXIX

Paris, *September*, 1805.

My Lord,—Three months before Brune set out on his embassy to Constantinople, Talleyrand and Fouché were collecting together all the desperadoes of our Revolution, and all the Italian, Corsican, Greek and Arabian renegadoes and vagabonds in our country, to form him a set of attendants agreeable to the real object of his mission.

You know too much of our national character and of my own veracity to think it improbable, when I assure you that most of our *great* men in place are as vain as presumptuous, and that sometimes vanity and presumption get the better of their discretion and prudence. What I am going to tell you I did not hear myself, but it was reported to me by a female friend, as estimable for her virtues as admired for her accomplishments. She is often honoured with invitations to Talleyrand's familiar parties, composed chiefly of persons whose fortunes are as independent as their principles, who, though not approving the Revolution, neither joined its opposers nor opposed its adherents, preferring tranquillity and obscurity to agitation and celebrity. Their number is not much above half-a-dozen, and the minister calls them the only honest people in France with whom he thinks himself safe.

When it was reported here that two hundred persons of Brune's suite had embarked at Marseilles and eighty-four at Genoa, and when it was besides known that near fifty individuals accompanied him in his outset, this unusual occurrence caused much conversation and many speculations in all our coteries and fashionable circles. About that time my friend dined with Talleyrand, and by chance also mentioned this grand embassy, observing at the same time that it was too much honour done to the Ottoman Porte, and too much money thrown away upon splendour, to honour such an imbecile and tottering Government. "How people talk," interrupted Talleyrand, "about what they do not comprehend. Generous as Bonaparte is, he does not throw away his expenses; perhaps within twelve months all these renegadoes or adventurers, whom you all consider as valets of Brune, will be three-tailed Pachas or Beys, leading friends of liberty, who shall have gloriously broken their fetters as slaves ot a Selim to become the subjects of a Napoleon. The Eastern empire has, indeed, long expired, but it may suddenly be revived."—" Austria and Russia," replied my friend, "would never suffer it, and

England would sooner ruin her navy and exhaust her treasury than permit such a revolution."—"So they have tried to do," retorted Talleyrand, "to bring about a counter revolution in France. But though only a moment is requisite to erect the standard of revolt, ages often are necessary to conquer and seize it. Turkey has long been ripe for a revolution. It wanted only chiefs and directors. In time of war, ten thousand Frenchmen landed in the Dardanelles would be masters of Constantinople, and perhaps of the empire. In time of peace, four hundred bold and well-informed men may produce the same effect. —Besides, with some temporary cession of a couple of provinces to each of the Imperial Courts, and with the temporary present of an island to Great Britain, everything may be settled *pro tempore, and a Joseph Bonaparte be permitted to reign at Constantinople*, as a Napoleon does at Paris." That the minister made use of this language I can take upon me to affirm; but whether purposely or unintentionally, whether to give a high opinion of his plans or to impose upon his company, I will not and cannot assert.

On the subject of this numerous suite of Brune, Markoff is said to have obtained several conferences with Talleyrand and several audiences of Bonaparte, in which representations, as just as energetic, were made, which, however, did not alter the intent of our Government or increase the favour of the Russian ambassador at the Court of St. Cloud. But it proved that our schemes of subversion are suspected, and that our agents of overthrow would be watched and their manœuvres inspected.

Count Italinski, the Russian ambassador to the Ottoman Porte, is one of those noblemen who unite rank and fortune, talents and modesty, honour and patriotism, wealth and liberality. His personal character and his individual virtues made him, therefore, more esteemed and revered by the members of the Divan, than the high station he occupied, and the powerful Prince he represented, made him feared or respected. His *warnings* had created prejudices against Brune which he found difficult to remove. To revenge himself in his old way, our ambassador inserted several paragraphs in the *Moniteur* and in our other papers, in which Count Italinski was libelled and his transactions or views calumniated.

After his first audience with the Grand Seignior, Brune complained bitterly of not having learned the Turkish language, and of being under the necessity, therefore, of using interpreters, to whom he ascribed the renewed obstacles he encountered in every step he took, while his hotel was continually surrounded with spies, and the persons of his suite followed everywhere like criminals when they went out. Even the valuable presents he carried with him, amounting in value to twenty-four millions of livres—£1,000,000—were but indifferently received, the acceptors seeming to suspect the object and the honesty of the donor.

In proportion as our politics became embroiled with those of Russia, the post of Brune became of more importance; but the obstacles thrown in his way augmented daily, and he was forced to avow that Russia and England had greater influence and more credit than the French Republic and its chief. When Bonaparte was proclaimed an Emperor of the French, Brune expected that his acknowledgment as such at Constantinople would be a mere matter of course and announced officially on the day he presented a copy of his new credentials. Here again he was disappointed, and therefore demanded his recall from a place where there was no probability, under the present circumstances, of either exciting the subjects to revolt, of deluding the Prince into submission, or seducing ministers who, in pocketing his bribes, forgot for what they were given.

It was then that Bonaparte sent Joubert with a letter, in his *own* handwriting, to be delivered into the hands of the Grand Seignior himself. This Joubert is a foundling, and was from his youth destined and educated to be one of the secret agents of our secret diplomacy. You may already, perhaps, have heard that our Government selects yearly a number of young foundlings or orphans, whom it causes to be brought up in foreign countries at its expense, so as to learn the language as natives of the nation, where, when grown up, they are chiefly to be employed. Joubert had been educated under the inspection of our consuls at Smyrna, and, when he assumes the dress of a Turk, from his accent and manners even the Mussulmans mistake him for one of their own creed and of their country. He was introduced to Bonaparte in 1797, and accompanied him to Egypt, where his services were of the greatest utility to our army. He is now a kind of under-secretary in the office of our secret diplomacy, and a member of our Legion of Honour. Should ever Joseph Bonaparte be an Emperor or Sultan of the East, Joubert will certainly be his Grand Vizier. There is another Joubert (with whom you must not confound him), who was also a kind of Dragoman at Constantinople some years ago, and who is still somewhere on a secret mission in the East Indies.

Joubert's arrival at Constantinople excited both curiosity among the people and suspicion among the ministry. There is no example in the Ottoman history of a chief of a Christian nation having written to the Sultan by a private messenger, or of His Highness having condescended to receive the letter from the bearer, or to converse with him. The Grand Vizier demanded a copy of Bonaparte's letter before an audience could be granted. This was refused by Joubert; and as Brune threatened to quit the capital of Turkey if any longer delay were experienced, the letter was delivered in a garden near Constantinople, where the Sultan met Bonaparte's agent as if by chance, who, it seems, lost all courage and presence of mind, and did not utter four words, to which no answer was given.

This impertinent intrigue, and this novel diplomacy, therefore, totally miscarried to the great shame and greater disappointment of the schemers and contrivers. I must, however, do Talleyrand the justice to say that he never approved of it, and even foretold the issue to his intimate friends. It was entirely the whim and invention of Bonaparte himself, upon a suggestion of Brune, who was far from being so well acquainted with the spirit and policy of the Divan as he had been with the genius and plots of Jacobinism. Not rebuked, however, Joubert was ordered away a second time with a second letter, and, after an absence of four months, returned again as he went, less satisfied with the second than with his first journey.

In these trips to Turkey, he had always for travelling companions some of our emissaries to Austria, Hungary, and in particular to Servia, where the insurgents were assisted by our councils, and even guided by some of our officers. The principal aide-de-camp of Czerni George, the Servian chieftain, is one St. Martin, formerly a captain in our artillery, afterwards an officer of engineers in the Russian service, and finally a volunteer in the army of Condé. He and three other officers of artillery were, under fictitious names, sent by our Government, during the spring of last year, to the camp of the insurgents. They pretended to be of the Grecian religion, and formerly Russian officers, and were immediately employed. St. Martin has gained great influence over Czerni George, and directs both his political councils and military operations. Besides the individuals left behind by Joubert, it is said that upwards of one hundred persons of Brune's suite have been ordered for the same destination. You see how great the activity of our Government is, and that nothing is thought unworthy of its vigilance or its machinations. In the staff of Paswan Oglou, six of my countrymen have been serving ever since 1796, always in the pay of our Government.

It was much against both the inclination and interest of our Emperor that his ambassador at Constantinople should leave the field of battle there to the representatives of Russia, Austria and England. But his dignity was at stake. After many threats to deprive the Sultan of the honour of his presence, and even after setting out once for some leagues on his return, Brune, observing that these marches and counter-marches excited more mirth than terror, at last fixed a day, when finally either Bonaparte must be acknowledged by the Divan as an Emperor of the French, or his departure would take place. On that day he, indeed, began his retreat, but, under different pretexts, he again stopped, sent couriers to his secretaries, waited for their return, and sent new couriers again—but all in vain, the Divan continued refractory.

At his first audience after his return, the reception Bonaparte gave him was not very cordial. He demanded active employment, in case of a Continental war, either in Italy or in Germany, but received neither. When our army of England was already on its march towards the Rhine, and Bonaparte returned here, Brune was ordered to take command on the coast, and to organise there an army of observation, destined to succour Holland in case of an invasion, or to invade England should a favourable occasion present itself. The fact is, he was charged to intrigue rather than to fight; and were Napoleon able to force upon Austria another Peace of Luneville, Brune would probably be the plenipotentiary that would ask your acceptance of another Peace ot Amiens. It is here a general belief that his present command signifies another pacific overture from Bonaparte before your parliament meets, or at least before the New Year. Remember that our hero is more to be dreaded as a Philip than as an Alexander.

General Brune has bought landed property for nine millions of livres—£375,000—and has, in different funds, placed ready-money to the same amount. His own and his wife's diamonds are valued by him at three millions; and when he has any parties to dinner, he exhibits them with great complaisance as presents *forced* upon him during his campaign in Switzerland and Holland, for the *protection* he gave the inhabitants. He is now so vain of his wealth and proud of his rank, that he not only disregards all former acquaintances, but denies his own brothers and sisters; telling them frankly that the Field-Marshal Brune can have no shoemaker for a brother, nor a sister married to a chandler; that he knows of no parents, and of no relatives, being the maker of his own fortune and of what he is; that his children will look no farther back for ancestry than their father. One of his first cousins, a postillion, who insisted rather obstinately on his family alliance, was recommended by Brune to his friend Fouché, who sent him on a voyage of *discovery* to Cayenne, from which he probably will not return very soon.

LETTER XL

Paris, *September*, 1805.

My Lord,—Madame de C——n is now one of our most fashionable ladies. Once in the week she has a grand tea-party; once in a fortnight a grand dinner; and once in the month a grand ball. Foreign gentlemen are particularly well received at her house, which, of course, is much frequented by them. As you intend to visit this country after a peace, it may be of some service to you not to be unacquainted with the portrait of a lady whose invitation to see the original you may depend upon the day after your arrival.

Madame de C——n is the widow of the great and useless traveller, Count de C——n, to whom his relatives pretend that she was never married. Upon his death-bed he acknowledged her, however, for his wife, and left her mistress of a fortune of three hundred thousand livres a year—£12,500. The first four years of her widowhood she passed in lawsuits before the tribunals, where the plaintiffs could not prove that she was unmarried, nor she herself that she was married. But Madame Napoleon

Bonaparte, for a *small* douceur, speaking in her favour, the consciences of the juries, and the understanding of the judges, were all convinced at once that she had been the lawful wife, and was the lawful heiress, of Count de C——n, who had no children, or nearer relatives than third cousins.

Count de C——n was travelling in the East Indies when the Revolution broke out. His occupation there was a very innocent one; he drew countenances, being one of the most enthusiastic sectaries of Lavater, and modestly called himself the first physiognomist in the world. Indeed, he had been at least the most laborious one; for he left behind him a collection of six thousand two hundred portraits, drawn by himself in the four quarters of the world, during a period of thirty years.

He never engaged a servant, nor dealt with a tradesman, whose physiognomy had not been examined by him. In his travels he preferred the worst accommodation in a house where he approved of the countenance of the host, to the best where the traits or lines of the landlord's face were irregular, or did not coincide with his ideas of physiognomical propriety. The cut of a face, its expression, the length of the nose, the width or smallness of the mouth, the form of the eyelids or of the ears, the colour or thickness of the hair, with the shape and *tout ensemble* of the head, were always minutely considered and discussed before he entered into any agreement, on any subject, with any individual whatever. Whatever recommendations, or whatever attestations were produced, if they did not correspond with his own physiognomical remarks and calculations they were disregarded; while a person whose physiognomy pleased him, required no other introduction to obtain his confidence. Whether he thought himself wiser than his forefathers, he certainly did not grow richer than they were. Charlatans who imposed upon his credulity and impostors who flattered his mania, servants who robbed him and mistresses who deceived him, proved that if his knowledge of physiognomy was great, it was by no means infallible. At his death, of the fortune left him by his parents only the half remained.

His friends often amused themselves at the expense of his foibles. When he prepared for a journey to the East, one of them recommended him a servant upon whose fidelity he could depend. After examining with minute scrupulosity the head of the person, he wrote, "My friend, I accept your valuable present. From calculations, which never deceive me, Mauville (the servant's name) possesses, with the fidelity of a dog, the intrepidity of the lion. Chastity itself is painted on his front, modesty in his looks, temperance on his cheek, and his mouth and nose bespeak honesty itself." Shortly after the Count had landed at

Pondicherry, Mauville, who was a girl, died in a condition which showed that chastity had not been the divinity to whom she had chiefly sacrificed. In her trunk were found several trinkets belonging to her master, which she *honestly* had appropriated to herself. His miscalculation on this subject the Count could not but avow; he added, however, that it was the entire fault of his friend, who had duped him with regard to the sex.

Madame de C——n was, on account of her physiognomy, purchased by her late husband, then travelling in Turkey, from a merchant of Circassian slaves, when she was under seven years of age, and sent for her education to a relation of the count, an abbess of a convent in Languedoc. On his return from Turkey, some years afterwards, he took her under his own care, and she accompanied him all over Asia, and returned first to France in 1796, where her husband's name was upon the list of emigrants, though he had not been in Europe for ten years before the Revolution. However, by some pecuniary arrangements with Barras, he recovered his property, which he did not long enjoy, for he died in 1798. Mistress of a large fortune, with some remnants of beauty and elegance of manners, the suitors of Madame de C——n have been numerous, and among them several senators and generals, and even the minister, Chaptal. But she has politely declined all their offers, preferring her liberty and the undisturbed right of following her own *inclination*, to the inconvenient ties of Hymen. A gentleman, whom she *calls*, and who *passes* for, her brother, Chevalier de M—— de T——, a Knight of Malta, assists her in doing the honours of her house, and is considered as her favourite lover; though report and the scandalous chronicle say that she bestows her favours on every person who wishes to bestow on her his name, and that, therefore, her gallants are at least as numerous as her suitors.

Such is the true statement of the past, as well as the present, with regard to Madame de C——n. She relates, however, a different story. She says that she is the daughter of the Marquis de M—— de T——, of a Languedoc family; that she sailed, when a child, with her mother in a felucca from Nice to Malta, there to visit her brother; was captured by an Algerine pilot, separated from her mother, and carried to Constantinople by a merchant of slaves; there she was purchased by Count de C——n, who restored her to her family, and whom, therefore, notwithstanding the difference of their ages, she married from gratitude. This pretty, romantic story is ordered in our Court circles to be officially believed; and, of course, is believed by nobody, not even by the Emperor and Empress themselves, who would not give her the place of a lady-in-waiting, though her request was accompanied with a valuable diamond to the latter. The present was kept, but the offer declined.

All the members of the Bonaparte family, females as well as males, honour her house with their visits and with the acceptance of her invitations; and it is, therefore, among our fashionables, the *haut ton* to be of the society and circle of Madame de C——n.

Last February, Madame de P——t (the wife of Count de P——t, a relation by her husband's side of Madame de C——n, and who by the Revolution lost all their property, and now live with her as companions) was brought to bed of a son; the child was baptized by the Cardinal de Belloy, and Madame Joseph and Prince Louis Bonaparte stood sponsors. This occurrence was celebrated with great pomp, and a fête was given to near one hundred and fifty persons of both sexes— as usual, a mixture of *ci-devant* nobles and of *ci-devant sans-culottes;* of rank and meanness; of upstart wealth and beggared dignity.

What that day struck me most was the audacity of the Senator Villetard in teasing and insulting the old Cardinal de Belloy with his impertinent conversation and affected piety. This Villetard was, before the Revolution, a journeyman barber, and was released in 1789 by the mob from the prison of the Châtelet, where he was confined for theft. In 1791 his *patriotism* was so well known in the Department of Yonne, that he was deputed by the Jacobins there to the Jacobins of the capital with an address, encouraging and advising the deposition of Louis XVI.; and in 1792 he was chosen a member of the National Convention, where the most sanguinary and most violent of the factious were always certain to reckon him in the number of their adherents.

In December, 1797, when an insurrection, prepared by Joseph Bonaparte at Rome, deprived the late revered Pontiff both of his sovereignty and liberty, Villetard was sent by the Jacobin and atheistical party of the Directory to Loretto to seize and carry off the celebrated Madonna. In the execution of this commission he displayed a conduct worthy the littleness of his genius and the criminality of his mind. The wooden image of the Holy Virgin, a black gown said to have appertained to her, together with three broken china plates, which the Roman Catholic faithful have for ages believed to have been used by her, were presented by him to the Directory with a cruelly scandalous show, accompanied by a horribly blasphemous letter. He passed the next night, after he had perpetrated this sacrilege, with two prostitutes in the chapel of the Holy Virgin; and, on the next morning, placed one of them naked on the pedestal where the statue of the Virgin had formerly stood, and ordered all the devotees at Loretto, and two leagues round, to prostrate themselves before her. This shocking command occasioned the premature death of fifteen ladies, two of whom, who were nuns, died on the spot on beholding the horrid outrage ; and many more were deprived of their reason. How barbarously unfeeling must that wretch be who, in bereaving the religious, the pious, and the conscientious of their consolation and hope, adds the tormenting reproach of apostasy, by forcing virtue upon its knees to bow before what it knows to be guilt and infamy !

A traitor to his associates as to his God, it was he who, in November, 1799, presented at St. Cloud the decree which excluded all those who opposed Bonaparte's authority from the Council of Five Hundred, and appointed the two committees which made him a First Consul. In reward for this act of treachery, he was nominated to a place in the Conservative Senate. He has now ranked himself among our modern saints, goes regularly to Mass and confesses ; has made a brother of his, who was a drummer, an abbé ; and his assiduity about the cardinal was probably with a view to obtain advancement for this edifying priest.

The Cardinal de Belloy is now ninety-six years of age, being born in 1709, and has been a bishop for fifty-three years, but, during the Revolution, was proscribed, with all other prelates. He remained, however, in France, where his age saved him from the guillotine, but not from being reduced to the greatest want. A descendant of a noble family, and possessing an unpolluted character, Bonaparte fixed upon him as one of the pillars for the re-establishment of the Catholic worship, made him an Archbishop of Paris, and procured him the rank of a cardinal from Rome. But he is now in his second childhood, entirely directed by his grand vicaries, Malaret, De Mons and Legeas, who are in the pay of, and absolutely devoted to, Bonaparte. An innocent instrument in their hands, of those impious compliments pronounced by him to the Emperor and the Empress he did not, perhaps, even understand the meaning. From such a man the vile and artful Villetard might extort any promise. I observed, however, with pleasure, that he was watched by the grand vicar, Malaret, who seldom loses sight of his Eminence.

These two so opposite characters—I mean De Belloy and Villetard—are already speaking evidences of the composition of the society at Madame de C——n's. But I will tell you something still more striking. This lady is famous for her elegant services of plate, as much as for her delicate taste in entertaining her parties. After the supper on this night, eleven silver and four gold plates, besides numerous silver and gold spoons, forks, &c., were missed. She informed Fouché of her loss, who had her house surrounded by spies, with orders not to let any servant pass, without undergoing a strict search. The first gentleman who called for his carriage was his Excellency the counsellor of state and grand officer of the Legion of Honour, Treilhard. His servants were stopped and the cause explained. They willingly, and against the protest of their master, suffered themselves to be searched. Nothing was found upon them; but the police agents, observing the full-dress hat of their master rather bulky under his arm, took the liberty to look into it, where they found one of Madame de C———n's gold plates and two of her spoons. His Excellency immediately ordered his servants to be arrested, for having concealed their theft there. Fouché, however, when called out, advised his friend to forgive them for misplacing them, *as the less said on the subject the better.* When Madame de C———n heard of this discovery, she asked Fouché to recall his order or to alter it. "A repetition of such *misplacings* in the hats or in the pockets of the masters," said she, "would injure the reputation of my house and company." She never recovered the remainder of her loss, and that she might not be exposed in future to the same occurrences, she bought two services of china the following day, to be used when she had mixed society.

Treilhard had, before the Revolution, the reputation of being an honest man and an able advocate; but has since joined the criminals of all factions, being an accomplice in their guilt and a sharer of their spoils. In the Convention, he voted for the death of Louis XVI. and pursued without mercy the unfortunate Marie Antoinette to the scaffold. During his missions in the departments, wherever he went the guillotine was erected and blood flowed in streams. He was, nevertheless, accused by Robespierre of moderatism. At Lille in 1797, and at Rastadt in 1798, he negotiated as a plenipotentiary with the representatives of princes, and in 1799 corresponded as a director with emperors and kings, to whom he wrote as his great and dear friends. He is now a counsellor of state, in the section of legislation, and enjoys a fortune of several millions of livres, arising from estates in the country, and from leases in the capital. As this *accident* at Madame de C——n's soon became public, his friends gave out that he had of late been exceedingly absent, and, from absence of mind, puts everything he can lay hold of into his pocket. He is not a favourite with Madame Bonaparte, and she asked her husband to dismiss and disgrace him for an act so disgraceful to a grand officer of the Legion of Honour, but was answered, "Were I to turn away all the thieves and rogues that encompass me I should soon cease to reign. I despise them, but I must employ them."

It is whispered that the police have discovered another of Madame de C——n's lost gold plates at a pawnbroker's, where it had been pledged by the wife of another counsellor of state, François de Nantes. This I give you merely as a report! though the fact is, that Madame François is very fond of gambling, but very unfortunate; and she, with other of our fashionable ladies, has more than once resorted to her charms for the payment of her gambling debts.

LIST OF ILLUSTRATIONS

NAPOLEON'S COURT AND CABINET OF ST. CLOUD

VOLUME I

	PAGE
EMPEROR NAPOLÉON . . . . *Fronts.*	
LE 18 BRUMAIRE, DECEMBER 25, 1799	32
THE JEST UPON CARDINAL CAPRARA	56
NAPOLÉON'S MOTHER	120
THE MIOT EPISODE	184
JEROME BONAPARTE AND HIS WIFE	240

www.ingramcontent.com/pod-product-compliance
Lightning Source LLC
Chambersburg PA
CBHW032023220426

43664CB00006B/340